JAMES DEAN

JAMES DEAN

little boy lost

BY JOE HYAMS
WITH JAY HYAMS

WARNER BOOKS

A Time Warner Company

Letters reprinted by permission of Curtis Management Group, Inc.
Copyright © 1992 by the James Dean Foundation Trust.

Warner Books, Inc., 1271 Avenue of the Americas, New York, NY 10020

w A Time Warner Company

Printed in the United States of America
First printing: November 1992
10 9 8 7 6 5 4 3 2 1

Library of Congress Cataloging-in-Publication Data

Hyams, Joe.
    James Dean : little boy lost / Joe and Jay Hyams.
        p.   cm.
    Includes index.
    ISBN 0-446-51643-0
    1. Dean, James, 1931–1955.   2. Actors—United States—Biography.
I. Hyams, Jay, 1949–   . II. Title.
PN2287.D33H9   1992
791.43′028′092—dc20
    [B]   91-51172
                                                                    CIP

Book design by L. McRee

To
Ortense and Marcus Winslow
and to Marcus Winslow, Jr.,
the keeper of the flame

CONTENTS

CONTENTS

My candle burns at both ends;
  It will not last the night;
But, ah, my foes, and oh, my friends—
  It gives a lovely light!

—Edna St. Vincent Millay

INTRODUCTION

His visits began with the distant sound of a motorcycle, and as the sound grew louder my son Jay would grow increasingly excited. When the roar of the motorcycle came down our street and then stopped in front of our house, Jay would shriek, "Jimmy's here! Jimmy's here!" Booted feet would stamp up the front steps, and then the door would burst open. James Dean never knocked or came in the way anybody else did: he always made an entrance. Most often he was carrying a paper bag full of ice cream containers.

He came to our house often because, he said, he missed Markie, the young cousin he had grown up with in Indiana, and Jay, then five, was about Markie's age. Jimmy had a remarkable ability to communicate with children, the younger the better. He listened attentively to Jay's stories about his school friends and asked the questions one youngster asks another: Why do you like so and so? Is he stronger than you? Are you afraid of the dark? He paid close attention to the answers and to the body language. I sometimes felt he knew more about my son than I myself did.

He and Jay would often break up with laughter, their sentences left unfinished, interrupted by conspiratorial giggles. My wife, Elly, watched with an indulgent smile: Jimmy was a favorite of hers, which was convenient for me because it meant she didn't object when I went out in the evening with him, something I did fairly often. She got along famously with Jimmy because he showed a simple, direct interest in her life, looked intently into her eyes, and seemed able to relate to her with effortless ease.

Jimmy occupied a special space in our family, seemed to truly yearn for that space, but sometimes as I watched him I wondered just who the real Jimmy was. I knew that before the night was out, after he'd finished a mixed pint of coffee and raspberry ice cream and helped Jay put his toy cars away, after he'd pecked Elly good night and hopped back on his motorcycle, he would probably prowl the town until the wee hours and would most likely end up having sex with someone, somewhere. Usually a starlet or a waitress, sometimes in his car or against his car or in her apartment or in someone else's apartment—he never went to his own home, as far as anyone knew.

I knew what he told me about women, and I had heard the rumors about Jimmy. But I knew the difference between rumor and fact, and I really didn't care what Jimmy did or who he did it with. Even had the rumors been true it wouldn't have mattered. What Jimmy did with his private life was his secret, and keeping secrets was my stock-in-trade as a columnist for *The New York Herald Tribune*. I was well aware of leading men, macho heroes of adventure films, who spent their afternoons admiring the tanned bodies of the boys who cleaned their pools, and the others who went out in the evening dressed in women's clothes. I also knew about the female sex bombs, the women all American men wanted to undress—or so their press agents claimed—who spent their evenings alone because most men were certain they were too popular to ask out, and the others who went out alone at night and picked up young men and paid for motel rooms. That was part of Hollywood then as well as now. I knew many of the secrets of the sunwashed community that was my beat, and I also guessed that the folks in Hollywood were no better or worse than the people in any other American city.

Jimmy was a friend. Not one I could ever depend on except possibly in a barroom brawl: he was gutsy and not afraid of getting hurt. He rarely picked up a tab. He didn't call when promised. Didn't give back what was borrowed, didn't do what he had said he would do. I never knew exactly what he wanted or hoped for from me, and I never knew what I wanted or hoped for from him.

In retrospect it seems to me that I felt by being around him something was about to happen or was already happening, but I just wasn't smart enough to get it. He was fascinating to be with and watch. There was the way he moved. He could lift a glass of water to his mouth with an intensity and grace that made it seem he had never before touched a glass, never carried that particular weight through the air. What he said wasn't especially smart or memorable: it was the way he said it that made it interesting, the delivery and the hand gestures. I never felt I was a disciple and should take notes because they would be valuable someday. Nor did I realize that I was lucky to be his friend until years later when he became a legend.

There was an afternoon, warm and sunny, and Jay was home from school and wasn't happy. "He's been like that all afternoon," said Elly. I realized my son was upset by something, but I had a column to write on deadline and left it to her to sort out. Then a few hours later there was the roar of the motorcycle, Jay's shrieks of joy, and Jimmy's arrival. Jimmy saw, even sooner than I had, that something was wrong with Jay, and he put aside the packages of ice cream, barely acknowledged my presence and that of Elly, and took Jay aside. I tried to listen to their conversation, not as a journalist but as a father, but I could make out little of it. Soon, Jay's smile was back, the packages of ice cream were opened, and we were all sitting on the floor, laughing at something.

Only a long time later did I learn that the mailman had been frightening Jay with stories about a boogeyman who came in the night and carried off children to eat them. That was how the mailman made it through his day—terrifying children. I don't know what James Dean said to Jay to do away with his fears, but he did so casually, effortlessly, and completely. What I do remember is what Jay said excitedly after he left. "Jimmy says he can go so fast on his motorcycle that no one can see him!"

On October 1, 1955, I was in Mexico City to interview the actor Cantinflas, who was filming a cameo role for *Around the World in 80 Days*. Bill Blowitz, press agent on the film, and I had just finished breakfast when we went by the hotel newsstand. I noticed a copy of the Saturday *New York Herald Tribune* on the rack, and glanced at the front page. In the lower right-hand corner was the headline: FILM ACTOR JAMES DEAN, 24, KILLED IN SPORTS CAR CRASH.

I must have turned ashen because Bill asked me if I was all right. "Jimmy Dean's been killed," I said and handed the paper to him. "He asked me to go with him to the race in Salinas yesterday just before we left L.A."

As Bill read the story I had conflicting thoughts. I wanted to call home and tell Elly to be careful how she broke the news to Jay, who I knew would be devastated. Then I realized that the news was a day old. I felt strongly that there was something that I, a newsman and friend, should be doing about Jimmy's death. I wanted to add something human and personal to the wire service report that my paper had put on the front page.

I called my editor in New York, who said, "Dean was really not that well known to warrant much more space than we've already given him."

I realized he was right. Of the three pictures Jimmy had starred in, only one, *East of Eden*, had been released, and although his performance was acclaimed by the critics, the general public was scarcely aware of him. There was no way that I or anyone else at that time could predict the impact his death would have on young people all over the world.

After Jimmy died, his second and third pictures, *Rebel Without a Cause* and *Giant*, were released and his fans grew posthumously to legendary proportions. Many of them refused to accept his death, and a worldwide James Dean cult began to develop.

It has been thirty-seven years since James Dean died, and over the years I often considered writing a book about him, but discarded the idea because I felt my memories might be too private, and I didn't want to betray a trust. My recollections of conversations and events have matured to the point, however, that I believe I have something to say about him that has not yet been said.

To buttress my own recollections and to write this book, I have interviewed most of the people who knew Jimmy, including myself. We are all past middle age (Jimmy would have been sixty this year) and our memories of Jimmy differ in many important ways. I have come to the conclusion that although we all knew Jimmy, each of us knew a different person, one who was a mass of contradictions and who presented a unique persona to each of us.

Depending on which of his ex-lovers I interviewed he was either heterosexual, asexual, bisexual, or homosexual. Friends describe him as generous and mean-spirited, moody and a party animal, macho and feminine, wise for his years and supremely adolescent. Film and television directors who worked with Jimmy referred to him in such contradictory terms as tractable, impossible, arrogant, and open to suggestion. Some who knew him claim he was a manic-depressive with a death wish while others believe he had a tremendous lust for life. Everyone agrees that he was a fascinating person and tremendously gifted actor who was able to tap into something deep inside of himself that resonates within all of us.

Chapter One

THE OUTSIDER

James Dean grew up in Fairmount, Indiana, a small Hoosier town with a population of 2,600 that had changed very little since the turn of the century. Business buildings extended for two blocks along Main Street, and the town's institutions included a weekly newspaper, *The Fairmount News*, a volunteer fire department, an elementary school, fifteen churches, including three Quaker meeting houses and one Baptist church, a railroad depot that had seen busier days, and a few quiet factories. Surrounding the town was rich farmland.

Beneath the prosaic surface, however, Fairmount differed from most other Midwestern towns. For every 230 persons in Fairmount, one had been listed in *Who's Who*—fourteen times the national average at the time. And of those natives, most were teachers or college presidents or writers. There were no actors, for the culture of Fairmount was not conducive to breeding them. The one movie house in town was closed because the townspeople, most of them Quakers, would not support it.

The first Deans to settle in Fairmount arrived in 1815 from around Lexington, Kentucky, and settled in Grant County. They were mostly farm folk, but Jimmy's grandfather Cal Dean, a drinking man before he got religion, was an auctioneer. The Deans were not poor people, but none of them were rich. Because so many of them lived in such a small area, the Dean family—and the families related by marriage—were closely knit.

Jimmy's mother, Mildred Marie Wilson, was a short, plump, dark-haired farmer's daughter from Gas City, a town near Fairmount. Like the Deans, her family had settled in Grant County around 1815. Mildred was just twenty years old when she was introduced at a dance to Winton Dean, a tall, thin, quiet bespectacled man two years her senior. Winton had been raised to be a farmer like three generations of his forebears, but instead struck out on his own and became a dental technician at the Veterans Administration in Marion.

After a few months of courtship, Mildred discovered she was pregnant. The only one way to solve such a problem in those days was marriage. Mildred was a Methodist, Winton a Quaker, so they applied for a marriage license on July 26, 1930, and were married three days later by the Reverend Emma Payne, a minister of the Wesleyan faith.

The wedding was so sudden that the newlyweds hadn't had time to make plans. On their wedding night they knocked on the door of the couple who had introduced them, Hazel and David Payne (no relation to the reverend). Winton explained that he and Mildred had just been married and had no place to spend their honeymoon night: could they spend it with the Paynes?

The frame house, which had once belonged to David's grandmother, was tiny, with two bedrooms, but both couples got along well together for two weeks until Winton found lodgings for himself and Mildred in a rambling house in Marion known as The Seven Gables Apartments.

When the time came for Mildred to have her baby, she ignored Winton's insistence that she go to a hospital. She preferred to deliver her firstborn at home with the family doctor in attendance. Winton's grandmother, Ella Turner, was a midwife, and arrangements were made for her to help out. On Sunday, February 8, 1931, at 2:00 A.M., after five hours of labor, Mildred gave birth to an eight-pound, ten-ounce baby boy.

Dr. Victor V. Cameron filled out the birth certificate, spelling out slowly James Byron Dean, the name Mildred and Winton had earlier selected for the boy they both wanted. It was a combination of the names of James Amick, chief dental officer at the Veterans Administration in Marion where Winton worked, and Thomas Byron Vice, Winton's best friend and a florist. Dr. Cameron's bill for the delivery was fifteen dollars.

From the very first, Mildred made Jimmy the center of her life. She nursed him for eight months and then bottle-fed him while rocking him on her lap. She devoted herself so completely to him that Hazel Payne, mother of a young son herself, protested that Mildred smothered Jimmy with attention. Mildred retorted, "He's all that I have, and I love him."

Mildred taught Jimmy how to draw, read classics and poetry aloud to him by the hour, and played games with him. For one of their games she built a cardboard theater; using dolls as actors, the two of them made up plays and stories. From time to time they put on skits for Winton and other members of the family. Both Mildred and Jimmy basked in the applause, and Mildred was fond of saying that one day her beautiful son was going to be a great actor.

The Deans were young and struggling to get by, but Jimmy had all the toys they could afford and, if anything, was spoiled beyond his parents' means. "He had a large anxiety to do many different things," Winton told me. "He had to try everything, and he soon outgrew most of the toys we bought him. He always seemed to be getting ahead of himself."

When Jimmy was a toddler Winton arranged to rent a cottage alongside Back Creek, a small stream that bordered the edge of the farm owned by Winton's sister, Ortense, and her husband, Marcus Winslow. The farm was in Fairmount, just a few miles from Marion, and in an idyllic setting. The typically Midwestern two-story white frame farmhouse resting on a stone foundation had been built in 1901 on the edge of a 178-acre lot. The house had fourteen rooms and an expansive front porch shaded by ancient oaks and sycamores with a porch swing suspended from chains anchored in the roof. Everything a youngster would like was there on the farm: horses, dogs, hogs, and cows. Marcus rigged up a swing on a tree for Jimmy, and when the chores were done, Marcus would play with him and take him for walks. A stream meandered through the property and widened into a pond where Marcus taught Jimmy to fish for shiners, red horses, and bream and where they swam in the summer and skated in the winter.

Faded photos taken when Jimmy was a child show the Deans to be a happy family. In most of the pictures Mildred is either holding Jimmy, a small, handsome, tow-headed smiling child, or standing with her arms on his shoulders.

When Jimmy had learned to write, his favorite game was the wishing game. When he went to bed each night, he'd write out a wish on a piece of paper and place the paper underneath his pillow. Mildred would slip in while he was asleep, read the wish, and, if possible, make it come true the next day.

In 1936 the Veterans Administration transferred Winton to the Sawtelle Veterans Administration in West Los Angeles, California. The Deans rented a five-room furnished flat in Santa Monica, and Jimmy was enrolled at the McKinley School on Santa Monica Boulevard. Mildred also scraped together enough money to pay for Jimmy to take violin and tap dancing lessons.

When Jimmy was nine, his mother, began to suffer terribly from stomach pains. X rays revealed that she had cancer of the uterus, and it was already considerably advanced. Winton wrote to his mother in Fairmount, telling her that Mildred was dying and asking her to come to California immediately.

Two days before Mildred's death, Winton, a taciturn man not given to easily showing emotion, tried to tell Jimmy that his mother would not be with them much longer. "Jimmy said nothing—just looked at me," Winton said. "Even as a child he wasn't much to talk about things close to him. He never liked to talk about his hurts."

Mildred Dean died in the hospital at the age of twenty-nine on the afternoon of July 14, 1940, with Jimmy and Winton at her bedside.

Winton had sold his car to pay for Mildred's medical bills and couldn't afford to go to the funeral in Fairmount. Two days after Mildred's death, Jimmy and his grandmother Emma Dean brought her body home to Fairmount on a train from Los Angeles. Each time the train stopped, Jimmy would rush out and run to the baggage car to make certain his mother's coffin was still there.

For two days Mildred's open coffin lay in the Winslow living room. Relatives remember how, just before the funeral, Jimmy went to the coffin for a final look at his mother and insisted on straightening out the hair on her forehead. He also snipped off a lock of her hair.

Funeral services were held in the house. Mildred was buried in Grant Memorial Park in Marion, only a few miles from her birthplace and the Winslow farm.

The next day a family conference was held in the Winslow home, and a telephone call made to Winton, who said that he had to remain at his job in California, and he had no one to take care of Jimmy during the day. "Is there anyone in the family Jimmy can stay with while I get my feet under me again?" he asked.

Times were tough and farmers were just beginning to recover from the Depression. None of the Deans were having it easy financially. Crops were poor, and business in general was bad. Jimmy was an extra mouth to feed and a young one at that. The only members of the family enthusiastic about taking him in were Ortense and Marcus Winslow. They had one child, a fourteen-year-old daughter named Joan, but they had always wanted a son. They agreed to raise Jimmy as their own until Winton was able to take care of him.

The Winslows were honest, hardworking, kindly people active in community affairs. Ortense, a plump, motherly woman, was a prime mover in the Women's Christian Temperance Union and played the piano for the Friends' Sunday School. Marcus, a slight, bespectacled man, was a graduate of Earlham College, a Quaker School near Fairmount, and in his youth had been a tennis player of some local repute. His nickname was "Rack," an abbreviation of racquet.

The Winslows accepted Jimmy as though he were their own child. They even gave up their bedroom and moved across the hall because he liked their maple bedroom furniture.

For the first two weeks in his new home Jimmy slept with Mildred's lock of hair under his pillow. But the wishing game had died with his mother. At first he was quiet and morose, and the Winslows left him alone to work out his grief, but they started him in school right away to keep his mind busy. A classmate of Jimmy's in the fourth grade recalls that Jimmy burst into tears at his desk one day during arithmetic class. When the teacher asked what was the matter, Jimmy sobbed, "I miss my mother."

During an interview I did with Ortense Winslow shortly after Jimmy's death, I asked if he ever talked about his mother in those early days. "Only rarely," she answered.

I always had the sense that Jimmy, like many young children who lose a parent, felt somehow responsible for his mother's death— otherwise why had his father sent him away? From conversations I had with Jimmy years later, I felt that he never forgave his father for sending him away, and carried that resentment with him all his life.

Pictures in the Winslow family album taken at the time reveal Jimmy to be sturdy but small for his age, with a handsome, almost beautiful face. He wears eyeglasses in most of the photographs because, even at that age, he was extremely nearsighted.

Jimmy easily and quickly adapted to the routine of farm life: Marcus grew corn, oats, and hay. He had his chores, such as milking, gathering freshly laid eggs, helping feed the stock, and in a few months he knew every detail of the farm machinery. On Sunday mornings he went to the Back Creek Friends Church with Ortense and Marcus. For Christmas that first year, Ortense and Marcus gave Jimmy a drum.

His days were busy with school, but there was plenty of time for play, especially in the summer, when Marcus turned the barn into a gymnasium, installed a trapeze, and instructed Jimmy in gymnastics. Many was the night Ortense had to go out to the barn to get her two "boys." "Jimmy had all the fun that could be had and then some," recalls Ortense. "He put more living into every day than anyone I ever saw."

During the winters Jimmy and his friends played hockey on the creek behind the barn where Marcus had rigged up electric lights so they could skate at night. Most of the boys had clamp-on skates and used branches for a stick, but Marcus bought Jimmy real hockey skates, a regular stick, and a puck.

Even as a child, Jimmy was attracted to danger and risk taking. He and his neighbor Bob Pulley made a ramp in the barn that ran from the hayloft out the barn door. At speed, they could almost make it to the street in a heavy dolly cart. Marcus soon put an end to the game, however, claiming it was too dangerous.

There wasn't much that Jimmy didn't try. He broke four front teeth attempting a trapeze stunt Marcus had shown him (during a rare trip to see his father in California, Jimmy received a dental bridge made by his father.) He was thrown while trying to ride a Brahma bull at a county fair. He discovered a book on Yoga and practiced holding his breath until he fainted.

Jimmy seemed to be a natural actor. At family gatherings he would entertain everyone with his mimicry. If his grandfather sat with his knees crossed, Jimmy crossed his. If someone said something with a particularly odd inflection, Jimmy was able to ape the pronunciation to perfection to the delight of his audience.

His talent did not go unnoticed by Ortense, who when Jimmy was ten and in the seventh grade asked him to read for a medal at the Temperance Union. Jimmy was unimpressed by the stories of vice and tragedy brought by liquor—"gory odes," he called them— but he knew that his recitations made Ortense proud. On his first outing he won a prize with his reading.

He soon won silver and gold medals for other readings before the WCTU, and Ortense looked forward to the day when he would compete for the coveted Pearl Medal.

Jimmy didn't want to read for the Pearl Medal because the reading was scheduled for the night of a track meet he wanted to attend, but Ortense insisted. Jimmy went to the hall, and when the time came he stepped up onto the stage before the audience. A baby was fussing and making noise. Jimmy stood still and seemed to be listening to it attentively. Not a word came from his lips. Then he walked off the stage, to the humiliation of Ortense. He later claimed his mind had gone blank.

"I was sure then what I had suspected all along," Ortense said. "You couldn't make James Dean do things he didn't want to do. He had a mind all of his own."

When Jimmy was eleven the Winslows had a son of their own whom they named Marcus Jr., but called Markie. Jimmy resented the baby because he took attention away from him. Instead of spending all his spare time with Jimmy, Marcus began dividing it between the two boys.

Despite the love and attention he got from the Winslows, Marcus and Ortense recognized that Jimmy was not a typical farmboy. In conversations with me years later, Jimmy said that he had considered himself an outsider in a town where the principal virtues were things he deemed unimportant.

Undoubtedly, the townspeople also sensed that he was different and nonconforming. He spoke his mind when he felt like it; he dressed as he pleased and disliked dressing up; he was interested in dramatics and was not afraid to admit it even though such an interest in a farm community held him up to ridicule. And he liked to be left alone.

He also bore the stigma of being virtually an orphan, since his father rarely wrote, called, or visited him. Despite the honest love of Marcus and Ortense, Jimmy was always aware that they were not his real parents.

In 1943 Jimmy enrolled in the seventh grade at Fairmount High School, a mammoth red-brick building almost in the center of town. Myrtle Gilbreath, one of Jimmy's teachers, was amazed at his fund of general knowledge. "He knew something about everything. He had a keen mind." Yet his marks were only fair. His average during the first few grades of high school indicated the trend his mind was taking. He got a D in algebra, a D in spelling, and a B+ in psychology.

Gurney Maddingly, his art teacher as well as a former Broadway actor, remembers Jimmy as a promising student. One painting of Jimmy's still stands out in his memory. "It was of people coming up out of the grave. I knew his mother had died when he was a kid, and he was always fascinated with the idea of meeting somebody after death. We talked about mediums who contacted the dead, particularly Harry Houdini, and we discussed whether the pyramids were built by the Egyptians or people from outer space. He said, 'When we finally die we'll know all those things but we'll have to wait until then.' "

Jimmy also joined the 4-H Club, more as a concession to the Winslows than out of any real love of farming. The first year he raised baby chicks, the second he grew a garden, then he tended cattle. The following year he prepared an exhibit of soils, a notion that stemmed from the fact that he had been watching a crew at work drilling a gas well on the Winslow property. He had watched the process from start to finish and had collected soil samples from every level, and these he mounted in a box he had made himself.

Hugh Caughell, Jimmy's biology teacher, recalls that the county agricultural agent had prepared his awards in advance but had nothing for a soil exhibit. "But the agent did have a grand champion rosette award for the Champion Guernsey Bull left over from the previous summer. He gave that to Jimmy, who had a sense of humor. He took it home and hung it in his bedroom."

But not all of his teachers remember Jimmy so favorably. John Potter, principal of Fairmount High, remembers Jimmy as a "troublemaker," but adds, "Kids like him are always telling you that they want you to involve them in something."

Marcus had always wanted to own a motorcycle as a youngster, and like many parents, he was determined that his "son" have some of the things he had missed. He bought Jimmy a Whizzer—a motorized Czech bicycle—for his thirteenth birthday. By his sophomore year in high school Jimmy traded the Whizzer for a small used motorcycle, and since he was one of the few students with one, he was somewhat of a local celebrity.

Jimmy's favorite hangout was Marvin Carter's Cycle Shop, only a few hundred yards down Fairmount Pike from the farm. The small one-room shop was crowded most every night with youngsters and adults tinkering with their bikes and authoritatively discussing such things as cams and headers. Like many young men, they were obsessed with their vehicles and speed.

Jimmy's real passion, however, was taking himself and his vehicle to the extreme limit or, as jet pilots put it, "pressing the envelope." He delighted in performing such daredevil stunts as racing along at fifty miles an hour while lying flat on the saddle. Dick Beck, a childhood friend who sometimes rode on the bike with Jimmy, recalls that he could do wheelies and lay a bike on the ground long before such stunts became popular.

When I visited Fairmount recently, Beck showed me an apple tree near Park Cemetery sitting on the inside corner of a sharp curve. "Jimmy would drive down the road flat out toward the curve and come so close to the tree that he could either reach out and touch it or kick it."

"If he'd only fallen once, things might have been different," Marcus told me with hindsight. "Trouble is, he never got hurt, and he never found anything he couldn't do well almost the first time he tried it. Just one fall off the bike and maybe he'd have been afraid of speed, but he was without fear."

Years later—just six months before another fast vehicle put an end to his life—Jimmy told columnist Hedda Hopper that he'd been riding motorcycles since he was sixteen. "I don't tear around," he told her, "but intelligently motivate myself through the quagmire and entanglement of your streets." Putting aside the stilted tone—he could fashion his speech to suit his listeners—I think Jimmy believed he was a good driver. And so did I. More important, motorcycles, like bongo drums, were part of Jimmy long before he arrived in Hollywood, long before they were a part of anyone's screen image. Shortly after Jimmy finished *East of Eden* I read somewhere—I honestly believe it was in Hopper's column—that as a boy Jimmy had herded cattle on his motorcycle. Since that didn't ring quite right to me, I asked Jimmy about it. His response was to roll his eyes, light a cigarette, and change the subject entirely.

Jimmy also had a passion for cars. One of his school friends had a '34 Plymouth coupe with a rumble seat that had been souped up at Carter's. All the boys took turns driving it from time to time. Dick Beck recalls that Jimmy held the record for going through Suicide Curve, an S curve on a gravel road near Park Cemetery. Jimmy was able to slide through it at top speed. Once he was challenged to a race by another boy driving a Chevy. The other boy tried hard to keep up with Jimmy, but he rolled over and crashed in the curve.

Dick Beck remembers Jimmy driving Marcus's old pickup truck onto the middle of the lake when it was frozen, and spinning around so fast that he ground a hole in the ice and barely made it to safety.

During summer vacations Jimmy did chores such as helping Marcus bale hay. He also worked part-time for ten cents an hour in a local factory canning tomatoes.

At night he and his friends would pile into a car and drive to the Hill Top Drive Inn in Marion to listen to the jukebox, drink frosted malts, and try to pick up the local girls.

Like most small Midwestern towns, Fairmount was basketball

crazy: games between Fairmount and Marion were major competitions and entertainments in the lives of the people in both communities. A star basketball player in a small town is a hero; even a nonconformist can be forgiven if he is a top scorer. Jimmy decided that he was going to make the high school basketball team despite his size.

Marcus, who had once wanted to be an athletic instructor himself, spent hours teaching Jimmy to dribble, pass, and shoot. In the school gym, the other boys soon found that the small youngster behind the ever-present spectacles was someone to reckon with. Because he was smaller than most of his teammates, he had to jump for most every shot, thus earning himself the nickname "Jumping Jim."

The first newspaper item ever published about James Dean appeared on the sports page of *The Fairmount News* in 1948. It called him "an outstanding threat on the High School team. . . . Dean accumulated forty points in three games."

Paul Weaver, coach of the Fairmount High School team, discovered that Jimmy, though a good player, had to be handled with kid gloves. "He wasn't too coachable," Weaver said. "I had to be careful about changing his style of play, and I soon learned not to embarrass him in front of the other boys."

Weaver had discovered early on what many directors would later learn, that Jimmy was just not tractable. He wanted to do things his way or he would not do them at all.

Around this time Ortense and Marcus arranged for Jimmy to go with them to visit a family where there was a young girl his age. Jimmy was polite all through the evening, and when they returned home Ortense asked him what he thought of the girl.

Jimmy went upstairs to his room and in a few minutes came down with a watercolor painting of a glass of red wine spilled on a tablecloth. "This is what the evening meant to me," he said, explaining that the wine on the tablecloth was like his time—wasted.

Marcus Winslow was the most important male in Jimmy's life until his junior year in high school, when he began to rebel against authority at school and at home. Like most teenagers he was aching for freedom of action and expression, and he was beginning to realize that there was a world outside of Fairmount where new sensations and people could be found.

"He became hard to handle, and we didn't know what was the matter," Marcus told me. "He didn't take any more stock in us and refused to help out. We were at wits' end. He was no longer one of us."

Jimmy began his senior year at Fairmount High in September 1948. By now a letter man in basketball and track, he decided to take up pole vaulting. Everyone told him he was too small, but his mind was made up. In his first big scholastic meet, Jimmy set a record for Grant County that was only recently broken. Having proven that he could do it, Jimmy never pole vaulted again.

Because of his superiority in athletics Jimmy experienced the sweet thrill of being a local celebrity. Important men like the superintendent of schools, Frank Gayley, would stop and chat with him, saying that the whole town was proud of him. And he soon became a role model for the younger students, who began to mimic the way he walked in a curious slouch as if perpetually waiting to straighten up and shoot a basket. The mimic was being mimicked and he liked it.

During his senior year several factors converged that were to determine the course of his life. During that one year he discovered that he had some real talent for acting, and he was introduced to an experience that was to start him on the road to sexual ambivalence.

Jimmy had a schoolboy infatuation for Dr. James DeWeerd, pastor of the Wesleyan Church in Fairmount. DeWeerd was something of a hero to most of the boys in Fairmount. During World War II he had served as a chaplain with the infantry at Cassino. He had come home with a Silver Star for gallantry in action, a Purple Heart with Oak Leaf Cluster, and a deep hole in his stomach plus a chest full of scars from shrapnel wounds. To Jimmy, DeWeerd represented everything he felt was missing in the closed culture of Fairmount.

DeWeerd was stocky and handsome, with full lips, a jovial laugh, and blue eyes. His conversation was liberally sprinkled with spiritual homilies, but as Jimmy was soon to discover he had a dark side.

The pastor was an educated man, and his combination of evangelism and genuine culture intrigued Jimmy, who considered De-Weerd the only man of the world in Fairmount, and the only one who understood him.

Although born and raised in the town, DeWeerd was openly critical of Fairmount and its limited ways of life. His soul-searing sermons fascinated the townspeople—and frightened them, too. In his business suit and tie, he was not one of them; no one had ever seen him wearing overalls. He was considered "prissy" by some of the townspeople, and was called "Dr. Weird" by others. It was no secret that he liked to take a group of the young boys to the YMCA gym in Anderson and suggest that they all swim nude together, a cause of some gossip in town.

Jimmy had never been in a home like the one DeWeerd shared with his aged mother. For one thing there was a flower garden outside the house, one of perhaps two homes in town with such an extravagance. At dinner there was white linen and gleaming silver on the table, and colored light bulbs in the lamps. They dined to the music of Tchaikovsky and talked about poets and philosophy. Jimmy had not been exposed to a sophisticated world except in the movies he saw, but he had a good mind and was aware that there was more to life than farming and Fairmount, the small parochial town that DeWeerd derided. The older man realized that Jimmy was different, that he had ambitions to get more out of life than was available in Fairmount, and he took on the role of mentor.

Jimmy soon became a welcome guest at the DeWeerd home, and he spent many evenings watching movies the pastor had taken of his vacations and bullfights in Mexico. DeWeerd introduced each new adventure by saying, "The more things you know how to do, and the more things you experience, the better off you will be." In the light of what was to come, that philosophy had ominous undertones.

A year after Jimmy's death, Dr. DeWeerd told me how he and Jimmy often went for long rides in the country in his convertible. During one of those drives, DeWeerd turned off the main road and parked under a tree. He had rarely talked with Jimmy about his wartime adventures, but on this day he told Jimmy how he had gotten the gaping wound in his stomach. He then asked Jimmy if he would like to put his hand inside the wound, which was almost deep enough for the boy's entire fist. The intimacy frightened and excited Jimmy.

To DeWeerd, Jimmy poured out his belief that he must be evil, or his mother would not have died and his father would not have sent him away. Jimmy confided that he was afraid that people would suspect how evil he was and not love him. DeWeerd confirmed Jimmy's beliefs. "I taught Jim that he was depraved and vile, that he had to seek salvation," DeWeerd said. And who better to offer salvation than the pastor himself?

On other drives there were more personal intimacies, and soon they had a secret bond that Jimmy was warned he must never reveal. It was the beginning of a homosexual relationship that would endure over many years, during which time DeWeerd came to consider Jimmy his protégé. "Jimmy never mentioned our relationship nor did I," the pastor told me. "It would not have helped either of us."

Forty-five years ago it would have been essentially impossible for a male in this country to grow up without feeling that any kind of homosexual contact was sinful or sick, in addition to being illegal. I can only imagine the mixed message Jimmy must have received when he was seduced by a religious person, a man above moral reproach. Some youngsters would have been so terrified of homosexual contact that they would have hit or run away from the pastor. There are others who would not have been overawed by their mentor, and would have said they didn't want anything to do with him. But Jimmy did neither of these things, presumably because he didn't have that strong an inhibition against male-male contact based on his acceptance of the pastor's philosophy that new experiences contribute to mental growth. And, of course, DeWeerd was only confirming what Jimmy had suspected about himself all along—that he was basically evil, for otherwise his mother would never have left him.

Jimmy once told me that, as a child, he had made up his mind not to be physically or mentally confined to small-town morality and thinking. Therefore it may have been easier for him to accept his relationship with DeWeerd, especially when he found the world didn't come to an end because of their "sinful" relationship.

It is likely that, because of his relationship with DeWeerd, Jimmy began to have doubts about his masculinity. Perhaps to put those doubts to rest, to prove that he was not "queer" or a "fairy," he started an affair with Elizabeth McPherson, a young physical education teacher at the high school who was also an art student.

Gurney Maddingly remembers that Jimmy was always in the church where Betty worked on her art. Sometimes while Betty was working, Jimmy would climb up into the belfry, where he carved his name on the wood rafters. "Every time I went by the church when they were together, the door was locked. He told me that he had asked her to marry him but she said there was too much difference in their ages. I got married when I was forty-three and my wife was twenty, so I wasn't the one to talk with him about age differences."

The simple reality that was to distinguish much of Jimmy's later life was being formulated—he was able to have sex with either a man or a woman, and with ease. But he was enough of a Quaker to believe that what he was doing was wrong. As a result I believe that he established a pattern, one that would characterize his later relationships with friends, male as well as female: he would never let anyone get truly close to him.

Toward the end of his senior year, Jimmy went with DeWeerd to Indianapolis to watch a race and was introduced to Cannonball Baker, a famous racing driver. A few days later the pastor and Jimmy talked about automobile racing and of the possibility of sudden death.

"I taught Jimmy to believe in personal immortality," DeWeerd told me many years ago. "He had no fear of death because he believed—as I do—that death is merely control of mind over matter." That must have been an intriguing philosophy to a young man who drove flat out whenever the opportunity presented itself.

In the spring of 1949, Jimmy was one of two Fairmount High students to win the state competition of the National Forensic League held in Peru, Indiana, which entitled him to enter the Nationals to be held in Longmont, Colorado. *The Fairmount News* ran pictures of Jimmy and the other student with the headline: F.H.S. STUDENTS WIN STATE MEETS. Marcus was dumbfounded at the news; Jimmy had never mentioned the league at home. The Winslows felt the gap widening between them and Jimmy.

With DeWeerd and Adeline Nall, his school drama teacher, as his mentors, Jimmy prepared for the national competition by memorizing "The Madman," from Dickens's *Pickwick Papers.* He lay upstairs in his bed at night reading the story by flashlight because he wanted to downplay the importance of the contest to Marcus and Ortense—on the chance that he failed to win. And he occasionally baby-sat for Gurney Maddingly's young son and daughter, using the occasion as an excuse to read his lines aloud into Gurney's wire recorder and then play the lines back. On weekends, when Maddingly visited his sick father in Muncie, he would leave the house unlocked so Jimmy could use the recorder.

Adeline Nall recalls that, from the start, Jimmy had a natural feeling for the mood contrasts required by the monologue, which opens with a scream and calls for the character to subtly drift from sanity to madness and back again.

One day in class, David Fox, a junior, began to make sarcastic remarks about Jimmy's reading. Despite Mrs. Nall's admonitions to David to quiet down, he continued heckling Jimmy.

"What're you trying to do, Dean?" Fox asked. "We know you're a great talent, a regular John Barrymore."

Jimmy's blue eyes blazed as he told Fox to shut up or he'd shut him up, but the taunting continued as the other students snickered.

After class everyone went to the playground where the two boys squared off and scuffled. Roland DuBois, the school principal, happened on the brawl and demanded to know who threw the first punch. Both boys were silent.

"You're both expelled," DuBois said with finality.

Then Jimmy spoke up. "I threw the first punch, sir." He was expelled from school but soon reinstated.

A year after Jimmy's death I dramatized the effect the suspension had on him and his family in a *Redbook* magazine article based on interviews with Ortense and Marcus.

The teenage boy sat slumped on his motorcycle and looked over the rims of his glasses at the words: Mildred

Wilson Dean, 1910–1940. A choking sensation crept into his throat. His mind hurled questions at the tombstone. Why did you die and leave me? Were you in much pain? How does it feel to be dead?

In the distance he saw a car entering the gate of the cemetery. He kicked at the starter pedal, gunned the motor, and left in a roar of speed. He hurtled down the country road and let the cold wind sweep the dark thoughts from his mind. Ahead of him was Marion, Indiana. Without being aware of it, he detoured to drive past the house where he had been born.

Back on the highway he sped toward Gas City. Within minutes he was in front of Charles Nolan's house. Charles was the uncle who had taught him to ride. He gunned the motor impatiently, waiting for a sign from the house. There was none. His calling card was a trail of blue exhaust.

From Gas City he headed toward Fairmount and home. It was supper time, and he knew Ortense would be waiting dinner for him. Before reaching the crossroads, he hesitated a moment but took the highway through town even though it meant he would be a few minutes later. He was in no hurry to face Marcus and Ortense, who must already have heard that he had been expelled from school.

In the distance he saw a car about to turn onto the highway. He quickly calculated the speed of the car and its distance from him. He could make it. Only a second of time was saved, but James Dean hated slowing down.

The roar of his coming preceded him. Marvin Carter, owner of Carter's Cycle Shop, said to his wife, Alice, "Here comes Jimmy Dean."

"There went Jimmy Dean, you mean," she said with a laugh.

"That boy sure is a pistol, ain't he," said a young man lounging in the shop.

"Yeah," said Carter. "He's got one speed—wide open."

Past the Back Creek Friends Church sped the boy on the motorcycle. Then, hardly slowing down, he skidded the machine into the driveway of his home.

He gunned the motor as he went past the front door on his way to the barn. The sound of the machine and the rumble of its wheels on the boards caused the cows underneath to move restlessly in their stalls.

He pursed his lips and mooed. The cows stopped their rustling to listen. He giggled with delight. Heavily stomping on the boards he shuffled toward the farm house.

There was no one in the dining area, but the table was set for supper. From the kitchen Ortense called, "That you, Jimmy?"

"Uh-h-h," he said.

Marcus was in the living room reading the evening paper, round spectacles on the end of his nose. To go to his room Jimmy would have to pass him. Rather than do that he sat at his place at the table and waited for Ortense to announce that dinner was ready.

It was a good meal, eaten for the most part in silence. He knew nothing would be said at the table, so he tried to prolong the minutes before Ortense would begin to clear off and Marcus would go back into the living room and the evening paper.

When Ortense got up with plates in hand Jimmy offered to help with the dishes. She was firm in refusing. There was nothing left to do but wait them out. Marcus was back in the living room so he decided to try for the stairs and his room.

"Jimmy!" Marcus had been waiting for him.

He paused at the foot of the stairs and murmured, "Yes."

"Why don't you take your gun tomorrow and spend the day hunting?"

The moment he was dreading had come and gone. That was all Marcus intended to say about it. He mumbled, "Okay," and climbed up the stairs to his room.

He left the door ajar slightly so he could hear what was said downstairs.

He heard Ortense put a dish down and go into the living room.

"What did you say to him?" she asked her husband.

"I told him to take his gun and go hunting."

"But, Marcus, he's been expelled. This is serious."

"What else can I do? I can't hit him, he's too big for that, and besides it would do no good, and you know it. I don't know how to reach him, let alone punish him."

Quietly Jimmy tiptoed to the door and shut it. He took off his boots and lay down on the bed. The empty, unsatisfied feeling was in his chest again. He hadn't wanted to come home and face the hurt he knew would be in the eyes of his aunt and uncle. But he didn't know whether he wanted to be scolded and punished, or hugged and kissed, or ignored. He wanted something that hadn't happened. Was it always going to be that way?

The school raised the money to send Jimmy and Adeline Nall by train to Longmont. On the night before the finals, when he was supposed to discuss strategy with Adeline Nall, she telephoned his host's home only to discover that Jimmy had borrowed a car and gone out on the town.

Although competitors were supposed to appear in suits and ties, Jimmy insisted on wearing an open shirt and jeans on the theory that he couldn't act crazy all dressed up. Also the entries were supposed to be no more than ten minutes, and despite Mrs. Nall's insistence Jimmy refused to cut his monologue down to less than twelve.

When the finalists' names were posted, James Dean was not one of them. There were only five finalists in Dramatic Declamation and he had placed sixth. Adeline recalls how miserable Jimmy was, huddled in his seat and heartsick that he was out of the running. She believes, however, that Jimmy learned the consequences of not concentrating, a lesson he was never to forget.

During Jimmy's tenure at Fairmount High, the school put on

about twenty plays, and Jimmy was in most of them, doing any odd job that was required if he was not onstage. His family attended most of the performances, but the one that convinced his grandmother Dean that Jimmy was an actor was his appearance in a church play called *To Them That Sleep in Darkness*. Jimmy played a blind boy so convincingly that his grandmother sobbed all the way through the performance.

In October of Jimmy's senior year, the Thespian Club presented *Goon With the Wind*, a spoof on the Frankenstein legend written in rhyme by Gurney Maddingly. Jimmy played Frankenstein, and David Nall, Adeline's son, was the narrator and hero. Jimmy relished the notion of being able to screech and howl and express his anguish at being trapped in an alien body in a strange land. He got in character quickly, so quickly that one day while Maddingly was making him up, Jimmy growled and bit the teacher's hand.

Maddingly also coached Jimmy with his role. "I told him that whatever you do, don't just stand still when you don't have lines. Anybody can act if they have something to say, but when you don't have lines you have to be in character and move around." Jimmy took Maddingly's advice and soon drove the other actors up the wall because he was constantly in motion during their scenes.

The play, put on in the school gym, was a big success. "Jim was thrilled with the fact that the kids didn't really believe it was him in the makeup," says Maddingly.

Money raised from the play, part of the school's annual Halloween festival, was used to send the senior class to Washington, D.C., in place of the class having their traditional graduation prom. The trip was memorable for Jimmy because Betty was one of the class sponsors. The group stayed at the Roosevelt Apartments at Sixteenth Street NW in the city. The girls and boys were on separate floors, but the boys soon found a way to tie sheets together so they could climb into the girls' bedrooms. As a result, Jimmy was able to spend his nights with Betty.

On his return home, Jimmy was asked by the senior class to read the benediction at commencement, May 16, 1949, when he graduated along with a class of forty-nine other students. In his Black and Gold yearbook, he wrote: "I bequeath my temper to Dave Fox." Underneath his picture in the yearbook the editors wrote: "Jim is our regular basketball guy, and when you're around him time will fly." Ironically, there was no mention of his acting ability.

After graduation from high school, Jimmy, who was eighteen, was eligible for the draft. DeWeerd told Jimmy he could get a deferment if he claimed he was homosexual, a suggestion Jimmy ignored. He registered for the draft, certain that he would get a deferment because of his bad eyesight.

Marcus originally had wanted Jimmy to attend his alma mater, Earlham College, but Winton, who had remarried and was presumably trying to make up to his son, wrote and suggested that Jimmy come live with him, and he would assume the costs of a college in California. Winton and Jimmy talked about the possibility of Jimmy considering sports as a career, with an eye to becoming an athletic coach. Jimmy agreed it might be a good idea, and said he'd think on it. He was determined to be an actor and thought that in Los Angeles he would have a chance to find out whether he had any real talent.

James Dean had no idea what California held in store for him, but he knew his future lay outside of Fairmount.

Since Jimmy's grades were not high enough for admission to UCLA—they were mostly Ds—it was decided that he would go to Santa Monica City College for a semester to prepare. In addition to being near his father's home, the school had a good basketball team and a theater arts course.

The night before Jimmy was to leave for Los Angeles, Marcus and Ortense held a farewell party for him at their home. *The Fairmount News* dutifully reported the party under the headline: JAMES DEAN WAS HONORED AT FAREWELL PARTY MONDAY NIGHT. Many of Jimmy's friends were there, with the notable exception of Dr. DeWeerd.

Years later Jimmy told me that before leaving Fairmount he stopped by his mother's grave in Marion where he knelt at her headstone and whispered, "If you are ever remembered it will be because of me."

Chapter Two

MACBETH, ST. JOHN, AND A BLOODIED CAPE

Jimmy was eighteen years old when he arrived in Los Angeles in June 1949 to live with his father and step-mother in a small apartment on Saltair Avenue near the Veterans Administration Hospital. During the nine years Jimmy had been in Fairmount he had seen Winton rarely, when his father visited him while on furlough from the army (in 1943 Winton had been drafted into the Army Medical Corps). Winton rarely wrote to Jimmy and sent only occasional small checks to the Winslows for his son's upkeep. Jimmy wrote to his father only when "Mom," his name for Ortense, insisted upon it, usually at Christmas or Winton's birthday.

Jimmy once told me that he resented his father for abandoning him, but it was always my belief that his feelings ran much deeper. I think it fair to say he disliked him intensely, but was enough of a pragmatist to realize that he was now dependent upon Winton for board and room, and he had no place else to go. Their first meeting was artificially cordial: it was the first real exposure to each other that they'd had in many years. Jimmy refused to call his father "dad," instead referring to him as "father," although Winton called him "son."

Nevertheless Jimmy and Winton arrived at an uneasy truce: the apartment was small and it was apparent to Jimmy that Winton was trying to make up for his past neglect by having Jimmy live with him and his wife, Ethel Case.

Winton had remarried four years earlier and worried about how Jimmy and his stepmother would get along. Those worries were unfounded, for Jimmy soon realized that Ethel was the power in the family, and he had always liked and been able to get along with older women, whom he allowed to mother him. On her part, Ethel was aware that her husband felt a substantial amount of guilt about his neglect of Jimmy, and she was determined not to come between father and son.

Winton courted Jimmy by spending as much time with him as possible those first few weeks: they went bowling together, and Winton tried to teach Jimmy to play golf but had minimal success since Jimmy didn't like the game and refused to cater to his father by acting as though he did.

Father and son were soon at odds over Jimmy's future and there were constant arguments. Jimmy wanted to go to UCLA as a theater arts major but Winton was not impressed with Jimmy's passion to be an actor. He did not believe Jimmy had any real acting talent and considered his successes in Fairmount as kid stuff, an adolescent bug he would get out of his system. Winton was determined that Jimmy study something practical that might lead to a real career, and since he was paying the bills, he wanted Jimmy to take prelaw courses at Santa Monica City College.

He promised to buy Jimmy a car as an early birthday present so he could commute to college. The used '39 Chevy sedan swung the day, and Jimmy enrolled as a prelaw student in January 1950, but he also signed up for all the available theater arts courses.

Gene Owen, chairperson of the college's drama department, had Jimmy as a student in her radio class. One day as part of an assignment, Jimmy read some scenes from Poe's "Telltale Heart," and Owen thought he was magnificent. Later, during the same class, she asked Jimmy to read some scenes from *Hamlet*. That night when she returned home, she told her husband that she had finally found the right student to play *Hamlet* as she felt it should be played.

Another person in the class who was impressed with Jimmy's

reading was Richard Shannon, a World War II veteran who was older than most of the other students in the class. Shannon remembers that he hadn't been much for Shakespeare until then. "But the day Jimmy read I suddenly saw the whole legend come to life."

After school and between classes Shannon talked with Jimmy about acting and life in general. "Jimmy had a tremendous curiosity about everything," Shannon recalls. "Ours was a kind of a father and son relationship, with me answering the questions but proud he chose me to be the one he talked with."

Shannon suggested that Jimmy seriously decide to become an actor "because it was the thing he wanted most to be."

Jimmy had a full schedule. Thanks to Owen, he became an announcer on the college FM radio station, and he played substitute guard on the college basketball team. But his heart was still in acting. The school basketball coach, Sanger Crumpacker, recalls a day that Jimmy came late to practice and, when pressed for an explanation, said he had failed a screen test at a local studio. "At that time he wanted more than anything else to get into acting."

After school and at night Jimmy hung out with friends at Ray Avery's Record Roundup on La Cienega Boulevard, listening to the latest jazz releases. And they cruised around the beach area, stopping off at coffee houses like the Cave and the Point.

At the end of his freshman term at Santa Monica Jimmy brought home As in gym and drama and Cs in prelaw. Faced with the realization that Jimmy was never going to make it as a law student, Winton reluctantly agreed that he could enroll at UCLA as a theater arts major.

Jimmy worked at a variety of part-time jobs that summer: he was an usher at a Santa Monica movie house several nights a week, and he worked as an athletic instructor at a boys' camp in Glendora, a suburb of Los Angeles.

At the end of summer Jimmy convinced Winton to allow him to register at UCLA. "I take a subject A English examination Monday," he wrote to the Winslows, and mentioned that he had joined the Miller Playhouse Theatre Guild, a summer stock company, but he hadn't been in time to be cast in any production. "My knowledge of the stage and the ability to design and paint sets won me the place of head stage manager for the next production of four one act plays," he wrote.

That summer Jimmy had a small part in a musical production of *The Romance of Scarlet Gulch*. On the playbill he is listed as Byron James.

At the start of the school year, Jimmy moved out of Winton's home, and because he needed a place to live, he pledged the Epsilon Pi chapter of Sigma Nu, a national fraternity that had a house just off campus. Manuel González, commander of the chapter, recalls that from the beginning there were signs that Jimmy was having difficulty in adjusting to the give-and-take of fraternity life. He remained aloof from chapter activities, and spent much of his time in his room, producing Salvador Dali–like sketches, such as a bloodshot eyeball suspended in midair and staring at a burned-over forest.

Because Jimmy most often wore jeans and a white shirt, some of the fraternity brothers derisively called him "plowboy" and made fun of the "hick" with the Indiana twang who wanted to be an actor.

Meanwhile, Jimmy had made another friend. He was Jim Bellah, son of the renowned novelist James Warner Bellah, and Jimmy's partner in fencing class. Jimmy confided his acting dreams to Bellah, who introduced him to an agent he knew named Isabelle Draesemer. Mrs. Draesemer wasn't convinced that Jimmy had any talent, but she took him on as a client as a favor to Bellah.

In October Jimmy wrote home to Marcus and Ortense, "The biggest thrill of my life came three weeks ago, after a week of grueling auditions for U.C.L.A.'s four major theatrical productions, the major one being Shakespeare's 'Macbeth' which will be presented in Royce Hall (seats 1600). After the auditioning of 367 actors and actresses, I came up with a wonderful lead in 'Macbeth' the character being Malcolm (huge part.)"

Bill Bast, another theater arts major at the time, saw Jimmy's last dress rehearsal from the audience, and attended opening night as well. Bast recalls wondering then how Jimmy got the role. Bast was also from the Midwest, having transferred to UCLA from the University of Wisconsin.

He thought Jimmy's opening-night performance was "like an agonizing dental extraction," a sentiment echoed by the critic of the theater arts newsletter, who reported that Jimmy as Malcolm had "failed to show any growth and would have made a hollow king."

After the play's opening Jimmy had coffee with Shannon and admitted that his performance was not good but he felt he was on the right track.

Soon after the play closed, Bast was introduced to Jimmy by a mutual friend, Jeanetta Lewis, a classmate from the theater arts department. Jimmy and Bill discovered that despite their differences—Bast was far more sophisticated than Jimmy—they got along well together. They became friends at about the time Jimmy was to be initiated into Sigma Nu.

The fraternity brothers had apparently decided that normal initiation rites, like stripping the pledge nude and letting him find his way back to the frat house at night, should be suspended in Jimmy's case and a special test of manhood devised. According to David Dalton, author of *The Mutant King*, "The idea was that Jimmy was to go down to the bottom of the pool and lay spread-eagle across the drainage vent. Then they would turn on the drain and he was supposed to escape its whirlpool. Jimmy went down and didn't come up. It became apparent that he was drowning, and it took longer than it should have for one of the 'lifeguards' to jump in and rescue him. He pulled Jimmy out and dragged him into the locker room to administer mouth-to-mouth resuscitation. . . . He glanced at the pale, still face coming to . . . he threw him his clothes from the locker room door and . . . walked out."

The last straw for Jimmy came when one of the brothers insinuated that anyone who spent all of his time talking and thinking about acting had to be a "fruit." In those days one man calling another a fruit was fighting words, and Jimmy obliged by punching his tormentor in the nose. He was shortly thereafter asked to leave the fraternity, and did so, leaving behind an unpaid bill of forty-five dollars.

Since Bast was then living unhappily in a dormitory, they decided to find a place they could share. After days of searching for an apartment, they finally found a furnished three-room Mexican-style penthouse on top of an apartment building in Santa Monica. The view from the living room with its high, slanted ceiling and Aztec furniture included the Pacific Ocean. Despite the relatively high rent of $300 a month, the boys moved in at once.

Bast soon found that his new roommate could be sullen, secretive, and uncommunicative for days, and then he would suddenly become warm, open, and friendly. The moods changed almost without warning and were usually dependent on whatever was going on in Jimmy's search for acting jobs. "Acting was his life, his whole reason for existence," recalls Bast.

"I don't even want to be the best," Jimmy told Bast. "I want to grow so tall that nobody can reach me. Not to prove anything, but just to go where you ought to go when you devote your whole life and all you are to one thing."

Jimmy's agent, Isabelle Draesemer, got him his first job—a Pepsi-Cola commercial for television. In one scene Jimmy dances around a jukebox playing and singing with a group of typical young all-American teenagers. In the second scene Jimmy wears a sailor suit and sings "Live it up with Pepsi-Cola" on a carousel in Griffith Park with five other actors. As the carousel turned, the youngsters grabbed rings. Jimmy can be seen in a close-up handing out the Pepsis. Since none of the youngsters was a member of the Screen Actors Guild, they were given lunch and a flat fee of ten dollars.

Two of the other actors in the carousel commercial would, within three years, have roles in *Rebel Without a Cause* with Jimmy. One was eighteen-year-old Beverly Long and the other was Nick Adams, fresh from the Appalachian coal-mining town of Nanticoke, Pennsylvania. Some years later, Nick told me that he and Jimmy "had a ball" making the commercial. "When the carousel came into camera and we were to sing the lyrics to the commercial, Jimmy started substituting bawdy lyrics and throwing us all off."

Jimmy made an impression on Jerry Fairbanks, producer of the commercial, and Fairbanks contacted Isabelle Draesemer asking her to have Jimmy audition for an episode of Father Peyton's *Family Theater*, a holiday special called "Hill Number One." Others in the cast were Gene Lockhart, Roddy McDowall, Joan Leslie, Ruth Hussey, and Michael Ansara, a first-rate cast for the time.

The TV drama was an allegorical tale that opened with a platoon of American GIs trying to capture an anonymous hill. The soldiers take a break while the army chaplain tries to cheer them up. "War is a crucifixion," he says. "It shakes the earth, darkens the sun, and makes men look for a meaning in life. Why don't we think a moment about the first hill—hill number one. It was taken by one man alone." At this point, bells begin to peal and the story flashes back through time to Joseph of Arimathea and Pontius Pilate, who are discussing what is to be done about the corpse of Jesus Christ.

Jimmy had only a few lines in the teleplay, in which he played the role of John the Apostle. Wearing a Hollywood version of a caftan with his hair in curls, Jimmy looks like a choirboy. In his first scene he is seated at a table with the other disciples who have gone into hiding and are discussing disbanding. Jimmy, seen in a close-up, rebukes them: "Was it for this we gave up our nets? Just to go back to our boats again?"

In a later scene when the apostles discover the stone has been rolled away from the tomb, Jimmy looks toward the heavens and announces, "He will bring us enlightenment. Come, we must spread these good tidings quickly."

Despite the small size of his role, Jimmy was terrified because the show, to be telecast on Easter Sunday 1951, was going out live. He also had laryngitis brought on by a bad cold, which made his voice sound deeper than usual.

He earned $150, his first big paycheck, thus enabling him to make his second rent payment on the penthouse. He also acquired his first fan club: the Immaculate Heart James Dean Appreciation Society. "Hill Number One" had been required viewing at the Catholic girls' school, and some of them thought that the young man who played St. John was a doll. The girls contacted Jimmy through his agent and asked him to attend a party in his honor.

Bill Bast went with Jimmy to the party, which he recalls as consisting of a lot of giggling. "The girls were between fourteen and eighteen and they had made a cake for the occasion. It was one of those embarrassing affairs where everyone just stands around a lot. Jimmy got to play the star to the hilt and he loved it, and don't think he didn't take advantage of the situation."

Jimmy was broke most of the time. He had to borrow money from Bill for food, and he was always behind with his share of the rent. Bill, too, was usually short of cash, and the two of them often ate nothing but oatmeal for dinner. During summer break, Bill, who wanted to be a writer, spent most of his days working on stories he hoped to publish or sell to films. As a result, he went to bed early at night. Jimmy, who was an insomniac as well as a constant worrier, often went out at night by himself. The Venice pier became one of his favorite haunts. He would hang out there with a ragtag crowd until dawn when he would come home and sleep off the cheap wine and his despondency most of the day.

Bill's mother came to stay for a week and filled up the larder as well as cooked for the boys every night. More than once, Jimmy managed to reduce the poor woman to tears—usually by ignoring her. Jimmy was constantly creating something, and Bill recalls a long rainy day that Jimmy and his mother spent alone together in the small apartment. Busy working on a mobile, Jimmy totally ignored her, leaving her almost a nervous wreck. She had also had the misfortune of arriving during what Bill calls Jimmy's Henry Miller period: all over the apartment were lewd drawings Jimmy had made in the style of Miller.

When Bill's mother left, Jimmy and Bill took her to the train station. Moments before the train pulled into the station, Jimmy disappeared, only to reappear with a box of chocolates and a photograph of himself inscribed "To my second mother." Taken aback, she burst into tears.

Bill soon got a job working after school at CBS in the radio workshop and was able to get Jimmy a part-time job as an usher. Jimmy liked watching and later criticizing the shows for Bill, but he refused to conform to the dress code and wear a suit and tie, and he didn't like taking orders. Within a week, he had another job at CBS, which he preferred because it dealt with automobiles; he became a car parker on the studio lot.

The one thing the roommates seemed to have in common was their interest in girls. Bill was dating a teenage actress named Beverly Wills (daughter of the comedienne Joan Davis), who played the role of Fluffy Adams on a weekly radio show called *Junior Miss*. Jimmy had just broken up with Diane Hixon, a slim, well-proportioned blonde, because, according to Bast, she was put off by the prospect of being a mother substitute. So Jimmy invited

Jeanetta Lewis to double with Beverly and Bill on a picnic. The girls would bring the food and the boys the wine.

"I thought he [Jimmy] was pretty much of a creep until we got to the picnic, and then all of a sudden he came to life," Beverly recalled. "We began to talk about acting and Jimmy lit up. He told me how interested he was in the Stanislavsky method, where you not only act out people, but things too.

" 'Look,' said Jimmy, 'I'm a palm tree in a storm.' He held his arms out and waved wildly. To feel more free, he impatiently tossed off his cheap, tight blue jacket. He looked bigger as soon as he did, because you could see his broad shoulders and powerful build. Then he got wilder and pretended he was a monkey. He climbed a big tree and swung from a high branch. Dropping from the branch, he landed on his hands like a little kid who was suddenly turned loose. He even laughed like a little boy, chuckling uproariously at every little thing. Once in the spotlight, he ate it up and had us all in stitches all afternoon."

The two roommates continued double-dating, and sometimes when Bill had to work, Jimmy drove Beverly to CBS. Bill recalls a hot summer night when Jimmy and Beverly picked him up from work. As soon as he got in the car, Beverly announced, "Bill, there's something we have to tell you. I mean, we're in love."

There was a long pause, during which Bill tried to imagine how he was supposed to react, but he couldn't think of anything to say. He wasn't upset by the announcement since he was not emotionally involved with Beverly. Also he seriously doubted that "love" would have been the word of choice for Jimmy. He knew his roommate better than that.

"We tried not to let it happen," Beverly continued apologetically, "but there was nothing we could do. These things just happen."

The matter didn't end there, however. Jimmy was still dating Jeanetta, who flew into a rage when she heard the news, creating a scene that ended with Jimmy shaking Bill, slapping Jeanetta, and then bursting into tears.

When Bill and Jeanetta left and had a chance to talk the situation over, she convinced him to move out of the penthouse as retaliation for the double cross.

There were no angry words between Jimmy and Bill on the day he moved out. Jimmy merely maintained a sullen silence. He stayed on at the apartment for another month and kept his job at CBS. When he was unable to pay the rent, he moved in with Ted Avery, an usher at the studio. But he soon had somewhere else to go. While parking cars one day, Jimmy met Rogers Brackett, a thirty-five-year-old advertising executive who worked for Foote, Cone & Belding, a prestigious New York ad agency. One of his accounts was the weekly radio show *Alias Jane Doe*, and in an arrangement that was then not uncommon, Brackett was also the show's director.

Brackett was tall, thin to the point of anorexia, with curly hair. A friend described him as the Noël Coward of the West Coast because of his flair for witty social conversation. According to the friend, Brackett was urbane and manipulative, in addition to being fifteen years older than Jimmy.

He was also homosexual. Then as now, there were many homosexuals in Hollywood holding important positions in the film industry. It was no secret in the film community that Henry Willson, a well-known agent, represented many homosexual actors, including Rock Hudson. Willson's private parties were a gathering place for the closet community. A pretty boy like Jimmy was undoubtedly a great prize for Brackett, who was a friend of Willson's. When Brackett offered Jimmy a place to stay, Jimmy immediately moved in with him.

I believe that Jimmy was drawn to Brackett because he viewed him as a sort of father figure who would take care of him, something his own father had not done. Jimmy was continually short of money and he was opportunistic enough to make the trade-off Brackett wanted. Also, thanks to his recent affair with DeWeerd, Jimmy was not an innocent. Undoubtedly it was a convenient arrangement: Jimmy needed a place to live and Brackett had many good contacts in Hollywood, homosexual as well as straight, who could further Jimmy's career.

The relationship soon worked out to Jimmy's benefit. Brackett got him work on *Alias Jane Doe* and *Stars Over Hollywood*, another radio show. Brackett also contacted his friend Sam Fuller, who was directing the film *Fixed Bayonets*, a Korean War story. As a favor to

Brackett, Fuller hired Jimmy to play a GI with one line, "It's a rear guard coming back." The line was later cut, but Jimmy's one scene remained.

That summer Isabelle Draesemer got Jimmy a bit part in the Dean Martin–Jerry Lewis comedy *Sailor Beware*. His role was small: he can just be glimpsed in a boxing scene. On the set of the film Jimmy met a young actor named Dick Clayton, who would later figure prominently in his life.

Brackett helped Jimmy get a job as an extra in *Trouble Along the Way*, starring John Wayne. Jimmy also had a small role as a smart-ass 1920s kid in *Has Anybody Seen My Gal?* with Rock Hudson. In a scene in which character actor Charles Coburn is being trained to work behind the fountain by soda jerk Rock Hudson, Jimmy, wearing a bow tie and straw boater, had one long sentence: "Hey, Gramps, I'll have a choc malt, heavy on the choc, plenty of milk, four spoons of malt, two scoops of vanilla ice cream, one mixed with the rest and one floating." Coburn's rejoinder got the laugh: "Would you like to come in Wednesday for a fitting? Thank you."

Jimmy learned that James Whitmore, a film star and Broadway actor, had a small informal group that met once a week in a rehearsal hall at Twenty-sixth Street and San Vicente Boulevard. The idea of studying drama with a recognized actor appealed to Jimmy. He joined the group and quit college.

One night he waited impatiently for the rest of the group to leave the room they used for an impromptu stage and classroom. Finally he was alone with the instructor.

"Mr. Whitmore," he asked shyly, "can I see you for a few minutes please?"

"Sure thing," Whitmore said. "Let's go get a cup of coffee."

Jimmy bided his time until the coffee was served, then he got straight to the point. "Mr. Whitmore, how do you get to be an actor?"

"There's only one way, Jimmy," Whitmore replied. "Stop dissipating your energy and talent. Go to New York. There you will find out whether you can take the uncertainty of an actor's life. And while you're looking for work you'll be rubbing shoulders with other actors, and that can be gratifying, too.

"Get to know yourself, and learn how to be yourself. Give it the total effort, and don't do it halfway. Learn to have the actor's disdain for convention. Learn to study. Learn to act—and above all, act. You get to be an actor by acting."

Jimmy looked over the rims of his glasses at Whitmore. "Is there any place I can go to learn? What's the best place?"

"Go see Elia Kazan at the Actors Studio," Whitmore said. "I don't know if they'll take you, but you can't do better."

When Jimmy wasn't working, which was often, he was either studying the Stanislavsky method of acting with Whitmore or dating Beverly, who picked up the checks or loaned him money.

In the spring of 1951 he took her to her Beverly Hills High School prom. Jimmy was working as an usher at the time, and although he was in debt, he managed to put aside a few dollars every week so he could rent a tuxedo.

"Although we sat out most of the dances, Jimmy was in wonderful spirits the night of the prom," Beverly told writer Bill Bast. "Some of the kids at school joined us and he laughed a lot and told funny stories. . . . My mother stopped by with some friends for a few minutes, and even she was fascinated by Jimmy's personality that night. He jumped out of his chair when she came to our table and even helped her with her stole. 'Good heavens, I've never seen him like this before,' said Mother, flabbergasted but charmed."

It was during the summer that Beverly saw another side of Jimmy, who was getting more and more despondent over not being able to get acting jobs. "I soon learned that it was nothing for Jimmy to run through a whole alphabet of emotions in one evening. His moods of happiness were now far outweighed by his moods of deep despair.

"He was almost constantly in a blue funk. He still couldn't get an acting job and he was growing increasingly bitter. I hated to see Jimmy become so blue. When he was happy, there was no one more lovable. When he was depressed, he wanted to die.

"These low moods became so violent that he began to tell me that he was having strange nightmares in which he dreamed he was dying. The nightmares began to give him a certain phobia about death."

Meanwhile, Jimmy was living a double life. He went with Brackett to exclusive parties often given by and attended by homosexuals, dined at the best restaurants such as Chasen's and LaRue, and went to film screenings at private homes. They occasionally drove over the border to Tijuana, Mexico, to see bullfights. On one such occasion Brackett introduced Jimmy to the Brooklyn-born matador Sidney Franklin—a one-time friend of Ernest Hemingway's—who gave Jimmy one of his bloodied capes as a souvenir. Jimmy cherished it.

Brackett later said of his relationship with Jimmy, "If it was a father-son relationship, it was also incestuous." Isabelle Draesemer saw the relationship in a different light. She believes that Jimmy was torn at this point between two different ways of life. "It was a question of marrying Joan Davis's daughter or going off to live with a studio director."

The romance with Beverly had to come to a head sooner or later, and it did late in the summer of 1951 when Beverly went to live with her father at Paradise Cove, an exclusive residential area near Malibu on the Pacific. Most of Beverly's friends were from well-to-do families, and they tended to patronize and look down on Jimmy, who stuck out like a sore thumb and responded to their slights by drawing deeper into his shell.

One night Jimmy objected to Beverly dancing with another boy, and he exploded. He grabbed the boy by the collar and threatened to blacken both of his eyes. Beverly ran out to the beach and Jimmy walked after her, scuffing angrily at the sand. They were both miserable, and both knew it was the end.

Later in the week Jimmy called Beverly to apologize and say goodbye. He said he was leaving with a friend for New York, neglecting to mention that the friend was Rogers Brackett, who was going there to direct a radio show and had asked Jimmy to drive across the country with him. The plan was for them to go together to Chicago, where Brackett had a short assignment.

David Swift, writer of the *Mr. Peepers* television show and a California friend of Brackett's, was in Chicago at the time visiting his wife, Maggie McNamara, who was starring in the play *The Moon Is Blue*. Brackett had telephoned Swift and invited him to come by the Ambassador East Hotel where he was staying. Swift recalls that when he knocked on the door of Brackett's hotel room it was slowly opened by a young man standing in a classical bullfighter's pose with an *espada* pointed at him as though going in over the horns for the kill, grunting, "Toro, toro." Brackett appeared and pushed the boy away, telling him to be nice. He then introduced the young man as Jimmy Dean.

Later in the week Brackett and Jimmy joined the Swifts at dinner, and as David recalls, "When Maggie and Jimmy met it was instant love. They just adored each other." Jimmy promised to call the Swifts when he got to New York.

From Chicago, Brackett called his friend and former lover Alec Wilder, a composer living in New York, and asked him to book a room for Jimmy in the Iroquois Hotel on West Forty-fourth Street. Brackett then put Jimmy on a bus for New York.

Chapter Three

SWISHY-SWASHY

When he arrived in New York during the first days of September 1951, Jimmy had less than $150 in his pockets: he had borrowed $100 from DeWeerd in Indianapolis, and the Winslows had given him $50. He had his letters of introduction and his plan to study at the Actors Studio, but during his first days in the city he rarely wandered far from his small room in the Iroquois. He found the city bewildering and overwhelming, intimidating and hostile—and ultimately thrilling and inspiring.

In a letter home to Marcus and Mom written soon after his arrival, Jimmy reported: "For the first few weeks I was so confused that I strayed only a couple of blocks from my hotel off Times Square. I would see three movies a day in an attempt to escape from my loneliness and depression. I spent most of my limited funds just on seeing movies."

Jimmy once told me that during his first few weeks in New York he sat through Marlon Brando's film *The Men* four times in two days, and he saw *A Place in the Sun* starring Montgomery Clift three times. He said that despite their different styles, Brando and Clift were the "greatest," and there was a lot he could learn from them. Later, when he was successful, many critics contended that Jimmy copied Brando. I think it more likely that Jimmy studied and admired Brando and took from him what he found useful.

When his money got low Jimmy took a room in the YMCA on

West Sixty-third Street and landed a job as a dishwasher in a bar on West Forty-fifth.

During the early 1950s, New York was an ideal place for aspiring actors because it was the center of television production, with more than thirty live drama and comedy shows being produced each week. The demand for actors was immense, and almost any promising actor could hope to find work. Mass auditions known as cattle calls were held weekly. Jimmy found himself together with as many as a thousand other young would-be actors at these open auditions where the routine was efficient, albeit dehumanizing, for the participants. Each actor would be given a number and called up on the stage, often in groups of ten, at which time he would file past the casting directors in the audience. If a casting director was interested in a particular individual, that person would be asked to come back for a reading, or would be dismissed with a curt "Sorry, thank you for coming."

Martin Landau, then one of New York's aspiring actors, met Jimmy after one such casting call instigated by CBS, which produced many live TV shows at the time. It was a rainy day, which meant that even more actors than usual answered the call at the Martin Beck Theatre because they couldn't make rounds anyway. The actors were usually in ethnic groups, and Landau, who was tall and darkly handsome, was generally with such "New York ethnics" as Sydney Pollack, John Cassavetes, Michael Toland, Paul Stevens, Ben Gazzara, and Tony Franciosa. Jimmy was usually grouped with such all-American types as Paul Newman and Steve McQueen. But on this day, Landau and Jimmy were in the same group. As they walked off the stage together Landau made a funny remark about the weather. Jimmy laughed and they walked out onto the street together and started talking about the humiliation of the experience.

"We started to walk around the streets," Landau recalls. "We stopped at a construction site and I said, 'Well, if we're gonna be out on the street, let's act like we belong on the street.' So we started to pretend we were construction foremen and shouted orders to the workmen. That lasted about twenty minutes. Then we went to Rockefeller Plaza skating rink. There was a cute girl skating and doing tricks; so we applauded her and cheered, and she became like a queen and turned to us and bowed and we applauded some more."

As they continued down the street Landau mentioned that he hadn't seen Jimmy before. Jimmy said he had just arrived from California where he had studied acting with James Whitmore. Landau suggested they have a cup of coffee at Cromwell's Pharmacy, in the lobby of the NBC Building at 30 Rockefeller Plaza. Known as the actors' drugstore or the poor man's Sardi's, Cromwell's featured inexpensive meals, booths where the habitually out-of-work actors could sit undisturbed for hours, and a bank of phones where they could make calls to their agents. Discussions ranged from critiques of shows or performances they had seen to tips on places where they might find employment.

Over coffee with cinnamon sticks, Landau told Jimmy that in addition to being an actor he was also a cartoonist: he drew the cartoons for Billy Rose's theatrical column "Pitching Horseshoes," and he did a hasty pen and ink drawing of Jimmy. Jimmy then sketched Landau. Before parting company they exchanged telephone numbers and agreed to get together again later in the week.

Meanwhile, Jimmy diligently followed up every lead that might get him an acting job. In Hollywood, Bill Bast had introduced him to Ralph Levy, a television director friend of his who used Jimmy as an extra on *The Alan Young Show*. When Jimmy left for Hollywood, Levy promised to write a letter to a friend of his in New York named James Sheldon who was supervising commercials on a variety of shows, asking him to help Jimmy if possible. Jimmy went to Sheldon's office and read a scene. The older man was impressed: "Jimmy reminded me of a young Brando, so I sent him to audition for a regular co-starring role on a television show I handled called *Mama*, based on the Broadway hit *I Remember Mama*. The star of the show was Dick Van Patten, who was being replaced because he had been drafted into the military. Jimmy got the part, but Van Patten received an exemption, and returned to the show."

Sheldon liked Jimmy and they became friendly, sometimes going out for dinners as a threesome with Sheldon's wife. "Jimmy attached himself to me," says Sheldon, "and I lent him money when he needed it, and sent him to see various producers, directors, and casting people. I knew he needed representation so I sent him to see Jane Deacy."

So it was that Jimmy met the woman who, probably more than any other person, made him a successful actor. When Jimmy first went to see Jane Deacy, she was working for the Louis Schurr Agency. Schurr himself didn't think much of Jimmy, judging him too short and too immature. Nor did Jimmy's glasses help. Things were different between Jimmy and Deacy: it was love at first sight. She signed him immediately, and when she left Schurr to form her own agency later that year, she took Jimmy along as one of her clients. She was more than just Jimmy's agent, for she believed firmly in him and his talent and looked after him like a personal manager. Like most of her clients, Jimmy called her "Mom." In his case there was more than a little truth in the word.

In November, Jimmy got his first real job thanks more to his athletic ability than his acting talent. He was hired to test stunts on *Beat the Clock*, a popular TV game show hosted by Bud Collyer in which contestants were challenged to perform stunts before the clock ran out. It was Jimmy's job—along with other young actors and actresses, including for a time Warren Oates—to prove that the show's stunts were in fact possible. They did so during so-called lab sessions before each broadcast.

Frank Wayne, one of the writers on the show as well as a creator of the stunts, recalls that Jimmy was determined not to let any stunt on the show beat him. "If Jimmy couldn't do a stunt in the lab session, he would stay on his own time doing it over and over again until he finally got it, and then he'd come over with this big grin on his face and say, 'Frank, I've got it.' And then he'd kind of giggle."

Meanwhile, Jimmy and Landau became friendly and spent a lot of time together. One of their favorite spots on sunny days was a flat rock in Central Park where they rolled up their pants and shirt sleeves so they could get a tan as they talked. Landau recalls how they used to discuss the careers of Marlon Brando and Montgomery Clift and their acting techniques. Sometimes they talked about making it before it was too late. "Jimmy often said that he had to make it as an actor while he was young," says Landau. "Although we were the same age I looked like a man but he would always look like a boy. He used to say that I would grow into myself but he would grow out of himself, so he had to make it before he was thirty. Sometimes we talked about the possibility of dying young but we never thought that would happen to us."

Jimmy and Landau also spent hours in Jimmy's room at the YMCA listening to music: Bach and Bartók and even the more difficult Schoenberg.

Music was part of Jimmy's life, one of his few enduring interests and one of the few things he could truly concentrate on: he often spent entire evenings working out a rhythm on his bongos or playing a penny whistle he had taught himself. Other interests came and went, sometimes passing in the space of an afternoon. In New York, Jimmy sensed the inadequacies of his Indiana education: there was so much he had to learn. Although curious about everything, Jimmy had neither the patience nor the time—he was always in a hurry—to study anything in depth. He loved books, particularly deep volumes of philosophy, but he rarely read them all the way through; he would read enough to get the gist of the work or a quote he could drop into a conversation. He put the books on display in his apartment or carried the weighty tomes around with him so he could give the impression of being an intellectual.

Although he was often moody and liked to spend time by himself, he also liked company, particularly at meals and in the evening. He telephoned David Swift and Maggie McNamara, and he soon became a regular visitor at their apartment on Sixty-first Street or at a small house they rented on Fire Island. David Swift recalls Jimmy as a gloomy, handsome little boy playing moody tunes on his penny whistle or sitting by himself in a corner at parties sitting with a cocked eye and listening to the conversation. But Maggie adored him, and through her he met Norma Crane, an actress. The three became inseparable and spent much of their days together endlessly theorizing about acting.

Because he was invariably broke, he moved in to Norma's apartment on Thirty-fourth Street and Eighth Avenue where, according to David, they lived like brother and sister.

Late in the year, Jimmy met Leonard Rosenman, who looked

and dressed like a long-haired beatnik, but was a true intellectual. Born in Brooklyn in 1924, Rosenman had first tried his hand as a painter, but after serving with the air force in World War II he'd turned to the study of music, learning theory and composition from Schoenberg, Copland, and Bernstein. Together with Howard Sackler (who would go on to win the Pulitzer Prize for *The Great White Hope* in 1969), Leonard was working on an opera. After one of the performances, Leonard and his wife, Adele, a petite brunette who was also an excellent pianist, went to a party at the home of one of the sponsors of the opera. There was a Steinway piano in the apartment, and the hostess eventually convinced Leonard to sit down with her and play some Mozart two-hand sonatas. The hostess played poorly, however, and after a few minutes Leonard said, "My wife plays beautifully."

Adele demurred, saying she didn't have her glasses with her, but Leonard insisted. Adele turned to a young man wearing glasses standing nearby and asked if she could borrow his. He handed them to her.

The Rosenmans played together, and then Leonard played some Carl Philipp Emanuel Bach with the young man hovering over his shoulder.

When Adele handed the glasses back to the young man, he introduced himself as James Dean. Adele, Leonard, and Jimmy started to talk about music, and after the party he walked back with them to their apartment on Central Park West, an enormous place with twelve rooms, including a forty-foot-long living room big enough for their children to ride bikes in.

Two or three months later, at about 11:00 P.M., there was a knock on the Rosenmans' apartment door. Leonard opened it to find a young man wearing a leather outfit who said, "My name is Jimmy Dean, and I don't know if you remember me. I'd like to learn to play the piano with you."

"Sure," said Leonard, mildly amused. "Come on in."

Jimmy came by the apartment a few times for lessons. Adele asked her husband how it was going. "He doesn't have any talent for the piano, and he's too lazy," Leonard said. "He just doesn't know why, without being able to play notes or scales, he can't play

Beethoven's Opus 100, and he just won't practice." Leonard also discovered that Jimmy had a crooked finger that kept him from making the proper spread with his right hand.

Leonard explained to his frustrated student that learning to play the piano is like working in a gymnasium. "You can't lift heavy weights right off, you have to build up to them. You have to practice."

Jimmy soon found that Leonard was not only a brilliant musician and composer, but he was also an accomplished artist. Leonard was everything Jimmy aspired to be. A friendship developed, with Leonard assuming the role of mentor and Jimmy the eager student. Soon Jimmy was a regular visitor at the Rosenman home. Adele and Leonard, aware that he desperately wanted to be a member of their family, adopted him.

"Jimmy was really interested in everything, including music and how we were with our children," recalls Adele, who early on realized that Jimmy was trying to make up for his lack of education. "He had the ability to absorb from everyone he met something that he could digest and that would later be useful to him as an actor. He discarded the things that were not of use to him.

"He mixed well with everyone and some of our guests were pretty intellectual—composers, musicians, artists, writers—but he was smart enough to never try to upstage anyone."

Adele soon discovered to her amusement that Jimmy never came over for dinner if he knew they were having chicken. He explained to her that he couldn't stand chicken because he had grown up on a farm and had to take care of them. For that reason he also refused to eat eggs. Aside from that brief glimpse of his childhood, Jimmy never discussed his past.

At one point that fall, Leonard was reading Kierkegaard's *Fear and Trembling*. To his amusement, he noticed that Jimmy bought a copy of the book and carried it around with him. "I am certain he never read it all the way through, but he had read enough to quote from certain sections, which gave the illusion that he had read it," Leonard claims.

The Rosenmans provided Jimmy with a kind of home, but he was lonely and in need of companionship. One night he went to the Rehearsal Club, a residence hotel for actresses and dancers on

West Fifty-third Street—a good place to meet girls. "There were two couches in the lobby, and I was sitting in one and this boy wearing jeans and a raincoat with a magnificent face was sitting in the other," recalls Elizabeth (nicknamed Dizzy) Sheridan. "We were both reading magazines, and for some reason he read aloud something out of his magazine. Like 'I admit in retrospect that my methods were unorthodox to say the least.' " Dizzy recognized his pickup technique for what it was, but amusedly replied by reading aloud a quote from her magazine.

They both laughed, and Jimmy invited her to go around the corner to have a Champale with him at Jerry's Bar and Restaurant, an Italian joint on Sixth Avenue near West Fifty-fourth where Louis de Liso, the waiter whose uncle Jerry Luce owned the place, often let young actors run up a tab. "I remember the red-and-white tablecloth and the way he looked at me across the table," says Dizzy. "We sat in a booth and talked for a while and then we started drawing pictures on a napkin. I was very impressed with the way he could draw.

"When we met I was ready to be involved and I guess he was too. He seemed very lost, which I found attractive, although he was shorter than I was. I can remember what we drank and how we sort of fell in love across the table, but I can't remember a thing about what we said."

Dizzy, a tall, sensuous brunette, was studying dance while trying to put together a nightclub act with two young men. She also worked part-time as an usher at the Paris movie theater on Fifty-eighth across from the Plaza hotel. When Jimmy visited her at the theater she would feed him the coffee and doughnuts set out for patrons waiting for the next feature. He often took her home after work, or sometimes met her after one of her dance classes.

They were in love, and within a few weeks they decided to move in together. They found a room they could afford at the Hargrave Hotel, on West Seventy-first off Columbus Avenue. "I washed his socks and underwear, and he introduced me to Shredded Wheat," recalls Dizzy. Jimmy had one habit that Dizzy found hard to tolerate, however: he used as a blanket the bloodied bullfight cape that matador Sidney Franklin had given him in Mexico. Dizzy complained constantly about the smell of the blood.

It was the second time that Jimmy had lived with a female, but his first romantic involvement. He was, however, barely able to pay his share of the rent, and was soon embarrassed because he had to borrow money for his meals and bus fare. He constantly went on casting calls, carrying with him a portfolio of pictures and a brief résumé. Across the front page of his portfolio, Jimmy had written, "Matters of Great Consequence," which, Dizzy explains, "was really Jimmy's way of saying it was a matter of no consequence at all; it was all bullshit."

Frank Wayne, the writer on *Beat the Clock*, discovered that Jimmy sometimes went without eating. "We had a sponsor that made tapioca pudding, and we always had gallons of it around because the commercials were live in those days. After the show we would throw it away. One day Jimmy came up to me and asked if he could have the pudding. I asked why he wanted it. 'Man, anything would taste good right now. I haven't had anything to eat in two days,' he said. So I gave him the pudding and took him out for dinner."

Having finished his work in Chicago, Rogers Brackett had arrived in New York and asked Jimmy to move in with him. Again Brackett offered Jimmy what he then needed: important show biz contacts that might lead to acting jobs, a better life-style, and a place to live rent-free. Jimmy was aware of what he would have to do as Brackett's roommate, but he was tired of being broke and struggling to make rent payments. He told Dizzy he was going to move in with Brackett. She realized that Jimmy was confused about his sexuality, and she rented a tiny room on Eighth Avenue, but stayed friends with Jimmy.

"I guess it was time for us to separate, because when we were together we were both hiding out," she says. "We stayed in a lot and clung to each other. But you can't live that way for very long."

Jimmy and Brackett spent New Year's Eve with the Swifts. The other guests were Grace Kelly, who was then in love with Gene Lyons, a handsome Irishman who was starring on Broadway in *Witness for the Prosecution*, actress Maureen Stapleton, playwrights Tennessee Williams and Bill Inge, and Norma Crane—all of them struggling at the time to gain a foothold in the theater. "Jimmy was cute as ever playing the little boy," recalls David Swift.

Jimmy celebrated his twenty-first birthday in February at Jerry's with some of his friends, who pitched in and picked up the tab for the party. The guests included Marty Landau, composer Alec Wilder, lyricist Bill Envig, Maggie McNamara, and Sarah Churchill, the rebellious daughter of Britain's prime minister, who promptly got drunk.

Twelve days later, Jimmy finally landed his first role in television. He was given the part of a bellhop who helps solve a murder in a mountain resort in an episode entitled "Sleeping Dogs" that was part of the CBS series *The Web*. The stars of the episode were Anne Jackson and E.G. Marshall; the producer was Franklin Heller.

Jimmy was lucky to get the part. When Heller first met him, he thought he was unkempt and arrogant. As Heller feared, Jimmy proved difficult to work with during the rehearsals and managed to so antagonize him that he wanted to fire him—Jimmy seemed determined to play the role his way and not as Heller wanted it. Only the intervention of another director, Lela Swift, kept him from being fired.

The following month he refused to take direction and was fired from an episode of the private eye series *Martin Kane*. That same month, however, he had two other parts for CBS, in "Ten Thousand Horses Singing," a segment of *Studio One*, and "The Foggy, Foggy Dew," part of the *Lux Video Theatre*. In May, Rogers Brackett got him a bit role in a *Kraft Television Theatre* episode about the young Abraham Lincoln. Later in the month he played a Vermont soldier who is court-martialed for sleeping on guard and is pardoned by Abraham Lincoln in "Abraham Lincoln," on *Studio One*. The next month he found himself on the other side of the historical fence, playing a Southern aristocrat in "Forgotten Children," a segment of the *Hallmark Summer Theatre*. Historical productions were popular television fare, and during those same three months Paul Newman—one of Jimmy's closest competitors for roles—was performing in such teleplays as "The Assassination of Julius Caesar" and "The Death of Socrates." The differences in the historical settings may reflect subtle typecasting, for Jimmy was to make his film debut as an American boy, and Newman would make his wearing a toga.

Jimmy was still living with Brackett and spending his evenings out with him and other advertising executives and television producers, most of them homosexuals. His feelings for these men alternated between resentment and friendliness, for although he disliked the role he had to play with them, they were a potential source of employment. Around his straight friends he joked about the situation, referring to Brackett and the others as his "mother hens" and making fun of the dressed-up, fancy life they led, with all its maitre d's and wine lists. He absolutely refused to attempt a pronunciation of vichyssoise, calling it instead "swishy-swashy."

Despite the parting scene he'd had with Bill Bast in California, Jimmy had stayed in touch with his old friend, who wanted to come to New York himself to try his hand at writing for television. Bast's arrival that summer gave Jimmy an excuse to leave Brackett's apartment, where he was beginning to rebel against being on call for parties and functioning as a sort of houseboy for Brackett, occasionally serving drinks to guests and cleaning up afterward.

On Bast's first day in the city, he and Jimmy got together and decided to rent a room at the Iroquois for ninety dollars a month. Room 802 was a sickly gray-green color, furnished with a chest, twin beds, a pitcher on a small wardrobe, and some faded lithographs.

After only a few months at the Iroquois, Jimmy and Bill teamed up with Dizzy, who had remained friendly with Jimmy. They moved into a tiny apartment in an old, sparsely furnished brownstone on West Eighty-ninth Street. The night they moved in, they were broke because they had to pay an advance of the rent. "We had between us less than a dollar on which to eat," Bast recalls. "So, like scavengers, we took all the leftovers from the refrigerator and made a stew into which Jimmy dumped half a package of old vermicelli." As they sat eating the concoction, all of them noticed tiny bugs floating on top of the meal, but none of them said a word.

Despite their poverty, the three friends had many happy moments together. They spent afternoons in Central Park where Jimmy would stand with his cape and challenge them to charge. But he continued to live a double life and remained in touch with Rogers Brackett, who still invited him to parties on the promise that he might meet influential people.

In July, Jimmy, who had only the meager wardrobe he had brought with him from Los Angeles and felt shabby when he went out with Brackett, wrote to Marcus explaining his plight.

"The hard part is the maintaining of a respectable social standing. Meaning clothes. You must be fashionable even in the heat. Shirt, tie and suit. Wow. You know how I love to dress up. . . . I would greatly appreciate it if you could spare ten dollars or so. I need it rather desperately. I'm sorry that when I write I always need something. Sometimes I feel that I have lost the right to ask; but because I don't write isn't an indication that I have forgotten.

"I shall never forget what you and Mom have done for me. I want to repay you by being a success. It takes time and many disappointments. I'll try very hard not to take too long. If I have asked for help at the wrong time please forgive me and I will understand."

He received a check for twenty dollars by return mail and bought himself a brown suit. Now when he went for interviews or out with Brackett to dinner or parties he would at least be presentable.

Late that August Jimmy met Rod Steiger, who, along with Marlon Brando, Montgomery Clift, and Paul Newman, was one of the Actors Studio's most talented students. Steiger had received a call from director Fred Zinnemann, who was then casting for the film version of *Oklahoma!* and wanted Steiger to audition for the role of Jud. Steiger agreed.

"I found I was to do the audition with an actor named Paul Newman playing the part of Curly," Steiger recalls. "Then Zinnemann told me that an actor who was scheduled had not shown up, and would I test with another unknown? I was delighted because it gave me two chances at my role. The other unknown turned out to be James Dean."

Steiger eventually got the role of Jud, and the role of Curly went to singer Gordon MacRae.

From then on, Jimmy and Steiger often met at Cromwell's, where they usually shared bitter jokes about how they weren't being discovered. A short while later they acted together in a teleplay, an episode of the popular ABC series *Tales of Tomorrow*, television's first science-fiction series. The episode was called "The Evil Within" and was about a scientist (Steiger) whose wife accidentally swallows a serum for patients with mental disorders. The effect of the drug is to make her murderous. Wearing a lab coat and glasses, Jimmy had the role of the scientist's assistant and appeared once in the first half of the program and then later, coming in to announce the good news that "the effects of the serum will wear off in twenty-four hours."

Director Don Medford found Jimmy frustrating at times because he never did the same thing twice. "He would do anything you wanted him to do, but he would never be able to repeat the same moment, and that, unfortunately, included the staging. In other words he was the antithesis of being mechanical. He was a very natural actor who didn't know how to separate physical acting from the role itself."

Chapter Four

RIPPING OFF LAYERS

One afternoon in September 1952 Jimmy dropped by to see Jane Deacy. He took a place in the waiting room alongside some of her other clients, and then noticed an attractive young blonde sitting behind the receptionist's desk using the typewriter. She was wearing a red jumper and a matching red baseball cap.

Jimmy got up and walked over to the desk, looked at the girl for a few moments—paying special attention to her cap—and then asked, "What are you writing?"

Without looking up from the keyboard, and with a brusqueness she half hoped would drive him away, the blonde answered, "I'm typing a scene."

The curt reply didn't work: Jimmy stayed put. "What's your name?" he asked.

Still looking down she said, "Christine White. And who are you?"

"James Dean." Then he corrected himself: "James Byron Dean," and saying "Byron" he performed a strange little dance.

Chris paused in her typing and looked up. With her first glance she thought Jimmy looked small but jaunty, agile and lean. She, too, was an actress and one of Jane Deacy's clients. She didn't have a typewriter at home and was using the receptionist's typewriter while she was off on her lunch hour. She had never used it before and was doing so now in order to smooth out a scene she was working on.

Since Chris kept on typing and not talking, Jimmy retreated to a filing cabinet about two yards away. He hoisted up one arm and draped it over the cabinet. From this safer distance he continued his attempts at conversation.

"That's one helluva outfit," he said, nodding toward her baseball cap. "Are you an actress or a baseball player?"

"I don't know. Maybe both. A writer, too."

Jimmy started to say something else, but she cut him off. "Look, you're going to cause me to make mistakes here," she said.

At this, Jimmy waved his hands in the air and stepped away from the reception desk, walking backward. He sat down again and was soon called in to see Deacy. When he came back out of her office he didn't leave but sat down again, this time in a far corner of the waiting room.

About twenty minutes later, Chris walked across the waiting room, her script in hand. She was about to leave but then spotted Jimmy sitting in his corner. She stopped near the door, turned, and walked back and stood in front of him.

"I'm sorry I didn't have time to talk to you," she said. "I was concentrating."

"Yeah," said Jimmy. "Well, can we talk now? How about getting a cup of coffee?"

They went to the nearby Blue Ribbon Cafe. For a while they exchanged the usual formula questions—beginning with "Where are you from?"—but neither paid much attention to the information obtained, and in fact both just barely listened. Instead, they found themselves relaxing, laughing and joking. Chris now had a chance to examine Jimmy more carefully and decided that his eyes were too close together, but that they were framed by well-shaped eyebrows and high cheekbones balanced by a firm jaw. His mouth intrigued her—it pouted or smiled or wavered unpredictably.

At one point he took his glasses off and squinted around the coffee shop. Without hesitation Chris stated, "I think you look better with your glasses on."

"That's good," said Jimmy, putting them back on, "because I can't see a damn thing without them."

Most of their conversation concerned acting. When Jimmy mentioned his interest in the Actors Studio Chris told him that she had an audition scheduled there and was writing a skit for herself to play with an actor. In fact, that was what she had been typing on the receptionist's typewriter. They said no more about it in the coffee shop, but as they walked together to the bus stop, Jimmy asked if he could read her skit, and Chris gave it to him.

It was then that Jimmy acted on James Whitmore's advice and put his name on a list for auditions to be held in November at the Actors Studio. He called Chris and said that he loved her skit and thought he might be able to help make it better. Almost as an afterthought, he said, "You told me that you have an audition at the studio coming up, but you're in the Ws. I already have my audition scheduled and I'm in the Ds, which means they'll get to me first, so I took the liberty of asking them if you can come up to the Ds with me and we can read together."

Chris was appalled as well as impressed with his effrontery. "But you're too young for the part," she protested. "I wrote it for a guy who is ten or twelve years older than the girl."

"Well," said Jimmy, "you don't have anyone else to play the scene with, so we don't have to stick with that. We'll just do a little rewriting."

Chris and Jimmy worked for five weeks rewriting her story about two young people who meet on an isolated beach at a turning point in their lives. They created new dialogue and expanded the characters. They decided to name the skit "Roots," a title that came from Jimmy's response to the question "What have you been doin' most of your life?"—"Ripping off layers to find the roots," answered Jimmy.

They worked at the scene constantly, often sitting in her apartment after her roommates went to work. They would rehearse on the roof of her building to feel the flavor of the "beach," at least the sense of open air. They ran the lines in buses, in taxis, at Rockefeller Plaza, in Central Park, on crowded Manhattan street corners, and, of course, they rehearsed at Jerry's, sitting at the bar or in one of the booths.

"We were the original American teenagers," recalls Chris. "We wore jeans all the time, and we believed that the world was ours and everything was possible. It was a time of growing up, of exploring all the possibilities. There was no limit. We were into the soul from Aristotle to Nietzsche. Jimmy told me of his many ambitions: he wanted to fight bulls, he wanted to be a director, he said that he and I would have a production company. All this despite the fact that we never had any money. Whoever was working would float the other a twenty—you could eat for a week on that.

"When we weren't working we talked about everything because we thought we knew all the answers. He told me about the Indiana farm where he had been raised and his appreciation of land and space. He told me how much he missed his mother, but he did so without any self-pity. He was an all-American boy, sometimes serious, often moody, mostly always driven to succeed.

"In those days sex was not as important in a relationship as it is today. You didn't always go for the physical right away, you could have a friend of the opposite sex and not sleep with them. Not that Jimmy didn't make passes at me. He did, but when he did, I wouldn't speak to him for three days, and then he'd call and say, 'Okay, let's just be friends.' Then we would be even closer as friends, friends who were not yet lovers. The expectancy was always the better feeling.

"When we were in the streets together, cars and traffic were no threat to Jimmy. He told me that he knew cars, and there was no way a car was going to hit him. He would fight make-believe bulls head-on in the traffic, using passing cars as bulls to cape with his coat. He loved bullfighting. The sport did a lot for him in terms of quelling fear. He believed that if you could face a live bull in a bull ring with people watching and hollering, a theater audience would certainly seem tame by comparison. He told me he had been to Mexico and 'danced with the bull in the ring.' He often used the rhythm of the matador, the measured footwork, in a scene. You have to look for it, but it's there. He would sometimes use that 'head-down, eyes-up look, staring at you dead-on,' which comes from staring down the bull."

Throughout this period Jimmy maintained his contact with Rogers Brackett, and one Sunday Brackett invited him to cocktails at the home of Lemuel Ayers. Brackett explained that Ayers was a big-time theatrical producer who had a production planned for the end of the year with a part that would be ideal for Jimmy. Jimmy charmed Ayers and his wife, Shirley, never mentioning the fact that he was an aspiring actor. After socializing a few more times with the Ayerses, Lemuel asked if he'd like to crew as a cabin boy on their yacht. Jimmy accepted with alacrity and joined them on a week-long cruise to Cape Cod that August. During the cruise back, he found a chance to casually mention to Ayers that he was an actor and was in fact going to study at the Actors Studio. By then, Ayers had become fond of Jimmy so he suggested he come in for a reading for his play, *See the Jaguar.*

Bill Bast remembers the night of the reading, which was held in a midtown hotel. Jimmy's nerves were showing and he rushed around the apartment in a state of panic, totally disorganized, trying to get dressed.

The play was centered around the character of Wally Wilkins, a sixteen-year-old innocent whose mother, trying to protect him from the bestiality of the world, has kept him locked up in an icehouse for most of his life. Before dying—and without explaining that she is about to die—his mother sends him out into the world barefoot and in overalls carrying only her letter to a benevolent teacher whom she asks to take care of him.

If ever there was a part written for James Dean, this was it, and his first reading of the script went well, so well, in fact, that the play's author, N. Richard Nash, asked him to come back again to read at the theater.

Nash recalls that Jimmy came to the theater wearing glasses with one cracked lens. Although he had read so well the first time, he read very haltingly and badly on the second occasion. Nash couldn't understand what was wrong and asked Jimmy to come see him.

"What happened?" asked Nash.

"I broke my glasses and can't see," explained Jimmy.

Nash promised him another reading and told him to go fix his glasses.

"I can't," said Jimmy. "I don't have any money."

Nash gave him ten dollars and set up the date for the reading.

"Two or three days later he came in and his glasses were still broken," recalls Nash. "But he'd memorized the entire thing so he didn't have to read. . . . Afterward I said to him, 'You son of a bitch, why didn't you get your glasses fixed?' He pulled out this vicious-looking knife and said, 'I saw this knife and I've been wanting one . . . I just had to have it. But I figured I couldn't betray you entirely so I memorized the script for the reading.' "

Late in October, Jimmy received a letter from Winton saying he would drive to Fairmount for a visit if Jimmy was there, and he would bring with him a partial dental bridge to replace Jimmy's old one, which was causing him problems, not a small gesture on Winton's part: he now seemed willing to go out of his way to be friends with his son. That was the only encouragement Jimmy needed to get away. He suggested to his roommates that they go with him to Fairmount for a visit. Bast then had a nine-to-five job in the public relations department at CBS and said he couldn't possibly go, but Jimmy refused to take no for an answer. He arranged for someone to call Bill's employers and say he was sick. The trip had one large attraction for all three: the promise of home-cooked meals. At dawn the next day, with only ten dollars among them, the trio began hitchhiking.

They got a ride: Clyde McCullough, a catcher for the Pittsburgh Pirates on his way to Des Moines, picked them up. By nightfall they were in Fairmount. The Winslows showered Jimmy with affection and made Dizzy and Bill feel welcome even though they were put off by the young people sharing Jimmy's bedroom.

Winton soon arrived and, as promised, had brought a new bridge to replace the one he had made years before when Jimmy was a child. Jimmy and Winton got along well, and Winton even congratulated Jimmy on the progress he was making in New York.

Jimmy delighted in showing his friends around the farm and Fairmount. When they visited Adeline Nall at the high school, she turned her drama class over to them.

The Fairmount trip was cut short by a telephone call from Jane Deacy with good news: Jimmy had a date for a proper audition for *See the Jaguar*, and had to return to New York as soon as possible. Ortense prepared an early Thanksgiving dinner, and with money borrowed from Winton and the Winslows, the three friends returned to New York by bus.

N. Richard Nash remembers the audition and the fact that Jimmy was "the only person in the play who caught the spirit of it from the beginning. There's a great difference between a simpleminded person playing a simpleminded role, and a complex person like Jimmy playing it. He brought a great richness to the part. There are scenes of great puzzlement, and you have never seen such puzzlement as portrayed by Dean. He had it. It was deep down and quite beautiful."

Director Michael Gordon agreed. Gordon had interviewed more than a hundred young actors for the role and was at his wits' end because it was a very difficult part to cast. When he saw Jimmy, he knew that he was the one actor who could handle the role.

Jimmy was signed and began rehearsing on October 20. One afternoon the director had difficulties with the leading lady. He berated her cruelly until Nash, who was in the audience, was unable to listen anymore—he jumped to his feet, told the director to leave her alone, and then stormed out of the theater.

Jimmy, who was onstage at the time, ran off to the front of the theater, where he stopped Nash. "You fight for her," he said. "Why don't you fight as hard for your play? They're ruining it and you say nothing." With that, Jimmy ran back to the theater.

Meanwhile, the boy who'd had too much time on his hands now never seemed to have time enough. Whenever he was not at the theater rehearsing his lines he was with Chris going over their skit, which they were due to perform at the Actors Studio within a few weeks. They tried to get the scene down to the required five minutes, but it always seemed to run between twelve and fourteen. They finally gave up trying to shave it down and resigned themselves to letting the judges blow the whistle on them.

At home Jimmy drove Bill and Dizzy up the wall asking them to read lines from *Jaguar* with him and kept them awake much of the night as he tried to master a folk song that Alec Wilder had composed for the show. Jimmy was tone-deaf and, as Bill recalls, "Nothing could help him with the singing."

Jimmy soon decided to move out on his own. Rather than try to find an apartment, he rented a room again in the Iroquois because even though he now had a Broadway role he still didn't have enough faith in his earnings to risk a monthly rent. It was cheaper to stay week to week in a hotel, and it was easier to bail out if he ran short. Besides, all he needed was a bed, his books, sketch pads, and the all-important telephone. He wore borrowed clothes and saved his money for movies, sandwiches, and getting around town. He also bought a lot of records. The fact that he didn't own a record player mattered very little—there was always someone somewhere who had one. He would show up at parties hauling records and explain that he just couldn't pass another day without hearing some of his favorites.

On November 12, 1952, only a few days before he was to go to Hartford for out-of-town tryouts of *See the Jaguar*, Jimmy and Chris performed their skit before Elia Kazan and the panel of judges at the Actors Studio.

Kazan—or Gadge, as he has always been known in the business—was born in Constantinople and was four when his Greek parents emigrated to the United States and settled in New York city, his father becoming a rug merchant. Gadge was drawn to the theater and then to film, becoming first one of Broadway's finest directors and then one of Hollywood's top directors. He had been one of the founders of the Actors Studio, home of the method style of acting, and by 1952, at the age of forty-three and at the height of his career, he had made ten films and won an Academy Award. He was considered a kind of wonderworker, particularly because of his preference for new, unknown talent. It had been Gadge who had discovered Marlon Brando—a fact of which Jimmy was very much aware. As Jimmy's actor friend Bill Gunn put it, "Kazan was gold. Every New York actor dreamed of being found anywhere doing anything by Kazan. Kazan was the ultimate. If Brando was the God, then Kazan was the Godfather."

Thus Jimmy was understandably nervous about performing in front of Kazan. In fact, he was so nervous that Chris was certain he would run out on her. "I can't do it," he said. "I'm not ready yet." Luckily, their props included four cans of beer, and these Jimmy quickly consumed. But then they were without props. Chris thought they could get by without the beer cans, but Jimmy refused and rushed out to buy four more, making them lose their place. But when Jimmy came back he was no longer nervous. "Physical energy is the answer," he said.

"Without his glasses on, Jimmy couldn't find center stage," recalls Chris. "He ended up almost in the opposite wing, away from both overhead amber lights, which didn't matter too much because the scene was supposed to be nighttime anyway. I ran out, stood for a moment, then sat down at center stage and didn't look at him. He was startled, but immediately made the adjustment. He rolled over twice on the floor toward me, laughed, and said, 'Hi,' which wasn't in the script, and we were on our way."

The scene went on past the allotted five minutes, but the bell never sounded: Jimmy and Chris were allowed to play out their scene, which ran for fourteen minutes. When it was over the studio fell silent. Then Kazan spoke. "Very nice," he said. "Very nice." Kazan later told Chris that it was a very sensitive scene and that everyone had wanted to see the end of it. Lee Strasberg, artistic director of the studio and its guiding force, also had good things to say about their effort, telling Chris that it was well written and that they could have seen even more of it.

After the audition, Jimmy and Chris ran down the steps of the Actors Studio and into the street, headed for Jerry's bar. There they scrambled onto bar stools, out of breath and already high with tension. Jimmy collared Jerry and asked, "Do you want to see the scene the way we just did it?" Jerry knew it really wasn't as much a question as an announcement and stepped back to get a better view. Jimmy and Chris went through the entire scene while sitting on the stools.

Out of the hundred-odd aspirants for entry into the studio, Jimmy and Christine were two of the twelve chosen as finalists, but they would not learn whether they had been accepted until the board announced its decision several weeks later. When Chris got the postcard informing her of both their acceptances, she called Jimmy and that night they again went to Jerry's, this time for a celebration.

A few days later Jimmy went to Hartford where an unpleasant incident occurred during rehearsal of the third act of *See the Jaguar*. Director Michael Gordon recalls: "The tension during that scene was pretty high, and Jimmy and the prop man had words. Suddenly Jimmy took out after the prop man. I was sitting down in the audience and when I heard a commotion I jumped up onstage, but by the time I got there it was all over."

Arthur Kennedy, who played the teacher in *Jaguar*, later told writer Ed Corley that Jimmy had pulled a knife, probably the same one he had bought with the money Nash gave him for glasses. According to Corley, Kennedy, who was a star on Broadway as well as in films, "supposedly took the knife out of Jimmy's hand and broke the blade, with stern instructions 'not to pull any of that crap in my show.' " The matter ended there, but the story circulated around Broadway for months.

It was the afternoon of December 3, 1952, and Jimmy was scheduled to open that night in *See the Jaguar*. He'd not had breakfast before the final dress rehearsal and he was hungry. Huddled alone at a table in Cromwell's he saw Marty Landau in a booth with Carol Sinclair and Rusty Slocum, actors he knew, and a brunette he had never met. He waved to Marty and locked eyes with the brunette, whose name was Barbara Glenn.

"Who is that incredible-looking man?" Barbara asked Marty.

"His name is James Dean," said Marty, "and he's a friend of mine. Do you want to meet him?"

"Yes," said Barbara.

Marty went over to Jimmy and asked him to join them.

"Got no one else to eat with," Jimmy mumbled.

"He was physically gorgeous with a lost quality about him that immediately touched me," Barbara recalls. "It was as though he was the only person in the world, totally unattached to anything or anyone. But there was something else in his demeanor that flashed red-light warning signals at me."

Jimmy was not in the mood for small talk and failed miserably at it, mumbling answers, asking only enough to find out that Barbara was a struggling actress. Nevertheless, something about her touched a chord in his psyche as well. He once told me that if he walked into a party he could, at a glance, spot the one girl he wanted to go home with, and Barbara appealed to him instantly because he sensed an intensity and neuroticism that was a match for his. Barbara was just sixteen years old with an incredible figure: an eighteen-inch waist held in by a four-inch-wide belt over a tight skirt and a thirty-six-inch bust barely concealed by a sweater. As she puts it, "I was waiting for someone to relate to me and wondered why men didn't look into my eyes."

See the Jaguar opened that night at the Cort Theatre on Broadway. Other shows playing at the time were *Guys and Dolls*, *The King and*

I, and *South Pacific*. In keeping with established tradition, the entire cast went to an opening-night party at Sardi's to anxiously await what *New York Times* theater critic Brooks Atkinson would say of their efforts.

Jimmy invited Dizzy to attend the party with him. "His feet never touched the floor," she recalls. "He just flew from table to table, talking, laughing. I watched people's eyes pouring adulation all over him; they loved him.

"But it was a very crushing night for me. We left together because we wanted to be together, but he was staying at the Royalton that night, and after we got upstairs they called and told him he couldn't have a woman in his room. So we ordered something to drink and then he walked me downstairs and put me in a cab. I had the feeling that things were starting to move for Jimmy and I would never be able to catch up. I saw him two or three times after that and then I left for Trinidad."

See the Jaguar closed after only five performances. Most of the reviews for the play were bad—Atkinson cited none of the actors and commented instead on the play's "tortured literary style and tangled craftsmanship"—but all of Jimmy's notices were good, commending his extraordinary performance in a difficult role.

Jimmy got a ticket for Christine White to attend the last performance. As she watched him, she felt that his jaguar gestures—an animal faster than a car—even his pacing back and forth were stealing the show.

Afterward they went back to his room in the Iroquois and went over his work, what she thought of it, what he thought of it—inexhaustible subjects. While on the road Jimmy had learned a lot of stage lingo and had picked up more street slang and long strings of obscenities. He had toughened up.

Because his hotel room was so small—really only a cell big enough to contain the bed—they moved out onto the fire escape. They sat on that metal grating until dawn, talking and drinking beer, punctuating their statements by letting the bottles slip through their fingers so they could hear the crash on the ground ten floors below.

For both Jimmy and Chris that night on the fire escape was like being in a great play without an audience: only the two of them facing the windowless brick wall of the building behind the hotel. They were both still unknown and were not yet sought after. Even so, they were excited, intoxicated with dreams and geared for the future. They concocted outlandish plots just for the fun of it; anything seemed possible. Thus when they were called in to read for a part, they had to come down, lower themselves to that other reality to read a nothing part of a prosaic bit. They believed themselves to be good competitors, hard to beat. But at the moment no one was beating a path to their doors.

A few days later, Jimmy called the manager of the Iroquois and got a room for Chris directly below his. She moved in immediately—she had no furniture to worry about—arriving with one suitcase and two plants, one of which she gave to Jimmy to cheer up his dark cell. They talked on the phone, visited each other's rooms, walked the streets together, went to interviews together, ate together, did scenes anywhere, anytime, for fun, for growth, just to feel alive. Although they were together constantly, Chris contends that their relationship was purely platonic.

Jimmy was depressed over the closing of the play, but his reviews gave him more confidence in himself as an actor and in his ability to earn a living at his chosen craft.

By then, too, Jimmy had begun attending the Actors Studio. He wrote to Marcus and Ortense telling them the news: "I am very proud to announce that I am a member of the Actors Studio, the greatest school of the theater. It houses great people like Marlon Brando, Julie Harris, Arthur Kennedy, Elia Kazan, Mildred Dunnock, Kevin McCarthy, Monty Clift and June Havoc. It is the best thing to happen to any actor. I am one of the youngest to belong."

The Actors Studio meant very little to Marcus and Ortense, but they responded to Jimmy's plea as they had on every other occasion when he had asked for money, and wired him twenty-five dollars.

Despite his excitement at being accepted to the studio, Jimmy attended classes only rarely because as part of the studio program students were called upon to perform before the class and were then criticized, sometimes caustically, by the entire group. For his first performance before the studio group, Jimmy adapted a character from Barnaby Conrad's novel *Matador*, and wrote a scene for himself in which, as a matador, he prepared for his final bullfight.

His props were Sidney Franklin's cape, a statue of the Virgin, and a candle. Lee Strasberg gave the scene a penetrating and harsh critique. Jimmy listened impassively, but the color drained from his face. When the critique ended, Jimmy slung the cape over his shoulder and left the studio, furious with the criticism. He never appeared before the class again.

"The desire to better himself was not as strong as his urge for independence," Strasberg told me some years later, adding that Jimmy never went to him for personal help. "He was sensitive about letting people in too close. He seemed to shy away from people. He was afraid they would get to know him. But he was a natural-born actor with an unusual sense of naturalness and integrity."

Jimmy told Chris White that he got bored when he had to watch the so-called organic scenes mounted by the beginners at the studio. Of course, he, too, was a beginner, but he didn't feel like one. He was also determined to dodge any storm rising up in his heart as a protest to the invasions of criticism. He spoke to her about the awful feeling of tottering on the brink of maximum retaliation when crossed. He believed that if he could be in charge of what he was doing, he would be as good as he could possibly be.

Shortly before Christmas Jimmy and Bill Bast had a last cup of coffee together at Cromwell's. Bill had decided to return to California and devote himself to being a full-time writer. "Just forget about the end results," Jimmy advised his friend. "Remember the gratification that comes in the work, not in the end result. Just remember who you are and what you are, and don't take any of their crap out there."

After his short speech, Jimmy suddenly got up and announced, "I've got to go."

Bast left the drugstore and was walking down the street when he heard Jimmy call out his name. Jimmy came up to him with three books in his hand, which he had apparently bought as a Christmas present.

"Here," he said, "read the one called 'Harpies on the Seashore' in the *Maurois Reader*." Bill looked down at the books. There were paperback editions of Virginia Woolf's *Orlando* and Carson McCullers's *The Heart Is a Lonely Hunter*, and a hard-bound copy of

The André Maurois Reader. On the inside of the cover was written: "To Bill—While in the aura of metaphysical whoo-haas, ebb away your displeasures on this. May flights of harpies escort your winged trip of vengeance."

The two friends were not to see each other again for more than a year. Meanwhile, Jimmy had run into Barbara Glenn again. She was with Billy James, an actor friend of his, and he invited them back to his room. Barbara recalls that "the room was heavy with the attraction between the two of us and I expected him to ask me for a date." Instead, Jimmy gave her a copy of a *New Yorker* magazine profile on Truman Capote and said he would call her to find out what she thought about it.

Jimmy did call, and within a few weeks he and Barbara were in love, a fact that surprised Barbara, who was usually attracted to much older men and considered Jimmy a boy. The glue in their relationship, the thing that held them together, was sex, and Jimmy became Barbara's first major love affair.

Jimmy once told Barbara, "You know what's going to happen to us? You're going to grow up and marry somebody, and I'm going to grow up and marry somebody, but we're still going to be having an affair until the day we die."

"The sexual attraction was so powerful," Barbara recalls. "There were a lot of people after Jimmy, men as well as women, but our physical relationship held."

Barbara came from a very traditional Jewish family in Queens and had to go home most every night, but the romance flourished.

Jimmy used part of the money he had earned on *Jaguar* to buy a used Indian 500 motorcycle. With Barbara reluctantly holding tight around his waist they cruised the city from Brooklyn to Harlem with Greenwich Village their favorite spot. In those days one could get a plate of spaghetti and meatballs large enough for two for seventy-five cents at any one of the Italian restaurants on Thompson Street. Twenty-five cents would buy an espresso at Figaro's on the corner of Bleecker and MacDougal, including a table for the evening shared with friends.

Although Jimmy loved his motorcycle, Barbara loathed and feared it. "I considered it an instrument of death," she says. "I remember half of my life with Jimmy was waiting for him because he was always late, and I was always wondering if he was going to make it. There was an inevitability about Jimmy's death from the day I met him, which frightened me because I always had the feeling that somehow, someway, someday he's not going to show up."

Chapter Five

THE LITTLE PRINCE

In 1953 Jimmy came of age as an actor. Jane Deacy, who had started her own agency, believed in Jimmy and his potential. Fortified with his good reviews in *Jaguar*, she was able to get him roles in seventeen television productions. He soon earned a reputation as being one of the better juvenile actors, especially good at playing young psychotics, but he also acquired a reputation for being difficult.

A director who worked with Jimmy in TV at the time recalls that at rehearsals he often sat aloof and moody on the set waiting for his cue. "At rehearsals he would mumble his words as though completely disinterested in them. But, like Brando, the moment the camera was on him he came across." One day Jimmy learned that NBC was planning to do a bullfight drama on television and needed an expert to coach Ray Danton, the star, in some traditional matador moves.

He went to see the writer, James Costigan, and introduced himself. "I studied bullfighting in Mexico," he said, "and I know all about it."

In recalling the incident, Costigan told me, "I didn't know he was also an actor, but we needed a coach for the bullfight scenes so we hired him after explaining that we had very little money to pay. He said it didn't matter.

"The next day he showed up in Levi's and a ragged jacket

with a cape and two swords under his arm. I found out later that everything he knew about bullfighting came from a book, but he taught Danton how to perform the movements. Later, when I offered to pay him, he said, 'Just remember me when you've got a part I can play.' "

Months later Costigan wrote a teleplay with a part ideal for Jimmy. He told him about it and virtually promised him the role. Unfortunately, the director on the project had worked with Jimmy before and considered him a brat. She told the producers that if Dean was in the teleplay she would quit. Costigan was out of town on vacation so Jimmy lost the part.

Barbara was working steadily that spring and Jimmy was jealous of the time they were apart. Their relationship was volatile, with a pattern of breakup and makeup that was ideally suited to both their temperaments. They invariably fought just before they were to be separated. While Barbara was emotional, Jimmy seemed fearful of losing his temper and would never shout back at her or really contend an issue, which frustrated Barbara even more.

Early in the summer Barbara got a role in a stock company that would take her away from the city for the summer. Friends decided to have a party for her. When Jimmy was told about it he snarled, "What the hell is this party crap? She's only going away for two weeks."

On the night of the party, Jimmy sat in a corner and sulked, making nasty comments until all the guests except for Carol Sinclair went home. Jimmy still refused to acknowledge Barbara, who finally said, "Okay, Jimmy, if you're around when I'm back, I'll see you."

Barbara and Carol went to Jerry's Bar and sat in a booth nursing drinks. The more Barbara talked about Jimmy and his behavior, the more she cried, and there soon were tears streaming down her face.

Jimmy walked in, looked around for Barbara, and sat down in the booth as Carol discreetly left. He reached for Barbara's hand and squeezed it. Nothing was said, no apologies on his part, but they left and went back to his apartment where they made love.

Thanks to Jimmy's good reviews in *Jaguar*, MGM had contacted Jane Deacy with an offer to test Jimmy for a role in an upcoming movie, *The Silver Chalice.* Jane had read the script and didn't feel the part was right for Jimmy, so she was holding the studio off, hoping for an offer for a better film for him.

That June, while discussions with the studio were going on and Barbara was away in summer stock, Jimmy performed a small part in an off-Broadway production of a play called *The Scarecrow*, directed by Frank Corsaro and starring Douglas Watson, Eli Wallach, and Patricia Neal. The performance took place in the Theatre de Lys on Christopher Street in Greenwich Village.

Jimmy had met Frank Corsaro at the Actors Studio, and they had become friends. Corsaro, who was five years older than Jimmy, had more acting experience and was already moving toward directing; he later became a theater director, opera director, teacher, and head of both the Actors Studio and the Juilliard School. Jimmy was fascinated by Corsaro's knowledge of music, and Corsaro found him an eager student: Jimmy studied Bach with him. Corsaro also played classical records for Jimmy, performed pieces for him on the piano, and gave him books to read. Jimmy absorbed it all with enthusiasm: he sincerely wanted to learn, and he enjoyed the lessons. The two friends also discussed literature, and spent hours discussing Kierkegaard and Kafka. Corsaro loaned Jimmy books and tried to teach him the necessary historical perspective.

Corsaro liked Jimmy and believed he had a wonderful raw talent, although Jimmy lacked technique and didn't believe he needed it. Corsaro also sensed something desperate in Jimmy and tried several times to have him go into therapy. But Jimmy, like many actors, feared if he undertook psychoanalysis—if he resolved his problems—it would dilute his talent.

Corsaro discovered that as a friend Jimmy could be fascinating but also trying. He played games with his friends and sometimes revealed a cruel streak. He drank, sometimes too much, but that was only one more kind of experimentation. He was, Corsaro believes, a young man in transition trying to find himself, trying to define himself.

Jimmy had similarly intense conversations with other actor friends and spent much of his time in Greenwich Village, hanging out in such local bars as the Minetta Tavern, Louie's Tavern, and Rienzi's. Such discussions were a fundamental aspect of being "hep." Another aspect was being flat broke. Jimmy was earning money from his television performances, but Jane Deacy was holding it for him and had put him on an allowance, which he quickly consumed. When low on funds, he often borrowed money from Barbara.

Toward the end of June he talked with Barbara on the phone, and she admitted she was upset about her role in the play she was doing. He then wrote her a letter.

"Don't be surprised if a lot of people like the Lindburger cheese. Whether the play is good or bad you will have had the chance to play a role quite outside yourself.

"I guess I'm alright. Got another cold. Have been staying with a friend of Frank's [Corsaro] in Manhattan. Will move to Frank's later when New Dramatist reading is finished. *Scarecrow* will resume its run in two weeks. That means Frank will not go to upstate NY and will commence rehearsals for *Scarecrow* next week because of some new people. He informed me that I could play the *Scarecrow* in August. . . I don't have a TV job yet. Still hoping $.

"Received your check. Haven't cashed it yet. Will tomorrow. Thank you. Sorry you had to go through all that trouble.

"I'm still holding MGM off while I see if I can get a play. Got a new pair of shoes honey. Black loafer *"Weejuns."* Shit! I'm so proud of them. Got a pair of pants too, not too good but alright. My uncle sent me $30.00 and besides I deserved it. Made me feel good just to go in and get something."

As Jimmy indicated in his letter, Douglas Watson, the lead in *Scarecrow,* was thinking of leaving the play, which had become quite successful, and Corsaro had offered Jimmy the lead. He thought Jimmy was right for the part, but nothing came of the offer: Watson stayed on, and Jimmy went off to do more work in television.

Jimmy soon wrote to Barbara Glenn again asking her to forgive him for "such a sloppy letter, little drunk, drink quite a lot lately. . . . In antiphonal azure swing, souls drone their unfinished melody . . . when did we live and when did we not? In my drunken stupor I said a gem. I must repeat it to you loved one. Let's see 'great actors are often time pretentious livers. The pretentious actor, a great liver.' (Don't get a headache over it) God Dammit!! . . .

You're terribly missing. Come back some day. Maybe I can come up and see you. When do you reckon? You think you need understanding? Who do you think you are. I could use a little myself. You're probably running around up there with all those handsome guys. When I get my boat, you'll be sorry.

"Hope you're OK up there. Working pretty hard. More than you can say for us poor thespians back in the city.

"Got to move out of this crappy old apartment next week. . . . Can't get along with nobody I guess. Makes you feel good when you're not wanted."

Alongside his signature Jimmy sketched a fat devil and pasted a collage of eyes and mouth. By the eyes he wrote, "to see you with," and by the mouth he wrote, "to kiss you with."

During this period Jimmy had no fixed home and stayed with friends. He roomed for a while with Frank Corsaro, and later he moved in with Leonard Rosenman. Leonard and Adele Rosenman were having domestic problems and had opted for a trial separation: Adele went with the children to her parents' home in Nogales, Arizona, and Leonard kept the apartment. Jimmy agreed to pay half the $300 a month rent and moved in with all his belongings: bongo drums, books, bullfighter's cape, hi-fi equipment, some record albums, and a small box. When Leonard asked what was in the box Jimmy opened it to reveal a .22 automatic. Leonard recalls asking why Jimmy needed a gun, and was told that it was only a gift.

While living with Leonard, Jimmy acted as his chauffeur and took him to his appointments on his motorcycle. "I was on the back all dressed up and carrying my briefcase, and he was wearing his black leather outfit," says Rosenman. "Sometimes when we arrived at an appointment I would still be shaking from the terror of the ride, but Jimmy was skillful with that cycle of his and we never had an accident."

For a short time Jimmy stayed in the apartment of an Englishman who worked for TWA. The offer was that he could stay in the apartment free if he took care of the man's dog, a big German shepherd. While walking the dog one morning around Rockefeller Plaza he ran into Christine White, whom he had not seen for weeks.

She smiled. He grinned and said only, "I'm a dog-sitter. Can you beat that?"

Chris, too, had recently come into a new place to live. A friend of hers, another aspiring actress, had gone to Europe "to look for lost golf balls," an explanation that was supposed to mean that no one needed an excuse to go to Europe: the rule then among Jimmy and all his friends was "Just do it." The sublet was near the East River and had three rooms; since it was on the fifth floor the rent was low. The girl who'd headed for Europe left her record player in her apartment, and Chris fell heir to it. She considered herself rich. Now she and Jimmy could listen to their favorite music: *Peer Gynt*, Mozart, Janáceck, jazz, and more jazz. And Billie Holiday. "When Your Lover Has Gone" drove Jimmy nuts. He was also fond of the tango, and since the apartment was big he finally had enough room to teach her that famous dance. Having been to Mexico, he knew the classic steps, and as she swept around the room he would call out, "No, no, go for the whole beat. Don't take little half steps . . . don't run . . . use your long legs . . . be broad . . . spread like you're flying . . . then stomp and dig in . . ."

Along with riding the motorcycle Jimmy had taken to wearing boots, and he would often clomp up the five flights to Chris's apartment, yank off his boots, and crash onto the sofa, his legs dangling over its arm.

Eventually the period of his apartment sitting came to an end. As he wrote to Barbara Glenn:

"I'm staying in a guy's apartment while he flies to London. No dear . . . by airplane! He's a TWA purser not a vampire. At least not a full-fledged one. That's why I have to leave tomorrow. He's coming back. I'm sure he considers me a victim. I do not wish to move to———'s apartment now. He has been staying here with me. He also considers me a victim. I refuse to be sucked in to things of that nature. Street urchin again."

Barbara knew exactly what Jimmy was writing about. She knew from what Jimmy occasionally told her that there were certain aspects of his life that he disliked, and she felt he was angry and upset with himself for his involvement with homosexuals who, he said, considered him as a victim.

Jimmy didn't remain a street urchin for long, for he finally found an apartment of his own, a tiny fifth-floor walk-up at 19 West Sixty-eighth Street.

The apartment was really a maid's quarters on the top floor of a brownstone. Some light came through the round windows revealing bookshelves crammed with records ranging from Schoenberg to Sinatra; an eclectic collection of books on a variety of subjects including treatises on bullfighting and jungle drums; books on theater from Stanislavsky to Shakespeare; children's books like *Charlotte's Web*; and novels ranging from Thomas Mann's *Death in Venice* to Saint Exupéry's *The Little Prince*, which Jimmy told everyone was his favorite book. He soon furnished it to his taste. On the bookshelves were a flute, a hot plate, a baseball bat, and a plant sprouting from a coffee can. A bust of Jimmy looked down on a new chrome music stand that held several sheets of music. Bull horns and a red matador's cape adorned one wall.

One day while making rounds of casting directors Jimmy, who was dressed in his interview outfit—a worn-out checked sport coat and brown corduroy pants—met up with a friend of his from the West Coast, an actor named Ray Curry whom he had once worked with as an extra in a film. They were both hungry and Jimmy suggested a drugstore on West Forty-seventh that served fresh orange juice and offered thick pats of butter with its muffins. Ray noticed a friend of his at the counter and started talking with him. Finally he said, "Hey, we're all bums from the Coast," and introduced Jimmy to Jonathan Gilmore, another actor. Until then, Jimmy had ignored Gilmore but then he noticed that he was carrying a copy of Barnaby Conrad's *Matador*. The three got into a discussion of bullfighting, and Jimmy told them about the bullfights he had seen in Tijuana, and the cape he had been given by Sidney Franklin, the matador from Brooklyn. Jimmy asked if he could look at the book. He opened it on the counter, and flipped through it with one hand. With the other he eagerly helped himself to all the butter on his plate as well as that on Curry's. He spread the butter on his muffin and giggled as he ate it, sucking his fingers to clean the butter off.

Jimmy learned that Gilmore had been in New York only a couple of months. Most important to Jimmy, Jonathan was not only a bullfight aficionado but he also owned an old Norton motorcycle.

Jimmy and Jonathan became friends. They loaned each other money and shared tips on where to find work. They saw each other regularly, meeting on the same street corner or getting together for meals at the drugstore. They started going to movies together, and spent one entire day watching George Stevens's *A Place in the Sun* over and over in a second-run theater.

One night Jonathan was surprised to hear a knock at the door of his apartment on West Forty-seventh Street. It was Jimmy, his hands covered with grease, who said he had dropped by and seen the Norton motorcycle chained to a water pipe on the street. He had smelled gas, and saw some leaking from the carburetor. He had fiddled with the bike for an hour until he had found the problem, which he explained in detail to Gilmore.

A few evenings later in Gilmore's apartment, after they'd both had too much cheap wine and were tipsy, Jimmy asked Jonathan, "You ever had something to do with a guy, or just fooling around?" Jonathan told him that when he was fifteen he had gone to a Hollywood party at the Garden of Allah and Tyrone Power, who was drunk, had kissed him on the mouth, squeezed his hand, patted him on the head, and told him that he was the most beautiful boy he had seen in a long time. Since then he had been approached many times but, no, he'd never had an *affair* with a man, he had just been experimental and trying to get around. Jimmy seemed satisfied by his friend's response and, for the moment, let the issue drop.

Near the end of August Jimmy again worked with television producer Franklin Heller, this time in an episode of CBS's *Danger* series called "Death Is My Neighbor." Jimmy had the role of a psychotic janitor who ends up being gunned down at a window. The star of the program was Walter Hampden. Then nearly seventy-five, Hampden was a famous Shakespearean stage actor who had also performed as a leading man in both silents and talkies. Heller had a great deal of respect for Hampden; Jimmy didn't seem to. At one point during the first reading, Jimmy suddenly threw his copy of the script to the floor and announced, "This is shit." Heller stopped the rehearsal and took Jimmy out into the hallway. He told him about Hampden's experience and reputation and asked him to show some respect. Back onstage in the rehearsal hall, Jimmy again threw his script to the floor and swore. The third time he did it Heller threatened to fire him.

But then Hampden spoke up and took Heller out into the hallway. "I've seen this young man on television," he said, "and I think he's very talented. As a matter of fact, I think he's going to be a big star. He's very rough around the edges, but he's going to be okay, and it's our duty to encourage people like that."

Back in the rehearsal hall Hampden took Jimmy aside and spoke softly to him for a few minutes. Then they went back to work, and Jimmy performed perfectly.

Also performing in the teleplay was Betsy Palmer, a Hoosier like Jimmy as well as a devotee of Stanislavsky. Betsy and Jimmy already knew each other—earlier that same month they'd performed together in "Sentence of Death," an episode of CBS's *Studio One*—and she and Jimmy started dating: Barbara Glenn was obviously not only out of sight, but she was out of Jimmy's mind. Neither of them had much money, so Betsy began to cook dinners for him in her one-room apartment. Most of their dates were spent walking the streets of New York together and going to movies. Betsy gave him a quilt, sheets, and bedding for his apartment, and they became lovers. However, she would later say that Jimmy displayed little interest in sex: "As a matter of fact, my assumption about Jimmy was that he was almost asexual."

That may have been true of his relationship with Betsy, but Jimmy apparently did have some interest in sex, as indicated by another evening he spent with Jonathan Gilmore. Jonathan recalls that on September 7, 1953, he and Jimmy were James Sheldon's guests at an inexpensive French restaurant. Jimmy was soon drunk on wine and started to act up; among other things he squeezed a crepe suzette until the filling came out, and then started to laugh hilariously. Sheldon said to Jimmy, "You're a knucklehead," and rubbed Jimmy's head. He paid the check and left.

By then Jimmy and Jonathan were both smashed. They walked back to Jonathan's apartment where Jimmy lay on the bed with his head hanging over the edge, looking upside down at Jonathan, who sat opposite him in a chair. They talked about old Hollywood—Jonathan's mother had been an actress in the 1930s and he knew many of the old-time stars. At one point Jonathan tried to stand up but he was too drunk so he ended up on the floor near Jimmy. He reached up and touched Jimmy's hair. "Man, you know more than just getting kissed by Tyrone Power," Jimmy said. "You know things like I do 'cause you've been through the same shit, haven't you, John?"

Jonathan, who had kept a daily journal for years, noted that on that night he and Jimmy talked for hours on subjects ranging from Sidney Franklin to homosexual producers in Hollywood who had made passes at them, with Jimmy saying, "You know I've had my cock sucked by some of the big names in Hollywood and I think it's pretty funny because I wanted more than anything to just get some little part, something to do, and they'd invite me for fancy dinners overlooking the blue Pacific, and we'd have a few drinks, and how long could it go on? That's what I wanted to know—and the answer was it could go on until there was nothing left, until they had what they wanted and there was nothing left [for me]."

The diary notes indicate that the undercurrent of the conversation was each other's attitude toward love for another man. As Jonathan recalls it, there was a strange intensity in the air as they talked. Their faces were close and Jimmy put a finger on Jonathan's lower lip and started to giggle, and then they kissed. It was the first time Jonathan had ever really been kissed by another man. Jimmy asked Jonathan, "Can you be fucked?" "Jesus, I don't think so," said Jonathan. "I want to try to fuck you," said Jimmy. They kissed then, and tried to make love.

Jimmy's first homosexual contact with DeWeerd had been experimental, his relationship with Brackett was opportunistic, but he and Jonathan apparently experienced a mutual physical attraction. "Jimmy was neither homosexual or bisexual," Jonathan said recently. "I think he was multisexual. He once said that he didn't think there was any such thing as being bisexual. He felt that if someone really needed emotional support from a man he would probably be homosexual, but if he needed emotional support from a woman he would be more heterosexual."

Jimmy once put it more succinctly when he said, "I'm certainly not going to go through life with one hand tied behind my back."

In September Jimmy was asked to read for a role in "Glory in the Flower," a drama by William Inge that was to be part of a CBS program called *Omnibus* scheduled to air in October. Inge himself suggested Dean to director Andrew McCullough for the important role of Bronco, a marijuana-smoking juvenile delinquent. Inge told McCullough that Jimmy was hard to handle but would be just right for the part, and McCullough, believing he could handle anyone, called him in.

Jimmy sat down and began reading the script. After a few lines he put his feet up on the table in front of him, then took a knife out of his boot and stuck it into the table. McCullough pulled out the knife and tossed it aside.

"Okay," he said to Jimmy. "Let's cut that out. I want to hear you read."

Jimmy read, McCullough thought him marvelous, and he got the part. The other actors in the drama were Jessica Tandy and Hume Cronyn. Cronyn—by then well known as one of America's most distinguished and versatile actors—played the role of the proprietor of a shabby bar with a small dance floor. Eager to protect his liquor license, he is forced to confront the dozen-odd rowdy teenagers, chief among them Jimmy, who crowd his premises. Cronyn had two major scenes with Jimmy, and neither went well in rehearsal.

In the first, aware that four of the teenagers were passing around a bottle of liquor, he had to confront them and demand the bottle. The scene had been rehearsed: he was supposed to ultimately find the bottle in Jimmy's hip pocket. During the final technical rehearsal Cronyn waded into the crowd, located Jimmy, but could not find the bottle. He fumbled around, looked under the table, behind cushions, under napkins, even among the plastic flowers on the table. No bottle. He finally gave up, and the camera stopped rolling.

"Where is it, Jimmy?" he asked.

"Why don't you just find it?" challenged Jimmy.

"Is it worth it?" asked Cronyn, aware that Jimmy was trying in his own way to make the scene more real. "I think I can *act* hunting for it."

McCullough came out of his booth, asked Jimmy where the bottle was, and Jimmy pulled it out of his jeans—he'd had it stuffed behind his fly. McCullough stuck it back in Jimmy's hip pocket and got everyone ready to start again, for time was running out, and there was still the dress rehearsal to do.

They finished the technical rehearsal with barely enough time for the dress rehearsal, the minutes ticking off before airtime.

Cronyn's second major scene with Jimmy was a climactic one near the end of the drama. He was supposed to again wade into the crowd of teens and break up a fight, with Jimmy, of course, one of the principal combatants. This scene had been carefully choreographed so that the camera could follow Cronyn through the crowd on the dance floor to the scene of the fight without being blocked by the swaying bodies. When the time came, Cronyn launched himself into the packed teens and was immediately lost. He couldn't find Jimmy, with whom he was supposed to have an exchange of dialogue. He looked around wildly, pushed teens aside, crouched down, and stood up on tiptoe, but he could see no trace of Jimmy. Finally, from somewhere behind him, he heard the words "I'm here."

Had Cronyn gone to where Jimmy was standing, they would both have been out of camera range and out of the light. From the director's booth McCullough called out, "Cut! Hold it! I'm coming down."

The normally composed Cronyn lost his temper. He grabbed Jimmy by the arm, spun him around, and pointed up to the studio clock.

"See that? It says twenty-two minutes to airtime, and we haven't yet finished the dress. I don't know about you, but I'd at least like to have time to take a pee before we do this for real. For Christ's sake, be where you're supposed to be!"

As the other people on the set fell silent, Jimmy responded, "I was trying something new. I wanted to confuse you. You should be confused."

"I was!" cried Cronyn, "I am! But I can *act* confused. Keep that experimental shit for rehearsal or your dressing room! You're not alone out here!"

By then McCullough had arrived. "Cool it," he said, "cool it, both of you! Jimmy, get your ass over here where you belong, and let's get on with it, now!"

The show went on without further incident, and then a few weeks later Cronyn ran into Jimmy on the street. Jimmy surprised him by throwing his arms around him in a warm embrace. Before Cronyn could say a word Jimmy said, "I forgive you—you were nervous." Cronyn was left dumbfounded, but smiled. Jimmy smiled back, and the two actors continued on their separate ways.

McCullough later saw another side to Jimmy when he worked with him on "The Little Woman," another episode of the *Danger* series. The script for the drama was written by casting director Joe Scully, his first experience writing. He wrote it with Jimmy in mind. "I used his personality to help me create the character of Augie," Scully recalls. "Jimmy was a bad-boy type, but no matter how bad he was, you would still want to help him and love him, and that's what we needed for Augie."

Augie is a small-time gangster who steals money from the mob and hides out. He meets a little girl who offers to let him hide in her playhouse. Although McCullough thought Jimmy was ideal for the role, he remembered the knife and was worried about Jimmy's growing reputation as a troublemaker. He told Jimmy he'd heard he was having problems and that he had no intention of putting up with anything. In particular, he explained that he had hired Lydia Reed, then just eight years old, to play the little girl and that if Jimmy was difficult it would ruin the texture of the program.

What happened instead is that Jimmy, as always, was immediately drawn to the child. He made fast friends with little Lydia: the two seemed to share a special chemistry and understanding.

"Wherever she went with the performance," remembers McCullough, "he was there, supporting her. His was one of the most generous performances I've ever seen."

Throughout the summer and into the fall of '53 Jimmy performed steadily in television dramas: in October he had roles in three, and he had three more that November. He had developed a reputation for being extremely difficult, particularly during rehearsal, but also for being absolutely brilliant in performance.

On the night of October 14, Jimmy appeared in "Keep Our

Honor Bright," an episode of the *Kraft Television Theatre*. The next morning he was awakened by the telephone. A girl on the other end said, "You don't know me, but I just saw you on television last night and I'd like to know you. I go to Performing Arts [high school] and Sidney Lumet is one of my teachers, but I think there's so much I could learn from you."

"How old are you?" Jimmy asked.

"I'm seventeen."

"Seventeen," repeated Jimmy. "You know you just woke me up."

"I'm sorry," said the girl, "but I'm calling between classes, and this is the only moment I have."

"Give me your name and number."

The girl's name was Arlene Sachs, and she gave Jimmy her phone number, never really expecting to hear from him.

Jimmy did call, however, and suggested they meet in front of the Museum of Modern Art later in the day. When Arlene arrived Jimmy was surrounded by schoolgirls who had recognized him. Arlene was too shy to approach him until the girls left and he was standing alone at the gift-shop counter by the sign DON'T TOUCH. He was picking up things, examining and toying with them, when Arlene turned the sign toward him.

"Why shouldn't I touch things?" asked Jimmy, who had recognized Arlene from her description of herself on the phone: she had long black hair, was interesting looking with big eyes, and was wearing a white angora sweater.

"Because I don't want to see you get thrown out," said Arlene.

"Oh," said Jimmy. "Do you like Bartók?"

"Yes."

"Have you ever read *The Little Prince*?"

"Yes, it's my favorite book."

"Do you like Italian food?"

"Love it."

After touring the museum Jimmy asked Arlene to join him for dinner at the Capri, one of his favorite Italian restaurants, on West Fifty-second.

Arlene remembers how impressed she was when they went to the restaurant because Jimmy was treated like a celebrity. She also recalls clearly the sexual excitement between them when Jimmy asked if she was a virgin and she said she was, but "ready."

They went to Jimmy's apartment, which was cold and drafty. Jimmy motioned her to the bed and then he kissed her, after which he excused himself and went to the bathroom. When he came out he was shirtless. He sat down on the bed next to her, and they began making love.

"I guess he didn't realize I was telling the truth until I screamed, and suddenly there was blood all over," said Arlene. "He said, 'Oh my God, you were telling the truth. I'm so, so sorry. I didn't believe you.' He was very shaken and thrilled at the same time, laughing and crying, and I certainly was in a state of shock."

Jimmy brought Arlene back to her apartment at 2:00 A.M. only to find her mother waiting up, stern faced with arms folded across her bosom. "You may be accustomed to bringing girls home at this hour," she said to Jimmy, "but this is my daughter, and she is very young, and this is not acceptable." Jimmy stammered an apology and left, promising to call Arlene the next day.

He did call to ask tenderly if she was all right and to ask if he could see her that night. From that day on Jimmy had a relationship with Arlene that would last almost until his death.

I asked Arlene what it was like to be courted by Jimmy. "We used to run in Central Park at night, and then go home and listen to Vaughan Williams's music and Ernest Bloch's 'Hebraic Rhapsody,' and he'd read me his favorite selections from James Whitcomb Riley, and we'd read books like *Steppenwolf*, by Hermann Hesse, aloud to each other. When we weren't together, we'd talk on the telephone from 2:30 to 6:00 A.M.

"We spent hours doing improvisations like being Negro. Jimmy identified himself with any minority because he felt his talent made him a kind of minority.

"He wanted to experience everything. Sometimes his thirst for knowledge stood in the way of living. He loved life so painfully.

"He talked to me a lot about the fact that his mother had died and left him. He said he never knew what he had done wrong to deserve losing his mother and father, and that's where the guilt feelings came from. He was going through a period of self-hate then. If you liked him, he had no use for you because you were unable to see him for what he really was."

One day when Jimmy and Arlene were walking down the street after he had done a TV show, they met some other actors, who congratulated Jimmy on his performance. He stuck his hands in his pockets and mumbled something. Later, Arlene asked him why he was so rude. "I felt guilty that I was working and they weren't," he said.

Arlene introduced Jimmy to her cab-driver cousin, Arnie Langer, who was amazed that Jimmy was an actor. "He didn't look like any actor I ever had in my cab or saw onstage," he recalls. One night Jimmy and Arlene visited Langer in his furnished room on Twenty-second Street. Langer had just gotten a new album of *Porgy and Bess* and played it for them.

"Jimmy had never heard of *Porgy and Bess* before, but he was crazy for my album," recalls Langer. "I taught Jimmy a lot about music and how to play chess, but I never got really close to him. We'd stay up until four or five in the morning talking about music, but all I ever learned about him personally was that his mother died when he was a child.

"He used to dress like me and talk like me but he wasn't like me. I couldn't reach him. At Arlene's parties I was never sure if he would give me a big greeting or ignore me and sit in a corner, but he knew everyone in the room was watching him. He was onstage all the time.

"He was always studying working people like me, and when I finally saw him on television I realized he used me in his acting as well as other people I knew."

Langer was undoubtedly right. Like many actors, Jimmy did study people, trying to get at their essence, hoping to pick up a gesture that might be useful, absorbing their speech patterns, and sucking from them anything that he thought he might later use in a characterization.

When she and Jimmy were alone in a room together, Arlene said she always had the feeling that she should open the windows and say, "Fly, bird!"

Life with Jimmy was not always fun or romantic: he had a dark side as Arlene soon discovered. Once when they were taking a drama class together, he pulled a pretty girl onto his lap, defying Arlene to say or do something about it. "It was shocking and cruel," says Arlene. "He was letting me know that just because he was my first lover, he wasn't mine."

Soon after the beginning of their romance, Arlene invited Jimmy to a party at her new apartment.

"What kind of party?" asked Jimmy.

"An orgy," said Arlene, thinking she would put him on.

"Be right over," said Jimmy.

Some of Arlene's friends overheard the conversation and decided to continue the gag. Before Jimmy arrived the boys rolled up their pants legs and took off their shirts. The girls removed their blouses and everyone got under a big blanket.

When Arlene let Jimmy in, he took one look around, opened his jeans, took out his penis, and began to masturbate. "That is not what I wanted to happen," says Arlene. He was calling their bluff, she believes, saying in effect, "Okay, if you want to stage a so-called orgy, I'll show you orgy."

Because Jimmy was an attractive, almost beautiful boy, Arlene knew he was sought by homosexuals, who sent him gifts and offered him entrées for jobs. She also knew that several of his friends were "queer." She once asked him if he was homosexual, and he told her, "I'm a man, but if they don't let up soon, I'm going to begin to doubt myself."

Arlene began to have doubts, too, because he sometimes called men from her apartment, and on one occasion he let her listen in to his conversation. The man on the other end of the phone was a prominent male star, an idol of Jimmy's, and Arlene heard the actor discuss his sex life and then say to Jimmy, "But I really want to cock you."

When Arlene asked Jimmy what the actor meant by that, Jimmy replied, "You're too young to understand."

Arlene began to understand a few days later when Jimmy came into her apartment complaining, "Oh, God, my ass hurts."

"What's wrong?" asked Arlene.

"It was Rogers, I shouldn't have been with Rogers," said Jimmy.

"Things started to come together," recalls Arlene. "I thought he was trying to hurt or taunt me, that it was part of his pattern of pulling me to him and then pushing me away. But I was terribly hurt and confused. I didn't want to believe that he would be having a homosexual experience at the same time he was making love to me."

Chapter Six

THE IMMORALIST

In December 1953 Jane Deacy sent Jimmy to audition for a role in the Broadway adaptation of André Gide's autobiographical novel *The Immoralist*. The play had been adapted by Ruth and Augustus Goetz and the theme, popular on Broadway at the time, was homosexuality (Robert Anderson's *Tea and Sympathy* was then in the middle of a long and popular run at the Ethel Barrymore Theatre). The main characters are Michel, a French archaeologist (played by Louis Jourdan), and his alcoholic wife, Marcelline (played by Geraldine Page). The plot was simple: while on her honeymoon in Africa Marcelline discovers, through the intervention of "a colorful, thieving, blackmailing, homosexual houseboy" named Bachir (to play the role Jimmy wore brown makeup on his face and a long, loose caftan) who arranges for the seduction of Michel, causing Marcelline to realize that her husband is a latent homosexual.

Jimmy went to audition for the role of Bachir in producer Billy Rose's office on the top floor of the old Ziegfeld Theatre wearing cowboy boots, a ten-gallon cowboy hat, and a bright green vest and jeans. "He looked like a little Irishman," Ruth Goetz recalled. But the moment Jimmy began to read, everyone involved in the production realized that he had the charm and nasty sexual undercurrent they were searching for, and he was signed.

"When he told me that he had been signed for the part I was thrilled," recalls Barbara. "But I knew that Jimmy was scared. He was always scared. That's why he had such an 'I don't give a damn' facade, to cover the fear, but it was an artist's fear of 'Can I do it?' It was joy and fear mixed together."

Rehearsals for the play began the week before Christmas, and Jimmy soon found he had two supporters in the production company. One was Geraldine Page, who admired Jimmy both for his talent and his pluck and whom Jimmy looked on as a mother figure, and the other was director Herman Shumlin, who was impressed with Jimmy and allowed him a lot of flexibility in his interpretation of Bachir. Perhaps for this reason, Jimmy liked Shumlin and enjoyed working with him.

These relationships were established on the first day of rehearsal. During the line readings for the first act, Jimmy sat slumped over in a chair in a corner of the stage and was hardly noticed by anyone. As each actor read his or her lines, Shumlin would say, "No, no, no, no," and then give what he considered the correct reading. One by one the actors failed their lines and were corrected. The actors had enormous respect for Shumlin, considered a masterful director, and they tried their best to please him, only to fail yet again each time. Daunted by the great director, they exchanged glances of pained commiseration.

Jimmy's character appeared in the second act, and when his first line came up, he mumbled it. No one onstage could hear him.

"I beg your pardon," said Shumlin. "The first line should be read this way," and he gave his version of the line reading.

There was a long silence, and then Jimmy said, "Mr. Shumlin, why are you insulting my intelligence?"

The other actors held their breath, convinced all hell was about to break loose.

Shumlin thought in silence for a while and then said, "I didn't intend to do that. How did I insult your intelligence?"

"Well," said Jimmy. "It's the first reading, and you want me to read the line in a certain way. I would like to have some time to get used to who the people are that I'm supposed to be talking to and have a chance to decide some things about it first."

The other actors again gasped, certain that Shumlin was now going to lash out and destroy Jimmy. Instead, he said only, "I'm sorry."

Geraldine Page and the other members of the cast onstage were amazed and full of admiration for Jimmy's courage.

Under Shumlin, Jimmy's role took shape, and he himself began to feel comfortable with it. But there were problems with the production, and Billy Rose, who had come to dislike Jimmy, finally fired Shumlin and cut down Jimmy's part considerably. He replaced Shumlin with Daniel Mann, a traditional theater director known for getting the best possible performances out of actors. Jimmy and Mann had a confrontation almost immediately. One day Jimmy came half an hour late for rehearsal and Mann scathingly asked him how long he had been in the theater. Jimmy glanced at his watch and said, "About four minutes." The other actors laughed, Mann was furious, and Jimmy's retort was bandied about by other actors for days.

Mann recalls one cold, rainy night when they were rehearsing at the Ziegfeld and the company ran out of coffee. He reached into his pocket, took out a fifty-dollar bill, and offered to buy some if someone would go out and get it. Jimmy volunteered. "I gave the money to Jimmy, but he never brought me back the change," said Mann, "and I never asked him for it. That was the beginning of him saying to himself that he was going to get me. He considered me some sort of an alien or parental discipline figure rather than someone who might help him help himself."

The production then moved to Philadelphia for three weeks of a pre-Broadway tryout. The producers had problems with Jimmy from the beginning. He was invariably late for rehearsals, and when he finally arrived he was dressed slovenly and was sullen to everyone. "He was the most exasperating young actor I had ever worked with," claims Ruth Goetz.

While in Philadelphia Jimmy and the director had a conflict that very nearly became physical. The problem occurred during a matinee. While Louis Jourdan was speaking in a scene, Jimmy reached into his pocket and took out an imaginary piece of candy. He held it between his thumb and forefinger for a while and then he tasted it and reacted to the taste. It was a completely spontaneous acting exercise on Jimmy's part, not called for in the script, and for its duration the entire play was stalled.

After the matinee, Mann, normally mild-mannered, went backstage with fire in his eyes to search out Jimmy, who saw him coming and dashed out of the theater with Mann running after him down Walnut Street, shouting, "You crazy son of a bitch, if I get my hands on you, I'll kill you."

Following that incident, Mann went to the Actors Equity representative and tried to get Jimmy fired and replaced with his understudy, Bill Gunn. Equity rules demanded that Jimmy be given two weeks' notice, however, so the matter was dropped.

In a letter to Barbara Glenn written during the Philadelphia tryout, Jimmy asked her to come see him. The letter was on St. James Hotel stationery. Under the hotel logo Jimmy drew a sketch of a minaret. Alongside the salutation he made a small sketch of a man with wires coming out of his head. The letter read in part: "Rehearsals are quite confusing at this point. Lighting etc. Can't tell much about the show yet. Looks like a piece of shit to me. Stereophonic staging and 3-D actors. Probably be a monster success."

Marty Landau called Jimmy at his hotel to ask what working with Louis Jourdan was like.

"Oh, Louis is great," said Jimmy, sarcastically. "He has really loosened up. He raised both hands at the same time."

The play received superb notices when it opened the second week of January in Philadelphia, a good omen as far as its Broadway reception was concerned. In the audience during one of the performances was Paul Osborn, then busy writing the screenplay for *East of Eden*. Osborn was impressed by Jimmy's performance and the next day called Elia Kazan in New York. Kazan remembered Jimmy from the Actors Studio and agreed to see the play when it opened in New York.

On January 10 Jimmy wrote to Barbara, who was ill with a cold in New York, letting her know that the play was well received in Philadelphia. He joked, "I am now a colorful thieving, blackmailing Arab boy played by James Dean. Don't know who the hell I am. They are rewriting a lot. In rehearsals I was working for the elements of tragedy—a real tragedians role, pathos etc. I turn out to be the comedy relief. The Leon Erroll of the show. . . . *This is the most boring dull cast and show I have ever seen.* . . ."

He ended the letter by asking Barbara to come see him, and promising to pay her train fare.

Jimmy must have still felt dissatisfied with the production when it returned to New York, for he made an attempt to switch plays. Calder Willingham's *End as a Man* was then on Broadway, with Ben Gazzara in the leading role. When Gazzara and the rest of the cast went on strike for more money, Jimmy spoke to the play's director, Jack Garfein, to see if he could get the lead. The notion wasn't outlandish: Jimmy already knew the play, having performed in an Actors Studio production of it in 1953, also directed by Garfein. The strike soon ended, however, and Jimmy went ahead with *The Immoralist*; the incident left Gazzara with a certain animosity toward Jimmy.

Because of the change in directors—and perhaps because of all the rewriting Jimmy wrote to Barbara about—Billy Rose decided to delay the previously announced opening and hold a week of paid public previews for what he called artistic reasons, asking critics to hold off during the production's first week of performances.

The week of previews began on February 1, 1954, at the Royale Theatre on West Forty-fifth Street. Disregarding Rose's plea, critics from the city's major newspapers came to see the play. Many of them were unimpressed; the *New York Times* reporter described the production as "often lifeless." But such reports were unofficial, and work went ahead tightening up the production.

After the week of previews, on February 8—Jimmy's twenty-third birthday—the play had its official opening. Marcus and Ortense had flown in from Fairmount to attend the performance. Jimmy was full of apologies that he couldn't spend much time with them, and he neglected to invite them to a party after the opening. But on opening night they were both seated in the theater, dressed formally in keeping with the spirit of the event. A few rows behind them was Barbara, who had met them earlier. Up on the stage, Jimmy parted the curtain and peered out over the rows of faces to make certain those three people were in their places.

At the final curtain the audience applauded wildly: to judge from their reaction, a hit was certain. One by one the other actors took their curtain calls, bowing to the applause and the shouts, but when Jimmy's turn came he stepped forward, spread his caftan, and curtsied like a girl. That single dramatic gesture almost brought down the house—because of the play's theme, the audience included more than a fair share of homosexuals. The curtsy also inflamed Daniel Mann, who had angry words with Jimmy backstage. Jimmy responded by giving his two weeks' notice.

Leaving a Broadway play after a successful opening is relatively unheard of. The Goetzes ranted and raved and said it wasn't right, but Jimmy was adamant. His friend Geraldine Page later cornered Billy Rose and screamed at him, "How could you let pure gold walk out on you like that?"

Jimmy was in an unsettled mood when Barbara went backstage to congratulate him. She found him putting on his torn jeans and T-shirt and assumed they were going back to his place. To her surprise, Jimmy announced they were going to Sardi's.

"You can't go to Sardi's dressed like that," she said, "they won't let you in."

"C'mon, they'll let me in," he said.

They wouldn't let him in. Even though he was one of the stars of the play, the restaurant management insisted he abide by their dress code. Jimmy told Barbara to wait at a table for him while he went home on his bike and changed into a suit and tie.

Barbara soon got irritated with the ugly gossiping and bitching around her, and by the time Jimmy walked in the door wearing his choirboy's suit she'd had enough. She stood up and announced, "I'm leaving."

They excused themselves from the table and went outside where they had a violent argument, ending up with their not talking to each other for two days.

The Immoralist did not receive great reviews. The phrases critics used included "strangely unfulfilling," "not much of a play," "clinical," and "not moving, not even touching." Billy Rose's ploy of preceding the official opening with a week of previews proved inadvisable, for critics and theatergoers alike did not have faith in a play that had postponed its opening.

Although the play got poor reviews, Jimmy was well received.

Broadway theater critics hailed what the *New York World-Telegram and Sun* called Jimmy's "sleazy impertinence and amoral opportunism." Later in the year Jimmy won the prestigious Daniel Blum Award as the year's most promising personality.

The play went on without Jimmy (he was replaced by Phillip Pine), but not very long: it closed on May 1, 1954, after a run of just three months.

By then Jimmy was long gone. Handing in his notice really hadn't been as bold and brazen as it had seemed, and it certainly wasn't a hasty act brought on by anger. Jimmy knew, as did his agent, Jane Deacy, that his time had come. As he had known all along— as Barbara Glenn and Christine White and everyone else who knew him well had known—all it took was one chance to finally show the world what he could do. *The Immoralist* gave him that chance. Deacy almost certainly supported his move when he quit the play— she probably sensed the play's ultimate failure, and the role of a conniving homosexual was not auspicious for Jimmy's future typecasting. Far more important, Jimmy did not leap from *The Immoralist* into open air: he was on his way to precisely where he had always wanted to go.

While he was still performing in the play, Deacy had arranged for Jimmy to test for a role in *Battle Cry*, a film to be made for Warner Bros. William T. Orr, the studio executive in charge of talent, had come in from Los Angeles to conduct the casting tests and had already looked at fifty-two actors during that one week. Although he had never seen Jimmy onstage, he'd had good reports about his acting ability and arranged for the Warner office, which usually closed at five, to stay open until his arrival.

Just before seven, Jimmy arrived on his motorcycle. He was unshaven and wore jeans, a dirty cap, and a torn army surplus jacket. Whether by design or accident, he was dressed for the part.

Orr introduced Jimmy to the actress with whom he was to read and handed him the script. "I don't need the script," said Jimmy. "Just tell me who I am."

"You're a young Polish boy being shipped off to war," said Orr. "You're leaving the next morning, and you have to say goodbye to your girlfriend, and her father hates you."

The actress sat on a chair with the script in her hand. Jimmy walked to her and put his arms around her from behind while peering over her shoulder so he could see his first line of dialogue. He then turned around with an agonized look on his face, walked to the window, turned back to her, and spoke the line. He held her and kissed her while peeking at his next line, and kept moving around nervously saying his lines.

"His reading," said Orr, "was the most electrifying of all the actors I had tested. It was a performance, not a reading at all. Just fantastic!"

Orr's notes on Jimmy, forwarded to the studio with his test, read in part: "Think you will see from this test even though we were dubious of his personal appearance . . . there is a trace of the Marlon Brando school in his work and also he is not a conventional actor. He brings more ability to scenes than the others I tested. He is gaining quite a reputation as a fine young actor."

When he returned to Hollywood, Orr learned that the studio executives had not looked at any of the tests he had made in New York. He insisted they at least look at the tests he had made with Jimmy, Paul Newman, and Walter Matthau. The executives wanted a name actor, however, and Tab Hunter was given the role.

But there was still Elia Kazan. Following Paul Osborn's advice, he had seen a performance of *The Immoralist*. Although he wasn't particularly impressed by Jimmy's performance, he called Jimmy the next day and asked him to come over to Warner Bros. New York offices.

Kazan had a hunch that Jimmy was right for a role in *East of Eden*. Among the actors he had originally considered for the parts were Marlon Brando, whom he had used in three previous films, and Montgomery Clift, another young actor drawing acclaim for his portrayal of troubled youths, but Gadge wasn't satisfied. He wanted young actors who could convincingly play troubled adolescents, and he wanted them hungry.

Although Jimmy was very much aware of the importance of his interview with Kazan, he showed up at the Warner Bros. offices in his usual sloppy attire. When Kazan went out into the waiting room he found Jimmy slouched at the far end of a leather sofa, a heap of twisted legs and denim rags, and a belligerent face. Kazan didn't like the look so he kept him waiting. He also wanted to see how he would react. It seemed that he had outtoughed him, because by the time he called Jimmy into the office the sullen pose was gone. Kazan tried to get some conversation going but failed. The two sat looking at each other. "How would you like a ride on the back of my 'sickle?" Jimmy asked finally. The experience was not pleasant for the director. Jimmy showed off, a country boy not impressed with city traffic, determined to scare the daylights out of the older man.

When Kazan got back to the office, he called Osborn and said there was no point in looking further: James Dean was Cal. Kazan then sent Jimmy to see John Steinbeck, who lived near him on East Seventy-second Street. Steinbeck phoned later to say that he thought Dean was a snotty kid. "That's irrelevant," said Kazan. "He is Cal, isn't he?" "He sure as hell is," agreed Steinbeck.

There were still other possibilities. When Kazan held preliminary readings for the lead roles, he also tested Paul Newman, who had attracted attention with his performance on Broadway in *Picnic*. Jimmy knew Newman; the two of them and also Steve McQueen had often competed for the same television and Broadway roles and were often compared. Today, the similarities among the three are no longer clear, but in the beginning, when all three were hungry young actors working their way up—when their public personalities had not yet been shaped by roles—they often found themselves being called for the same parts. Kazan decided on Jimmy over Newman for the role of Cal because he felt Jimmy was more believable as a teenager.

The other actors and actresses Kazan tested were a mixture of Actors Studio products, young actors who had earned recognition through Broadway roles, and absolute unknowns. Competing for the female lead were Joanne Woodward, who had been an understudy in *Picnic*, and Julie Harris, who had starred on Broadway to great critical acclaim in *The Member of the Wedding* in 1950 and had made her screen debut in Stanley Kramer's film version of the play two years later. She had just finished performing on Broadway in Jean Anouilh's *Mademoiselle Colombe*.

Jimmy and Julie had met before, at a party in Greenwich Village. When they were introduced, Jimmy asked her how she enjoyed working in *The Moon Is Blue*. "I've never been in *The Moon Is Blue*," she retorted, certain that Jimmy was just putting her on.

When they met again for the test at Gjon Mili's studio Jimmy was still needling her, this time about her age—she was six years older. At one point Julie rested her chin on her hands.

"Do you do that because you think you look too old?" he asked her.

"Well," she replied, "I am older than you."

Nevertheless, their rapport was easygoing and friendly; Kazan was pleased. He then tested Jimmy together with Dick Davalos, whom he was considering for the role of Jimmy's brother. Davalos had been working as an usher at the Trans-Lux Theater in New York before showing up at a Warner screen test.

They, too, got along, and precisely as Kazan had foreseen: he sensed sexual tension in the air during their test.

Jimmy was in his apartment on West Sixty-eighth Street when he got a phone call from Kazan confirming him in the role. He was elated. His first act was to call Christine White, his kindred acting spirit. "Chris," he shouted, "get over here right away!"

It was the first time she'd seen his new apartment. She was dressed for an interview she'd had that day, and as she trudged up the three flights of steep stairs she tore her stockings. Jimmy was jumping and hopping at the top of the stairs. When she reached the landing she noticed a naked light bulb shining out of the hall bathroom.

"Come on," he urged, "this is really a room!"

As she stepped into the tiny space she wondered what he meant by that. The room was a square, about eight feet by nine with a corner closet. The double bed was piled high with dirty laundry. Along the shelves was a stunning assortment of unrelated objects: a half-full jar of peanut butter, sheet music, a sculptured head, many books (in some cases three lying open one upon the other), a Chianti bottle with a candle stuck in it, bullfight paraphernalia, notebooks of his pen drawings, sketches and letters, a small globe, a glass ashtray, a flute, and a copy of Steinbeck's *East of Eden*.

She expected him to explode with his news. Instead, he lifted his eyebrows, made a sweeping gesture to take in the surroundings, and mumbled, "What do you think?"

"I think the attic windows lend a lot of atmosphere."

"Yeah," he said. "Aren't they great?"

She looked around the room, saw there was no place to sit, so cleared a space on the desk under the windows and sat there. "Fantastic," she breathed. "How did you get so lucky to find this pad?"

"You don't like it," he said. "I am immediately bored."

"Come on, Jimmy," she said. "You and I are far more important than this crazy room. Immediately tell me about *East of Eden*."

"It's so exciting!" he said. "My head is going to fall off." He was beaming.

"What is Hollywood going to do with you?" she asked. "You've still got hayseed in your hair from Indiana."

"It's good for the part. But I'm holding on to this room because I'll be back," he said. Then suddenly standing, he said, "Let's go to Forty-second Street and see movie after movie." He ran out the door and sprinted down the stairs. She came down behind him, and they both ran into the street.

In the middle of a crowd Jimmy suddenly turned to her and said, "Come on, do it."

"What? What?"

"Billie. Come on, do it."

It didn't usually take much persuasion to make Chris go into her imitation of Billie Holiday: "My man don't love me, treats me oh so mean . . ."

Jimmy laughed and laughed and leaned against a building to hold himself up. "You're as white as this building. You're so unlikely, but you can do that. Now do Marlon."

Chris was in the middle of the crowd, her audience the faces of strangers swirling around and past her. She couldn't do Marlon while moving, so she stayed still and pulled everything into slow motion. Finally, in her best Marlon tone, she said, "Screw you, Gadge. I don't care if fifty thousand people go through this *pause* . . . that's the way I see it."

Jimmy hollered, "Cut! Print!"

They ran on toward the movie theaters along Forty-second Street.

"It's just as much fun to direct as it is to act. Don't you think so?" sputtered Jimmy, out of breath.

"Oh, definitely," Chris answered.

They were very happy sitting in the dark theater eating hot dogs and popcorn and watching Humphrey Bogart. Jimmy threw his legs over the seat in front of him, put his hand on her knee, and rested his head on her shoulder. For a while they watched the film, but the excitement, the running and jumping, had tired them, and soon they both were asleep. Jimmy awoke about halfway through the film and asked her if she wanted to leave.

They bolted back into the street. It was nearly midnight, and they headed for Jerry's Bar, Jimmy pulling her by the hand through the late-night crowds.

As they went along Chris called out at random to the passersby. "*East of Eden*! Here he comes! Did you know that this guy is going to be in a movie? Does he look like a movie star? Get serious!"

It was Jimmy who suddenly got serious. "Gadge says I have to go to the gym and build up," he said in a confidential tone. Then he became even more serious; the fun was over.

"Gadge told me that he told you he thought I was great in our audition. You didn't tell me that."

"You were on the road," Chris said.

"He also said he liked you. But he's going to use Julie Harris."

"So that's why you're stalling and not really telling me about your sensational break," she said. "You didn't think I boosted you to Kazan? I certainly did! But, of course, he could see for himself."

Jimmy was quiet.

"Are you scared?" she asked him. "Just follow direction. Gadge will loosen you up. Have fun. It's a dream come true, isn't it?"

Near the entrance to Jerry's Bar, Jimmy pulled her aside. "I was very pissed that you didn't tell me Kazan said I was great in the audition. I worked so hard. Both of us were exactly right."

"I thought I did tell how much he liked you when I called you. He liked both of us and the scene as well."

"Yeah, but you didn't tell me he said the word *great*."

Chris looked at Jimmy's mouth: he was pouting. "Well, if the ultimate director, Gadge Kazan, said you were great, then he must see it in you. Right?"

"But you don't." Jimmy wasn't angry, but he was very serious.

"I think the seed . . . that indefinable whatever . . . is there."

"Well," Jimmy said, "I'll tell you a secret. I can't see it myself. It's just a gut thing." He was staring at her in his head-down bullfighters' pose. "I want you to know that if anyone says anything against you, I'll stick up for you. So make sure you always root for me. It's very important. And I'll do the same for you. Where I come from, a person's word is supposed to mean something."

Chris was genuinely touched. "I'm with you. I agree."

"Now let's go inside, have a beer, and talk about Humphrey Bogart," said Jimmy. The pout had left his mouth.

"Excellent," said Chris, giving him her best smile. "That's a wrap."

They celebrated in Jerry's as they had so often before, and once again it seemed to Chris that the good times would never end, but she knew that something important had happened and that something was indeed going to change.

Meanwhile, Jimmy stayed in touch with Arlene, who had gotten an apartment of her own. One day she called him and invited him over for dinner. Jimmy said he was working on a scene with Barbara and could he bring her? Arlene was agreeable.

Jimmy and Barbara showed up just as Arlene arrived home from her job as a hat-check girl at Birdland, a venue for jazz and be-bop, and she let them into her apartment while she went out shopping for groceries. When she returned it was clear to her that Barbara and Jimmy had made love in her absence. "I went into the kitchen and thought I was going to faint and throw up at the same time," says Arlene.

I can only assume that Jimmy knew that he was hurting her deeply, and that his actions were specifically designed to repel her.

Nevertheless, although no longer Jimmy's girlfriend, Arlene still wanted to be his friend, and shortly after *The Immoralist* opened, she invited him to meet a friend of hers, a photographer named Roy Schatt who took pictures of actors and actresses. Schatt had a studio on the ground floor of an old brownstone on East Thirty-third Street.

When Arlene and Jimmy came into his studio, Schatt was not impressed by Jimmy—he seemed unkempt and squinty—and paid attention instead to Arlene. While Jimmy sat at the far end of a couch, his hands pressed between his knees, Arlene talked to Schatt about Jimmy. "He's magnificent," she said, "doing that dance in *The Immoralist*. You should see him use those scissors."

At this, Jimmy came to life. "Castanets!" he exclaimed. "Like this!" And with that he jumped off the couch and performed the dance. Doing so he changed from a fidgety kid to a thing of beauty. Schatt was astonished. Now that he had his audience, Jimmy went into one of his favorite routines. He stooped over, took out his dental bridge, and lumbered around the room holding it out and lisping, "Wanna buy thum gold, man? I need thum thoup."

Schatt was enthralled. Later, when the conversation turned to Schatt's work, he mentioned that he gave lessons in photography. That was all Jimmy had to hear: by the time he and Arlene left the studio, Jimmy and Schatt were friends and Jimmy had asked to become one of Schatt's students.

Schatt soon learned that Jimmy was not the kind of friend one could count on when in need, but he was fun to be around, full of a rare sense of life. Schatt also realized that Jimmy was a good actor: everything seemed to come naturally to him. He always knew where the camera was and where the lights were, and he was very much aware of his persona in front of the camera, but he did so naturally, without ever posing. Schatt never saw any of Jimmy's films while Jimmy was alive, but he never doubted that his new friend was a true actor.

Jimmy's photography lessons were casual and were held when both Jimmy and Schatt had some free time. Like most photographers at the time, Schatt did his own darkroom work (to this day he still does), processing and printing. Jimmy thought that most of the darkroom work was boring and would quickly lose patience with it, but he did enjoy making prints.

Schatt soon found that Jimmy not only wanted to learn how to take pictures but he also had a good instinct about what made a good picture of himself. "I never posed him, and he soon discovered that he had better not pose," recalls Schatt.

Jimmy and Schatt often went out on the street where Jimmy,

under Schatt's tutelage, took candid photos with the used Leica he had bought. Jimmy took to carrying the camera everywhere with him and, to the consternation of his friends, constantly snapped shots of them when they were unaware. He entered a picture he had taken of Marty Landau mugging for the him in a photo show put on by Rienzi's restaurant in the Village, one of Jimmy's favorite haunts. The photo was awarded a prize, and was hung on the wall. The entire gang went to Rienzi's to celebrate Jimmy's coming of age as a photographer.

Jimmy gave Arlene and Schatt tickets to see *The Immoralist* on the night of his final performance, and made a date to meet them, along with Geraldine Page, outside the stage door after the show. They would then all go to Schatt's studio for coffee.

It was a rainy, bitterly cold February night, and when Jimmy appeared he was on his motorcycle.

"No, Jimmy, not in this rain," pleaded Page, but Jimmy only smiled and gunned the motor. Looking at Arlene, he yelled, "Get on the back."

Arlene hesitated a moment, exchanged glances with Schatt and Page and looked up at the rainy sky, but she got on the back, and she and Jimmy disappeared with a roar into the night.

Schatt wondered why Jimmy was risking his life just when his career was taking off. He and Page took a cab to the studio.

Jimmy and Arlene were nowhere in sight when Schatt and Page got out of the cab, but they soon appeared out of the rain and raced by on the motorcycle, Jimmy calling out, "See you." When they came back—having driven around the block—Jimmy pulled up near Schatt and Page. Rainwater was running down his face, and he was laughing. Looking at Schatt, he asked, "Want to go for a ride, teach?"

Schatt knew better.

A charming, gregarious, and intelligent man, Schatt soon became a father figure for Jimmy as well as a friend, and Jimmy soon became a regular at his brownstone. In the evenings, there was often a party with lots of food, talk, and music, usually favorite jazz records. Jimmy often accompanied the records on his professional bongo drums, a gift from Cyril Jackson, a renowned musician who was teaching him to play. Sometimes they would all just sing songs, with a kazoo as their only accompaniment.

Although girlfriends, guests, and total strangers fleshed out these get-togethers, the core group remained the same: Jimmy, Schatt, Marty Landau, Bill Gunn (Jimmy's understudy in *The Immoralist* who had taken over after his departure), and Bobby Heller, an actor who had become a friend of Jimmy's. These five were always together.

One evening, during one of these get-togethers in Schatt's apartment, Jimmy, who was sitting in a big armchair, suddenly disappeared along with the chair. A few minutes later there was a tremendous honking of horns in the street. Someone ran to the window and opened the venetian blind. There, holding up traffic in the middle of the street, was Jimmy, smoking a cigarette and sitting cross-legged in the chair.

Everyone ran out the front door. Marty and Roy grabbed Jimmy, who acted like a rag doll when he was pulled from the chair, his arms and head flopping around, and the rest of him just dead weight. They carried him back to the apartment.

"What the hell do you think you're doing?" shouted Schatt.

Jimmy lit a fresh cigarette and giggled. "Don't you sons of bitches ever get bored?" he asked derisively. "I just wanted to spark things, man, that's all." He got up and began to beat on the dining room table as if it were a bongo drum. "Look at you. Before I did it, we were all sitting quietly eating and drinking, and outside a lot of nine-to-fivers were going home to their wives like they do every night. Now you're all juiced up, and so are they, man. They'll talk about it for years."

Jimmy was obsessed with Marlon Brando and occasionally, for no apparent reason, he would begin quoting from *A Streetcar Named Desire*. One evening during a party at Schatt's, he took off his shirt and ripped his undershirt to shreds, yelling "Stella."

Jimmy rarely saw Brando in person, but did have contact with him. Leonard Rosenman recalls that Jimmy was particularly fond of Elvis Presley's "You Ain't Nothin' but a Hound Dog." He would listen to that song all night and into the wee hours of the morning, and sometimes he'd share his pleasure by calling someone on the phone, waiting to hear the voice at the other end, and then holding out the phone to his hi-fi speaker blaring the refrain. He'd hang up without saying a word, but the recipients of these calls soon learned the identity of the perpetrator. On at least one occasion Jimmy performed this stunt with Brando, and Montgomery Clift complained he'd received several of the nocturnal calls.

All three men are slightly mistaken, but in an understandable and even revelatory way. Presley made his first appearance on national television four months after Jimmy's death and didn't record "Hound Dog" until 1956. Even so, Jimmy may well have owned a record of the song—it was performed by at least two other singers before Presley (Big Mama Thornton and Freddie Bell and the Bellboys)—and the connection to Presley is valid. Jimmy loved music and listened to everything from African tribal music to *Madame Butterfly*, but he died too soon for rock and roll. That Rosenman—and few if any people know musical history better than Leonard—Brando, and Clift remember Jimmy listening to Presley shows how thoroughly Jimmy has become embedded in popular culture and myth. I've even heard that Jimmy learned to grind his hips like Presley and once did so in front of astonished Warner Bros. executives: an anachronism that seems so true it's hard to let go.

Meanwhile, Elia Kazan had made arrangements to take Jimmy to California for more screen tests.

The week before his departure for Hollywood, Jimmy took a bad spill on his motorcycle. Leonard Rosenman asked him why he was so suicidal.

"Death is always there," responded Jimmy, "and I want to conquer it."

Chapter Seven

HOLLYWOOD

On the morning of March 8, 1954, Kazan came to pick up Jimmy. He came in a black Cadillac limousine. As the long car turned into West Sixty-eighth Street Kazan found himself hoping that Jimmy would be ready: they had just enough time to reach Idlewild Airport for the 9:00 A.M. flight to the West Coast.

Kazan breathed a sigh of relief as the front door of the building opened, and his new discovery came down the stairs dressed like a homeless immigrant, his only luggage two packages wrapped in paper and tied with string, one in each hand. An inch of ash dropped from the cigarette in his mouth.

Kazan leaned over and opened the door. Jimmy dropped the cigarette on the pavement, bent over, and slid onto the backseat. He glanced at the director and the expansive interior and said, "Whoosh. Never thought I'd ride in one of these."

"Get used to it," Kazan said.

"I'd planned to drive out to the Coast on my 'sickle," said Jimmy. "But I had an accident."

Remembering his own ride with Jimmy, Kazan gave a little laugh. As the driver took them through the morning traffic toward the airport, Jimmy and Kazan exchanged only a few words. Jimmy seemed lost in thought, and Kazan was happy to leave him there.

The airlines were in the business of pampering celebrities in the early 1950s. The limousine drove straight onto the tarmac and stopped a few yards away from the steps leading up to the interior of the American Airlines DC-4 Constellation, one of the biggest and fastest nonstop coast-to-coast passenger planes in service at the time. Flight One would be leaving on time.

A stewardess at the top of the steps showed them to their seats forward in the cabin. Kazan stowed his luggage in the overhead rack and helped Jimmy with his two paper bags. He then asked him whether he would prefer a window or aisle seat.

"Window. I've never been in an airplane before," Jimmy said as he pressed his nose against the window.

The director had fortified himself for the flight with magazines he'd not had time to read, some books, and a draft of the filmscript. Jimmy was content with scrunching around in his seat like a little boy and looking out the window, busy with his own thoughts. From time to time Kazan studied him, his director's eye catching the nuances of the boy's face as the light changed. What he saw pleased him: Jimmy's face was formed with exquisite subtlety; a straight, narrow nose, high cheekbones, a mouth curved and mobile as a girl's. The camera will love him, Kazan thought.

The flight, dubbed the "noon saloon" by experienced travelers because so much booze was served in mini-bottles, was uneventful. Kazan watched as the boy wolfed down his lunch and then lit one of the endless chain of Chesterfield cigarettes he had smoked since the flight began. He also noticed with some amusement that Jimmy took two extra mini-bottles and stuffed them in a pocket.

The big Constellation touched down on schedule in Los Angeles, nine hours after leaving New York. When the hatch door opened a young man wearing a suit and tie, a big smile spread across his face, bounded down the aisle directly to Kazan. Tom Stout, the official airline greeter, had met Kazan many times before. "Welcome to Mike Lyman's," Stout said.

"Mike Lyman's?" repeated Jimmy.

"We refer to the Los Angeles airport by the name of the diner on the edge of the field," said Stout grinning.

Warner's transportation department had another limousine waiting for them on the tarmac. When Dean asked if they could stop on the way into town where his father worked, Kazan was agreeable. He looked forward to seeing the interaction between father and son.

Jimmy directed the driver to the Veterans Administration Hospital where, he told Kazan, his father worked as a lab technician. Jimmy hopped out of the limo and ran into the building. He soon came out with a tall, dour-faced man wearing spectacles he introduced to Kazan as his father, Winton Dean.

Father and son stood next to each other, and for a brief moment they talked. Then they fell silent, having quickly reached the end of anything they might have to say. Winton made little impression on Kazan. What did impress him was the fact that there was an obvious tension between Jimmy and his father. He sensed that Winton disliked Jimmy, and that Jimmy was uncomfortable with Winton. Kazan realized that his film about a boy who sought but could never have a good relationship with his father was probably Jimmy's story, too. He was right.

The Hollywood that greeted James Dean in 1954 holds a very special place in my memory: I had arrived there just three years earlier in the winter of 1951. I came with my mentor, Hy Gardner, then the Broadway columnist for *The New York Herald Tribune*. My original assignment was to send items and gossip to New York as fodder for Gardner's column, but by the time Jimmy arrived in 1954 I had my own column and was West Coast Bureau Chief for the newspaper.

I remember well the film capital as it was then. Beverly Hills, the residential area where most stars lived, still had the flavor of a charming village, not unlike Santa Barbara or Carmel today. On most days the air was crystal clear, and life was leisurely. Rodeo Drive, now celebrated as the street for shopping and expensive boutiques, had only a few clothing stores, a hardware store, and some restaurants. Strangers on the street acknowledged one another with a smile and a nod. Shopkeepers were friendly and on a first-name basis with most of their customers. Movie stars could walk the streets recognized but undisturbed: it was their expensive foreign cars that drew gawking stares.

During one of my first weeks in Hollywood a *Tribune* editor suggested I interview some stars. Having no idea of how to set up an interview, I dropped by the pool of the Beverly Hills Hotel in the hope I might see someone well known. While I was sitting morosely alongside the pool smoking my pipe a tall man dressed like an Easterner in gray flannels and a tweed sport coat, and also smoking a pipe, came over and asked me what brand of tobacco I was smoking. One thing led to another, and he finally asked what I was doing at the pool.

I explained that I was hoping to see a star I might interview. He then asked if I'd like to talk with Humphrey Bogart. I was delighted at the prospect. It turned out that my newfound friend's name was Bill Blowitz, one of the premier publicists in Hollywood, and he happened to be Bogie's press agent at the time.

Bogart and his wife, Lauren Bacall, were living on Benedict Canyon, only a few miles north of the Beverly Hills Hotel in a ranch house that had been built by Hedy Lamarr. Blowitz was waiting at the front door of the Bogart home when I drove up. After quieting down a pair of boisterous boxer dogs, he led me into the den.

Bogart soon arrived and after introductions asked me what I wanted to drink. "A Coke, please," I said.

"You don't drink?" Bogart asked, adding hopefully, "You AA?"

"No," I said. "I never drank."

Bogart, who was behind the bar, looked at me thoughtfully. "I don't trust any bastard who doesn't drink—especially a pipe-smoking newspaperman. You must have something to hide. People who don't drink are afraid of revealing themselves.

"Furthermore," he continued, "I don't trust any man who has more hair on his head than I have."

My heart sank. My first interview with a star was turning out to be a disaster. I had no rejoinder other than to leave, so I picked up my note pad and pencil and started for the door.

"Where are you going?" Bogart asked.

"How are we going to do an interview if we start out with your not trusting me?" I asked. "I don't drink and I certainly have more hair on my head than you do, but then so do most men."

Bogart thought that over for a moment. "You're just going to have to work that much harder to make me trust you," he said, and shooing the boxers off a seat, he gestured for me to sit down.

I had never interviewed a film star before and I was not impressed with Bogart's celebrity, nor was I chary of telling him that some of the answers to my questions were too glib. I don't recall the interview in detail but I do remember that when he needled me I needled him right back. Bogart was probably amused by my interview technique, or lack of it, and he apparently thought it might be fun to sic me on some of his friends because within the week he and Blowitz arranged for me to interview Frank Sinatra, Katharine Hepburn, Spencer Tracy, and Gary Cooper. My editor in New York was astounded. "I don't know what you're doing, but whatever it is, keep doing it," he told me, and so Hollywood became my permanent assignment.

Life in those days revolved around the major studios—20th Century-Fox, Columbia, MGM, Warner Bros., and many of the men who had founded those studios were still alive and active—Samuel Goldwyn, Cecil B. DeMille, Jack L. Warner, Louis B. Mayer. Each studio had its own distinctive style, determined in large part by the men at the top. Warner was known for turning out exciting but unadorned—if not grim—melodramas (Jack L. Warner was infamous for his tight-fisted finances); MGM was renowned for glamour; 20th Century-Fox had a reputation for bright and brassy productions with wonderful color. Each had its roster of contract actors. Of course, one studio might hire another studio's actor for a role in a film—at a high price.

Each studio had its own commissary where cast, crew, and featured players ate lunch. The specialty at MGM was an excellent chicken soup named after Louis B. Mayer, one of the founders of the studio. Almost every entrée on the menu at Paramount was named after a star: Turkey and eggs à la Crosby, $1.50; English kippers and eggs à la Danny Kaye, $1.25; Spanish omelette à la Alan Ladd, $1.25. In addition to a commissary, the Warner studio had its Blue Room, where writers and directors gathered. Top stars, directors, and studio executives ate in Jack L. Warner's bungalow dining room around a table set for fifteen with J.L. himself at the head of the table. The two places nearest to Warner were rarely occupied: no one wanted to be close to the Chief if a question was asked that could not be answered, thus incurring Warner's wrath and probable dismissal from the studio. Warner charged his favored diners fifteen dollars a month for the privilege of eating with him.

Lunches were also held off the lot at nearby restaurants. The Formosa, directly across the street from Goldwyn Studios, served superb Chinese food; the Retake Room alongside of MGM offered good sandwiches; most of the Warner stars, including Bogie, liked to lunch at the Smoke House, a stone's throw from the studio main gate. Lucy's El Adobe, opposite the Paramount studio gate, featured Mexican food and privacy in secluded and curtained booths along the walls of the restaurant. It was dark inside, a favored trysting place for studio executives and others hoping to have a "nooner" or "matinee." The restaurant was packed with beautiful, seemingly available extras wearing their screen wardrobes, ranging from period costumes to skimpy harem outfits. The atmosphere of blatant sexuality was palpable enough to be nerve tingling.

There was a profusion of restaurants away from the studios favored by film folk. When he was not working, Bogie regularly spent his lunch hours at Romanoff's, an elegant establishment on Rodeo Drive.

At Romanoff's, waiters in red jackets busied themselves around tables crowded with some of the best-known faces in the world. The regulars included Jack Benny, Peter Lawford, Frank Sinatra, Gary Cooper, and Groucho Marx. The maitre d', Kurt Niklas, seated tourists against the far wall where they could see but not be heard.

Mike Romanoff, proprietor of the restaurant he named after himself, was one of the more colorful figures in Hollywood. A self-styled prince, his antecedents were vague and certainly not royal, but he was beloved of the ultrasnobbish film crowd, which actually accepted him as its social arbiter.

Every night stars could be found dancing at one of Hollywood's many nightclubs: the Mocambo, the Trocadero, the Cocoanut Grove at the Ambassador Hotel, and Ciro's on the Sunset Strip.

Ciro's had been in the news only months before James Dean's arrival when Darryl F. Zanuck, the mustached buck-toothed vice-president in charge of production at 20th Century-Fox threw a party for his daughter Susan and starlet Terry Moore. One of the acts consisted of trapeze artists. After their show ended, Zanuck stripped to the waist and successfully chinned himself to the cheers of the delighted guests. He then tried to do a one-arm pull-up on the trapeze. He strained hard, the muscles in his throat bulging as the crowd held its collective breath, many hoping he would succeed while others hoped he would crash to the floor—which he did. Zanuck's act was later referred to as "The Darryl Old Man on the Flying Trapeze."

Such antics were common. Hollywood in the mid-1950s was a multiring circus with something zany constantly taking place on or off the sets. It was fun, and most of the people in the business seemed to be truly enjoying themselves.

There were things they could have been worried about, of course, but Hollywood's relationship to the real world has never been clear, and most of the people in the movie business don't trouble themselves too much about it. The mid-1950s were difficult times. Although the Korean War was over, each day's newspaper brought news of new bombs and new and faster bombers. The first nuclear submarines had been put in the sea, and all over the country more and more missiles were being put in the ground. Just before Jimmy's arrival, President Eisenhower approved a plan to send B-26 bombers and supporting ground crews to Indochina to aid the French in their struggle against the communists. As he did so, he proclaimed that it would be a tragedy for the United States to ever become involved in a "hot war" there.

By the time Jimmy arrived, a milestone had been passed with the fall of Dien Bien Phu. That event's meaning for the nation was not immediately clear, but Jack L. Warner knew what to make of it and rushed into production *Jump Into Hell*.

Hollywood was exciting during those years, but it was nothing like what it had once been. By 1954, the so-called Golden Age of films had ended. No longer thriving, the movie business was facing the greatest crisis in its history.

All those studios had become great and rich and glamorous as the result of a controlled market. Each owned theaters all across the country that showed its films. There were some independent theaters, but they could buy only what the studios offered, and what the studios offered was so-called block booking: one or two popular movies along with a collection of B pictures, whatever the studio wanted to sell. The theaters had to buy the films sight unseen.

This was nothing other than a trust, of course, and in 1948 the government finally acted, separating the studios from their theaters. Thus the studios found themselves without guaranteed box office sales. For a few years the studios pretended that nothing had changed, but by the early 1950s the effect of the antitrust case was becoming painfully clear.

Added to this was television, then coming into its own as a prime competitor for leisure time. Jack L. Warner forbade television sets to appear in scenes of his studio's films, but television could not be denied. More and more Americans were staying home at night; the lines in front of cinemas were growing shorter.

And there was the blacklist. Many of Hollywood's most talented actors and writers had been blacklisted since 1947, suspected of being communists or communist sympathizers. The blacklist—and printed alphabetical lists actually existed—was an insidious reality. Actors suddenly found their contracts canceled, bought up, or simply not renewed. Writers could find no studio willing to hire them. Original screenplays—and stories dealing with anything even vaguely controversial or socially relevant—were rare. For their films, nervous producers turned to such safe subjects as successful Broadway plays, biblical epics, and popular novels. As money for production became scarcer, this practice only grew.

The star system—whereby studios would take an actor and through publicity turn him or her into a national personality—was coming to an end. On the day that James Dean arrived in Hollywood, MGM, which once boasted that it had "more stars than there are in heaven," had dropped Clark Gable from its contract list after twenty-three years. People in the business joked, "The old gray Mayer, he ain't what he used to be." Many of the established older males, such as Bogie, Gary Cooper, and James Stewart, had formed their own production companies, but none of them would consider acting on television, which was looked upon as a second-class entertainment medium. There was a shortage of new young actors, and a shortage in general of performers whose names meant anything to the dwindling film audience.

Around Christmastime 1953, film production in Hollywood reached the lowest point in its history: throughout town, only five pictures were being shot. But then things started getting better, and by the time Jimmy arrived, most of the studios were again churning out films. Hollywood was fighting back.

They fought back with projection systems designed to dwarf the home television screen: Cinerama, with its three screens, Fox's CinemaScope, Paramount's VistaVision, Warnerscope, Todd-AO, Vistarama, SuperScope, Naturama, MGM's Panavision. To fill those big screens, the major studios turned more and more to blockbuster epics. For a while, the big stories on the big screens worked, and the mid-1950s are sometimes called the "CinemaScope rebound."

They also fought back by stealing talent—actors, writers, and directors—away from television. These people brought new ideas to Hollywood, and eventually they changed the themes and attitudes of America's films.

The change was long overdue, and when it finally came there was an entirely new audience ready to receive it. In making their musicals and westerns, biblical epics and comedies, the movie moguls had overlooked a potential audience: America in the 1950s suddenly found itself populated by teenagers.

They had always been there, of course, but no one had ever thought of making films for them as they really were. In films, teenagers had remained stuck in gooey Victorian mush. In the midst of domestic tranquility, teenagers behaved themselves, dressed properly, and learned important lessons of life from their elders. The best example was the MGM series of fifteen Andy Hardy films—beginning with *A Family Affair*—starring Mickey Rooney as the cocky son of a small-town judge. The films were great favorites of Louis B. Mayer.

Mayer loved the Andy Hardy films, took them quite seriously, and had strong feelings about their contents. Once, to demonstrate how Andy should pray for his sick mother, Mayer got up from his desk and lumbered down onto his knees, clasped his hands in prayer, and looked up at the ceiling of his office. "Dear God," he prayed, his eyes shiny with tears, "please don't let my mom die, because she's the best mom in the world. Thank you, God." In the film, the mother rose from her sickbed, smiled, and tenderly kissed her loving son.

But the young people sitting in theaters and watching such films came from the real world, the one in which mothers die and leave their children alone forever. On film, at least, no one had ever spoken to those young people in words they could understand. No one had ever moved the way they moved or thought the way they thought. Not until James Dean.

Chapter Eight

EDEN

W hen Jimmy first showed up on the Warner Bros. lot in March 1954 the film crew took one look at him and decided he was a stand-in for the film's real star, who was yet to appear. No one knew who Jimmy was, and many who saw him judged him an unlikely candidate for success: he was too short, too bespectacled, too intense, nothing at all like a leading man.

Kazan had arranged a screen test on a Warner soundstage to see how Jimmy behaved in front of a camera. This wasn't Jimmy's first time before a movie camera—behind him were all those live television shows in New York as well as his bit parts in films—and he wasn't at all nervous, but he was just as twisted and fidgety as ever. When Kazan told the crew this strange kid was indeed the star, they thought he was crazy. After all, this was Warner Bros., homeland of gangsters, rogues, and hardcase private eyes: Jimmy Cagney, Edward G. Robinson, Errol Flynn, Humphrey Bogart. Jack L. Warner probably saw Jimmy's screen tests but he kept whatever opinions he might have had to himself. When Kazan had told the studio head he intended to use newcomers in *East of Eden*, Warner said, "Cast who you want." The film was to be made in color and CinemaScope, so its budget was high for that period— $1,600,000—but Warner had no intention of interfering with Kazan, who was then the hottest director in films.

Kazan had arranged for Jimmy to share a one-room furnished apartment with Dick Davalos, who had also just arrived in Los Angeles from New York. The apartment was over the Olive Drug Store, directly across the street from the Warner Bros. Studio. The rent was low, less than $100 a month.

Kazan didn't put Jimmy and Davalos together to save money: he wanted them to establish a relationship before he put them together in front of his cameras, and he wanted that relationship to be complex and ambivalent, something beyond any ordinary sibling rivalry. He wanted that certain sexual tension he had sensed between the two young actors during their New York tests to grow. He also had a hunch that Jimmy wasn't the easiest person to live with. By having Davalos room with Jimmy in tight quarters, Kazan hoped they would end up disliking each other as thoroughly as the script required.

Kazan was right. Shortly after Jimmy and Davalos settled into the apartment they became, just as Kazan had foreseen, Aron and Cal. Within a few days they were at each other's throats.

Since he had not yet been signed to a studio contract, Jimmy was given $300 a week as pocket money from the studio. One morning when he was not on call he rented a car and drove to Santa Monica City College to look up some of his old friends. He prowled around the campus and finally went to see Mrs. Gene Owen. When he appeared before her he had a four-day growth of beard and was dressed, she thought, very much like a bum. Owen was ashamed to take him into the faculty café for lunch, and the meeting was stressful for both of them.

His reunion with Richard Shannon was equally unsuccessful. He had called Shannon, given him his address, and made a date to meet at his apartment. When Shannon arrived Jimmy was wearing dirty duck pants, a dirty shirt, and old cowboy boots. Jimmy let Shannon into the room, but it was clear that he was in the middle of a telephone conversation, and he only barely acknowledged his old friend. While Jimmy talked on the phone—in a low voice close to a whisper—Shannon looked around the room and was not impressed with what he saw. Clothes were lying everywhere, most of all on the floor, and the air was heavy with the smell of cigarettes. When Jimmy finally finished the phone conversation he hung up, belched, and scratched himself. Shannon was not amused and within minutes excused himself, saying he had another appointment. He had quickly discovered that he and Jimmy had little to say to each other.

But Owen and Shannon were willing to give Jimmy another chance. He called and invited them both to dinner at a café in Santa Monica. Jimmy showed up shaved and dressed neatly, but his behavior throughout the meal distressed both Owen and Shannon. He insisted on tearing down Shannon: no longer father and son, their roles were reversed, with Jimmy the teacher and Shannon the pupil. When dinner was over, Shannon, who had been doing a slow burn, finally had had about enough.

"Jimmy, what are you trying to prove?" he asked.

Jimmy looked up, startled and hurt. "I don't know," he said and started to cry. When he had regained control of himself he said, "I'm sorry, Dick," and ran out of the restaurant. He jumped into his car and drove off leaving his two friends puzzled, wondering what was going on in Jimmy's life.

Jimmy also got together with James Whitmore, the man at least partly responsible for his journey to New York. Jimmy invited Whitmore to lunch with Kazan in the studio commissary. For Whitmore, the lunch was uncomfortable. Jimmy seemed full of himself and was obviously proud to be with Kazan. Throughout the meal, he kept attributing his success to Whitmore. Jimmy had been in Whitmore's class for a long time, but Whitmore hadn't seen any great talent in him. Indeed, Whitmore thought Jimmy was immensely neurotic and that he had psychological problems. He was glad when the lunch was over.

Jimmy's closest friend in Hollywood during the brief period before work on *Eden* began was Dick Clayton, whom he knew from *Sailor Beware*, the Martin and Lewis comedy in which they'd both had bit parts. Clayton had since given up acting entirely and was working for the Famous Artists Agency, which had agreed to represent Jimmy for Jane Deacy.

"I was on trial the first few times we were together," Clayton later told me, "but Jimmy soon began to realize that I had his best interests in mind." In fact, Clayton took good care of Jimmy, looked after him and saw to his every need. Jimmy came to trust Clayton and even talked to him about some of his dreams for the future: he wanted to buy a car, an MG he had fallen in love with, he wanted to go to Europe, and he wanted to have enough money to buy a place, any place, as long as it was his own.

Clayton had a car, and the two often went for drives around the city. One afternoon Jimmy announced, "I want you to meet the goodest man alive." He directed Clayton to an apartment in Westwood near UCLA on South Bundy Drive—his father's home. Jimmy introduced Clayton to his father and stepmother, Ethel. The conversation was light and friendly. Winton had a scrapbook of Jimmy's childhood pictures, and father and son pored over them, laughingly recalling early events in Jimmy's life. Clayton was delighted to see Jimmy so open and happy. He had heard that Jimmy disliked his father, but assumed that time had healed the old wounds.

When not on the soundstage across the street from his apartment, Jimmy was restless, bored, irritable, and lonely. He usually had breakfast alone at the drugstore below his apartment. His glasses had broken at the frames, and he had patched them carefully with tape, but they slid down his nose, giving him a scholarly look. Sitting at the drugstore counter, he would study the script intently. Many people, most of all people from Warner Bros. who had seen him on the lot, wanted to meet him, but if anyone approached him he would peer up over his glasses as if to say, "What the hell do you want?" and then go back to the script. As a result he earned a reputation with many of the studio secretaries for being rude and standoffish.

After studying all the test footage he had shot, Kazan decided that his original instinct about Jimmy was right, he was indeed perfect for the part of Cal. The director instructed Warner Bros.' legal department to draw up an agreement, making Jimmy the first actor to be signed for *Eden*. The forty-five-page boilerplate contract, dated April 7, 1954, called for Jimmy to be paid $1,000 a week for a period of no fewer than ten weeks for his exclusive services to Warner Bros.: a very good starting salary for an unknown actor. If he was wanted for a second picture his weekly salary would be increased to $1,250. For his tenth film he was guaranteed a weekly salary of $4,000.

Mildred Marie Dean.
(David Loehr Collection)

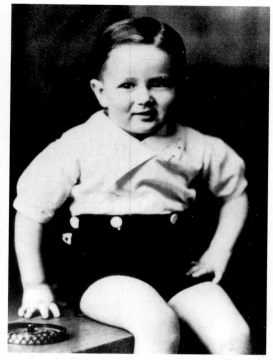

Jimmy, age four. One of the
earliest known photos.
(David Loehr Collection)

Ten-year-old Jimmy with neighbor
Anthony B. Kelley on the Winslow
farm. That's a cat Jimmy's got
by the tail in his right hand.
(Dene Kelley and Family Collection)

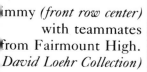

immy *(front row center)*
with teammates
from Fairmount High.
David Loehr Collection)

Girlfriend Arlene Sachs,
New York, 1953. *(Courtesy
of G. Maillard Kesslere)*

Christine White, nicknamed
"Face" by Jimmy. It was with
Christine that Jimmy auditioned
for the Actors Studio in 1952.
(Courtesy of Christine White)

John Gilmore, one of Jimmy's
close friends in New York, 1953.
(Courtesy of John Gilmore)

Twenty-one-year-old Jimmy *(in cage)* with Constance Ford and Arthur Kennedy in *See the Jaguar*, his first Broadway play. *(David Loehr Collection)*

As Bachir, the homosexual houseboy in *The Immoralist*, Jimmy's second (and last) role on Broadway, February 1954. *(David Loehr Collection)*

With Geraldine Page, in *The Immoralist*. *(David Loehr Collection)*

At the Villa Capri with Ursula Andress and maitre d' Nikko Romanos. Summer 1955. *(David Loehr Collection)*

In the Sherman Oaks apartment that he rented from Nikko Romanos. *(David Loehr Collection)*

Director George Stevens roped on the set of *Giant. From left to right*: Mercedes McCambridge, Elizabeth Taylor, Rock Hudson and Jimmy. *(David Loehr Collection)*

With Elizabeth Taylor during the filming of *Giant*.
(David Loehr Collection)

mmy as Jett Rink.
David Loehr Collection)

By the time he starred in *Giant*,
Jimmy was determined to make movies
of his own. *(David Loehr Collection)*

Jimmy and his silver Porsche, the car in which he died. *(David Loehr Collectio...*

Little Boy Lost. *(Dennis Stock / Magnum Photos)*

EDEN

East of Eden was scheduled to begin shooting in mid-May, and Kazan wanted to get Jimmy out of Hollywood to keep him from being impressed with the fact that he was, as the Hollywood press was reporting, "Kazan's new discovery, an unknown New York actor." He wanted Jimmy to keep a patina of innocence and feared that too much attention would spoil him. The director was also concerned that Jimmy—a farmboy from Indiana—was too pale and thin to play a farmboy, so he arranged with his assistant director, Horace Hough, to send Jimmy to live on a ranch in Salinas where much of the film was to be photographed.

"He can listen to the local accents, learn how to ride a horse, and maybe soak up something of the life-style there. He's too pale and needs some sun. And make him drink a pint of cream every day. I want him to gain a few pounds," Kazan told Hough. "And hopefully he'll get some sleep. You'd need two-by-fours to prop up the bags under his eyes." His last instruction was: "And get his hair cut."

Hough called Marvin "Monty" Roberts, a young man he had met on previous films. Roberts was four years Jimmy's senior and already the veteran of about ninety films made for Warner. A superb horseman and rodeo rider, he had doubled for many stars, including Roddy McDowall in *My Friend Flicka*, and had even stood in for Elizabeth Taylor in some long shots in *National Velvet*. As Hough knew, Monty was a third-generation Californian and had grown up in Salinas with John Steinbeck's children.

"We've got a kid here from New York who Kazan thinks is a tremendous actor," Hough said. "He's going to star in *Eden*, but we want him to learn about the life-style in Salinas, what vegetable growing is all about, and what people are like in a farming community. You take him, keep him with you twenty-four hours a day for a few weeks, and we'll work out a fee. But he's not to know we're paying you."

"You've got to be kidding," Monty said. "I've got thirty horses of my own in training, and I'm busy rodeoing. I've got a girlfriend, and I don't need some New York actor tagging around with me everyplace."

Hough, a veteran negotiator, interrupted. "How does two thou a month sound?"

Monty sighed. "Tell me what plane to meet."

And so Jimmy flew to Salinas to absorb the local color along with some sun. When Monty met him at the airport, Jimmy was carrying a small overnight bag he had borrowed from Davalos. He was dressed for Salinas in jeans, shirt, and boots.

Monty's folks had a two-hundred-acre spread in Salinas, and Monty lived in a bunkhouse on the property. No sooner had Monty assigned Jimmy a bunk than Jimmy shoved his bag underneath it, announced he was exhausted, and curled up on the small bed in a fetal position. He promptly fell asleep. Looking at him all curled up, Monty judged him to be about the size of a basketball.

During the first week Jimmy was with Monty, the young cowboy found it difficult to get his unwanted guest out of his shell. Jimmy was unlike any actor Monty had ever met. He was timid and reserved, overly polite, and determined not to impose on the Robertses. "I'm not a motion picture actor, and I'm frightened to death of being one," he confided to Monty. Such candor endeared Jimmy to Monty, who had always wanted to act in films himself, rather than just working as a horse wrangler or stunt double.

Hough had told Monty some of the locations that would be used in the film, so Monty took Jimmy to the train depot in Salinas, drove to the Gabilan Mountains, and toured Monterey and Cannery Row so Jimmy could become familiar with some of the buildings and the kind of people who lived in the area.

By the end of the first week Jimmy broke loose and was no longer a meek little mouse. Monty began to think of him as a brother he had known all of his life. They wore each other's clothes and dressed alike. Monty took Jimmy out to buy a hat and then showed him how to shape it so he would look like a local and not a tourist.

They rode horses together with Jimmy on a gentle animal. "Get some teeth in your ass, bite the saddle, and don't just sit there," Monty would shout. Although Jimmy was never comfortable on horseback and was not a good rider, he was persistent. Monty also showed him how to do rope tricks: the Butterfly, the Lazy Butterfly, and the Drunken Butterfly. Jimmy was slow to learn but practiced whenever he had a spare moment.

Everyplace Monty went, Jimmy went, too. They attended family gatherings and barbecues, and at such events there was music, dancing, roping, and riding. Jimmy usually found himself a place to sit on the ground, his legs bent up to his chest. He listened carefully to what was being said and carefully observed everything taking place. Within a month Jimmy had absorbed the unique central California rural attitude and accents so well that Monty, who received daily calls from Hough in Hollywood wanting progress reports, was able to give glowing accounts. Older people in the community meeting Jimmy for the first time were of the opinion that he had grown up in the Salinas area.

Despite Monty's encouragement, Jimmy showed no interest in the local girls and was angry when Monty pushed him to date one of them. Jimmy was enamored of Monty's fiancée Pat, however, and spent most of his evenings with the two of them, even making a toast to their happiness at their engagement party.

But Jimmy wasn't entirely happy. Toward the end of his stay in Salinas, on April 26, 1954, he sent a letter to Barbara Glenn. Handwritten on Famous Artists stationery, the letter read: "I don't like it here. I don't like people here. I like it home (N.Y.) and I like you and I want to see you. Must I always be miserable? I try so hard to make people reject me. Why? I don't want to write this letter. It would be better to remain silent. Wow! Am I fucked up.

"Got here on a Thursday went to the desert on Sat, week later to San Francisco. I DON'T KNOW WHERE I AM. Rented a car for two weeks it cost me $138.00. I WANT TO DIE. I have told the girls here to kiss my ass and what sterile, spineless, stupid prostitutes they were. I HAVEN'T BEEN TO BED WITH NO BODY. And won't untill after the picture and I am home safe in N.Y.C. (snuggly little town that it is) sounds unbelievable but that's the truth I swear. So hold everything stop breathing, stop the town all of N.Y.C untill (should have trumpets here) James Dean returns.

"Wow! Am I fucked up. I got no motorcycle I got no girl. HONEY, shit writing in capital letters doesn't seem to help either. Haven't found a place to live yet. HONEY. Kazan sent me here to get a tan. Haven't seen the sun yet. (fog and smog) Wanted me healthy looking. I look like a prune. Don't run away from home at too early an age or you'll have to take vitamens the rest of your life.

write me please. I'm sad most of the time. Awful lonely too. (I hope you're dying) BECAUSE I AM." Jim (Brando Clift) Dean .

A few days after sending that despairing letter, Jimmy said his goodbyes to Monty and his family and returned to Hollywood and the small apartment he shared with Dick Davalos.

Jimmy went to the Warner bookkeeping department and asked for a $700 advance against his first paycheck. Cash in hand, he rented a car and drove to the nearby Pickwick Stables, where he examined the horses for sale. A two-year-old buckskin caught his eye. The price was $300. He asked if he could use a phone and called Monty in Salinas. Jimmy described the horse to him and then called the stable's wrangler over and put him on the phone. After a brief discussion about the mare's bloodlines and general health, the wrangler handed the phone back to Jimmy.

"Jimmy, I've got to say that from the description the price sounds fair to me," said Monty, "but try to get it for $250."

After a few minutes of bargaining, Jimmy bought the horse for $250. He then posed for a picture with the horse and the wrangler.

A few days later he wrote another letter to Barbara. Dated May 19, this one read: "I haven't written because I have fallen in love. It had to happen sooner or later. Its not a very good picture of him but thats 'Cisco the Kid' the new member of the family. He gives me confidence. He makes my hands and my heart strong . . . May use him in the movie. I'm very lonely. Your card smelled so good, please don't do that. (dirty trick, I'm still a Calif-virgin. I *hate* this place."

Jimmy was so excited about Cisco that Kazan arranged for him to keep the horse at the studio corral.

The news that Elia Kazan was going to film *East of Eden* was greeted by the press with enthusiasm principally because it was an Elia Kazan film. Next to nothing was known about James Dean other than that he was Kazan's discovery, which, in light of the fact that Kazan had discovered Marlon Brando, aroused much curiosity about him. Kazan had complete control of his films, however, and preproduction publicity was kept to a minimum, with the usually assiduous studio publicity department giving out only the barest casting notes.

EDEN

While Jimmy was in Salinas getting tanned, toughened up, and acquainted with the area, Kazan was busy rounding out the cast of *Eden*. Press agents and the Warner publicity department kept me up to date on Kazan's progress, and I noted each new confirmed role in my column. Most of the actors Kazan chose had never worked in films and were unknown in Hollywood, so it was difficult to determine what Kazan had in mind. But there was nothing haphazard about his selections. He was assembling his cast with a chemist's sensibility: he somehow knew how the actors he chose would react to one another. And by choosing young, inexperienced actors he knew he would be able to mold them to fit his vision.

On April 15, Julie Harris was confirmed for the role of Abra in *Eden*. That casting note was followed up by others as Kazan signed on more Broadway actors for roles. Next to come was Jo Van Fleet to play Kate, the mother. Van Fleet had nearly ten years of Broadway experience and had won many awards for her acting, but as with most of the actors Kazan chose for *Eden*, this was her first film. The role of Ann went to an unknown actress named Lois Smith. For three important supporting roles Kazan turned to actors with film experience: Burl Ives, Albert Dekker, and Timothy Carey. Ives was quite a character, with a background that included playing professional football and getting by as an itinerant worker. Tall and heavyset with a goatee, he had an imposing physical presence. A musician and singer—and authority on folk music—he'd had several small parts singing and strumming his guitar in outdoor films and was just beginning to make his mark as a dramatic actor. Dekker had begun acting in films in 1937 and—often cast as the villain—had appeared in more than thirty. He'd already worked once with Kazan in 1947's *Gentleman's Agreement*, and while working on *Eden* he had a role in another film before the cameras at Warner Bros., *The Silver Chalice*. Carey, a tall and angular former baseball pitcher, had had roles in three films before *Eden*. Like Dekker, he was a character actor usually cast as a villain.

In late June Kazan signed his eleventh Broadway actor for *Eden*: Lonnie Chapman. Chapman, who had last acted on Broadway in *Ladies of the Corridor*, was given the role of Roy. A few days later I noted in my column that Mick Frank, a New York actor who had studied with Kazan at the Actors Studio, had hitchhiked to Los

Angeles on the long-shot gamble of landing a role in *Eden*. Kazan signed him up.

One day during lunch at Romanoff's with Bogie I mentioned the roster of New York actors Kazan had signed for *East of Eden*. "They're all from the Actors Studio," Bogie snorted. "Mumblers all. You'll need an interpreter to understand them."

There was one part Kazan didn't cast: the role of the father, Adam, went to Raymond Massey for purely contractual reasons. Massey had agreed to act in the war movie *Battle Cry* on condition that he be given a role in the more prestigious Kazan film.

On June 18 the studio announced that Leonard Rosenman had been signed to write the score for *Eden*. In New York, Barbara Glenn heard the news; Jimmy somehow missed it.

Around the time he'd met Jimmy in New York, Leonard had been interviewed by Kazan to write film scores. Kazan had heard about his work from Aaron Copland and Leonard Bernstein and had considered asking him to write the score for *On the Waterfront*, an assignment ultimately given to Bernstein. When Kazan first asked Leonard to write the score for *Eden*, Leonard had hesitated, saying he didn't have any experience. "I won't allow you to make mistakes," Kazan assured him.

Since his arrival in Los Angeles, Jimmy had been driving rental cars, but now that he was getting a regular paycheck he went out and bought himself a used Triumph T-110, a very loud and very fast motorcycle. Although he lived across the street from the studio, he rode the big bike to work the next day, attracting much attention from the guards at the gate, the actors and crew on the narrow streets of the lot, and most of all from Kazan. The director was furious: he had personal experience of Jimmy's motorcycle antics and was not about to risk losing his major star.

Even before Jimmy could get off the bike, Kazan was standing by him and yelling. "Just what do you think you're doing?"

Having anticipated something like this, Jimmy only smiled.

Kazan was still yelling. "I don't care what you do to yourself when this film is in the can, but until then you are to stay off that thing." He gave Jimmy a choice: garage the motorcycle or return it.

Jimmy garaged it and made a down payment on a new MG TA,

a small, fast, red convertible sports car that seated two, with some discomfort.

His first stop in the new car was Julie Harris's apartment. She had just arrived in Hollywood and had barely finished unpacking. "C'mon," Jimmy said to her, "I'm going to take you for a ride in my new MG."

She had misgivings. With its top down, the car looked too small for two people and too small for a safe ride at any speed—and she didn't think Jimmy intended to go slowly. But there he was at her door, so spirited and full of contagious enthusiasm. She agreed to the ride.

She thought it would be her last. He took her through the Hollywood Hills, up and down the winding roads at his usual alarming speed—so fast that for most of the trip her heart was in her throat. But she never objected, never even said a word. She knew that as long as she didn't complain about the speed, she was Jimmy's comrade. Around Jimmy, no one wanted to seem square.

That night he wrote a letter to Barbara Glenn, who had earlier written to him about a party she was going to attend for Kazan in New York. It was clear he was still feeling homesick for the city.

"Honey!!! I'm still a Calif. virgin, remarkable no. I'm saving it—H-Bomb Dean. A new addition has been added to the Dean family. I got a red 53, MG (milled head etc. hot engine). My sex pours itself into fast curves, broadsliding and broodings; drags etc. You have plenty of competition now. My motorcycle, my MG and my girl. I have been sleeping with my M.G. We make it together. HONEY

"Have been very dejected, and extremely moody last two weeks. Have been telling everybody to fuck off and that's nor good . . . Everyone turns into an idiot out here. I only have one friend, one guy that I can talk to and be understood. I hope Lennie comes out here. I need someone from New York cause I'm [acting] mean and I'm really kind and gentle. Things get mixed up all the time. I see a person I would like to be very close to . . . then I think it would just be the same as before, and they don't give a shit for me. Then I say something nasty or nothing. Or I walk away. The poor person doesn't know what happened. . . ."

Leonard Rosenman and his family arrived a few days after Jimmy sent the letter. One by one, the New York actors Kazan had hired arrived in Los Angeles. Jo Van Fleet moved into an apartment in a building on Riverside Drive near the Warner Bros. studio, and Burl Ives took a room in the Beverly Wilshire Hotel. Many members of the cast—including Lois Smith, Jimmy Whitehead, and the Rosenmans with their two daughters—moved into apartments over the Olive Drug Store, across the street from the studio.

The small band of New Yorkers got along well. The Rosenmans soon resumed their roles as surrogate parents for Jimmy, and their apartment became the nightly mealtime rendezvous for the other members of the film's cast.

While the Rosenmans were settling into their apartment, Jimmy came by to take them for a ride in his new car. Always fond of Gabrielle, he wanted to take her along, too. Leonard and Adele could see that Jimmy was thrilled with his new car and didn't want to turn him down.

Finding room in the tiny car for Gabrielle wasn't difficult: she sat on Leonard's lap in the passenger seat. Adele was another matter, and she ended up sitting on the folded-down top. Thus arranged they took off for Bob's Big Boy for hamburgers. Both Adele and Leonard were aware and appreciated that Jimmy drove carefully with Gabrielle in the car.

Faster and more eventful was Jimmy's drive alone with Leonard a few days later. Racing along Mulholland Drive, they did a spinout and piled into some garbage cans in front of a home. Their arrival was noisy, and while they examined the damage to the car—and Jimmy cursed—the lady of the house came out to see what was happening. This was Jean Howard, the actress-photographer wife of Charles Feldman, the man whose agency, Famous Artists, employed Dick Clayton, agent for both Jimmy and Leonard.

Howard recognized her husband's clients, rushed back inside to get her camera, and took some photographs of Jimmy and Leonard and the dented red MG.

Jimmy swore Leonard to secrecy and never mentioned a word to anyone about the accident. The next morning he took the car to a body shop and had the damage repaired.

On Wednesday, May 26, the cast and crew of *Eden* flew to

Mendocino to begin shooting the Monterey scenes of the film. Jimmy and Leonard sat together on the plane—Leonard slept most of the way—and in Mendocino the two friends shared a bungalow at the Little River Inn. One night while they were wandering around the grounds, they passed Jo Van Fleet's bungalow and saw the actress through one of the windows, naked from the waist up.

"I didn't realize she had such nice tits," remarked Rosenman.

"Those aren't tits," retorted Jimmy, "they're poison sacks."

When the conversation got dull at mealtimes, Jimmy would liven things up by dislodging his dental plate with his tongue. He would then take out the plate and deliver unintelligible insults.

Leonard Rosenman had suggested to Kazan that they work the way Prokofiev had worked with the great Russian film director Eisenstein: have the film score played for the actors before they performed their scenes. A piano was brought to the location, and Rosenman played his score in the open air to help the actors get in the proper mood. Some scenes, such as Jimmy's famous beanfield scene, were actually filmed to the music.

One night the entire cast was invited to hear some of the complete score for the film. This was the first time Leonard had heard his score played by a full orchestra. Jimmy went along with the Rosenmans. When they had finished playing the music, the members of the orchestra stood up and applauded. Adele turned to look at Jimmy and saw that his face was white and that he was crying.

Kazan forbade the actors to see the dailies or rushes, but Rhea Burakoff, the director's secretary, went with the costume designer one night to see the first week of filming. The following morning Jimmy showed up in her office.

"Well, what did you think of the dailies?" Jimmy asked anxiously. "How was I?"

"The scenery was beautiful," Rhea said, deciding to tease him a bit.

"I know," said Jimmy, urging her on. "But what else?"

Rhea went on about how wonderful Jo Van Fleet and some of the other actors were until she realized Jimmy was becoming truly upset. "You weren't bad, Jimmy," she finally told him. "In fact, you were quite good."

The following week the company moved to Salinas for a week of shooting. Jimmy called Monty Roberts, and he came to visit the set. They worked on rope tricks for a few hours.

After Salinas, the film company moved back to the studio in Burbank for two months of indoor shooting on soundstages. Meanwhile, Barbara Glenn had met a man she really liked and who wanted to marry her. She considered the proposal carefully because, as she said recently, "As much as I loved Jimmy I never anticipated marrying him and living with him for the rest of my life. That was just not a possible option because we could not live together or be together for any length of time without exploding in some way or another. Our personalities just did not allow for it." So, early in June 1954, she wrote to Jimmy telling him about the man she had met who wanted to marry her and whom she really cared about.

Jimmy wrote back to her immediately urging her to get married. In his letter, he claimed he wanted her to have a home and children and someone to love her devotedly. Much as he seemed to care for her, it was clear Jimmy did not feel himself capable of making this sort of commitment.

Although Barbara's relationship with the other man soon ended, her relationship with Jimmy was clearly over. By then, Jimmy was dating. For a while he was going with a waitress named Connie, but she soon disappeared from his life, to be replaced by a succession of starlets and other girls he met while prowling around Hollywood at night. He never seemed to date anyone for longer than a few days. Like a dutiful son, he brought most of his dates "home" to meet his "folks," which meant he showed up with them at the Rosenmans' apartment. Adele thought Jimmy brought the girls by to get her and Leonard's approval. She sensed that Jimmy was proud of having the Rosenmans as his friends and wanted to show them off to the girls—especially if they had brains.

Sometimes Jimmy treated the Rosenmans too much like parents. One day he went to Leonard and said, "Let's go out and shoot some baskets."

Leonard, who was trying to work, ignored the request and told Jimmy to stop bothering him. Finally, he said, "Why is it so important that I go out and play basketball with you? I'm not your dad, he's living in Culver City. Why don't you call him and ask him to play ball."

"Arghh," said Jimmy.

It was through the Rosenmans that Jimmy met Lew Bracker, a young man four years his senior who was to become one of his closest friends in Hollywood. Lew, who was about Jimmy's height and build, was, unlike Jimmy, a dapper dresser, probably because he was an insurance salesman. (I had bought insurance from him, and it was through him that I met the Rosenmans.) He was also Adele's cousin, and she and Leonard had spent their honeymoon at the Bracker family ranch, El Capitán, in Santa Barbara. Leonard invited Lew to lunch at the studio, and he was delighted at the prospect of meeting future clients.

While Lew and Leonard were having lunch, Jimmy came over to say hello. A few nights later, Adele and Leonard were invited to a party but couldn't find a baby-sitter. When Leonard suggested Jimmy, Adele objected. She didn't think he was reliable enough and feared that if something more interesting came up he would simply take off. After a moment's thought she suggested Lew, who just happened to be available.

No sooner had Lew put the girls to bed than the door opened and Jimmy came in.

"Where are Lenny and Adele?" he asked.

"They're out for the evening," said Lew.

"What are you doing?"

"I'm baby-sitting."

Jimmy sat down, and he and Lew spent the evening talking about their respective girlfriends and soon discovered they had a common passion: fast cars.

The evenings in the Rosenmans' apartment ended late, and Jimmy was usually the last to leave the festivities. He didn't go to his apartment to sleep, however, and most often drove around Hollywood into the early-morning hours. Always an insomniac, he was having even more trouble getting to sleep because he was so concerned about his role in the film.

Kazan noticed: when Jimmy showed up for work he had big circles under his eyes and looked pooped. Worried that the exhaustion might affect his work, Kazan decided to put Jimmy where he could keep an eye on him. Kazan was in Hollywood alone and was staying in a hotel. He moved out of the hotel into one of the big dressing rooms on the Warner lot and moved Jimmy into the adjoining dressing room. The dressing rooms were luxurious, each two rooms with a bathroom and small kitchen.

As Jimmy was unpacking his things in his new quarters, a studio guard noticed the .22 automatic he'd brought from New York. Jimmy was ordered to relinquish the weapon.

During much of the time Kazan was filming at the studio he ordered the set closed, which meant that no one—including studio executives—was allowed on. This only whetted the appetite of the press, which was determined to write about Jimmy, who was being touted as "another Brando." The label infuriated Jimmy, who said, "I have my own problems."

Although the set was closed, I prevailed on Ted Ashton, the studio press agent assigned to the film, to get a message to Kazan saying I wanted to come by for a visit. I had been one of the few newsmen allowed to sit in on Actors Studio rehearsals in New York, and I knew Kazan, who was a reader of the *Herald Tribune*. Kazan sent word back that I could watch filming with the proviso that I not try to interview anyone on the set or write about anything I saw.

What I saw of James Dean that day on the set was not impressive. He had only one scene, in which he was supposed to break in through a door, and it took countless takes before Kazan was satisfied. During a break in filming I asked the director why he had chosen an unknown actor for the film.

"I chose him because he is Cal Trask," replied Kazan. "There is no point in attempting to cast it better or nicer. Jimmy was it. He has a grudge against all fathers. He is vengeful; he has a sense of aloneness and of being persecuted. And he is suspicious. In addition, he is tremendously talented."

A few days later when Lew said he wanted me to meet an actor he knew, I was surprised. Lew, who had a no-nonsense attitude toward himself and life, had grown up around Los Angeles—his parents lived in Beverly Hills and owned a large ranch in Santa

Barbara—and he had a native's scorn of most film people. But this actor, he explained, was different.

"You'll like Jimmy Dean," said Lew. "He doesn't take any shit from anyone, and even though he's an actor, he's one of us." We drove out to the Warner lot to meet Lew's new friend.

Lew and I stood in the sunshine outside the commissary and waited. Then Jimmy sauntered over to us, wearing faded jeans held up by a silver-buckled cowboy belt, scuffed cowboy boots, a short-sleeved sport shirt, and a red cotton-twill golf jacket. Jimmy gave Lew a hug. Turning to me he rocked back on his heels, cocked his head to one side, and squinted for a long moment while I sized him up, too.

I must have passed his test because he finally grinned, and at that moment his face lit up, the sullen look was gone, and I liked him.

"I like you," he said. "I didn't think I was going to because you're a newspaperman."

I laughed. "I was about to say the same thing to you because you're an actor."

It was his turn to laugh. "That's what you think," he said. "You haven't seen me act yet."

That afternoon the three of us went up to Mulholland Drive and raced against one another. Jimmy drove his MG, Lew his Buick, and I lumbered around in a Bentley convertible. Although Jimmy had the fastest car on the curves, Lew had sufficient skill to give him a good run. I came in last, shaken but exhilarated.

One day Kazan invited Marlon Brando to drop by the set for a visit. It was a difficult moment for Jimmy. Brando was Jimmy's idol—Kazan was amused that when Jimmy spoke about Brando he did so "in a cathedral hush." Jimmy had met Brando in New York, but they hadn't become friends. In a sense, they were too similar, both of them famous for riding motorcycles, playing bongos, and mumbling dialogue. Brando himself didn't make things easier by treating Jimmy like a younger brother, taking him aside and giving him tips. He cautioned Jimmy not to ride his motorcycle too much, telling him that he was only risking his greatest asset—his face—

and he advised Jimmy to see a psychiatrist. He seemed to consider Jimmy an awkward imitation of himself, which was neither fair nor true.

Comparisons to Brando were inevitable—all young actors were then compared to him, including Paul Newman. What they all had in common wasn't Marlon Brando's real character but the characters they played on screen. A new kind of hero was beginning to take shape in films. Brando was that hero's first embodiment; Jimmy was to be its full realization.

Kazan put no stock in the comparison. "They weren't alike," he told me sometime later. "Marlon was well trained by Stella Adler and had excellent technique. He was proficient in every aspect of acting, including characterization and makeup. He was also a great mimic. Dean had no technique to speak of. He would either get the scene right immediately, without any detailed direction—and that was ninety-five percent of the time—or he couldn't get it at all."

It was painful for Jimmy to watch Kazan joyfully put his arms around Brando and to see even Julie Harris—Jimmy's closest friend on the set—treat Brando with obvious admiration.

Harris was especially important to Jimmy. Kazan has said that Jimmy might not have gotten through *Eden* had it not been for her. "She was goodness itself with Dean, kind and patient and everlastingly sympathetic. She would adjust her performance to whatever the new kid did."

Sometimes, even Harris's presence wasn't enough. Jimmy had one scene with Harris on a slanting roof outside a second-story window. Jimmy complained that he couldn't do the scene, and he was right. He did it poorly; but it was an important scene, so Kazan took Jimmy and Harris to a nearby Italian restaurant and loaded Jimmy up with Chianti. That did the trick.

Through the Rosenmans, Jimmy got to know Burl Ives, who often dropped by the Rosenmans' house, and when the music started he'd play his guitar and sing. Jimmy was enchanted by Ives, and Ives responded to Jimmy, who turned on the country boy charm for him.

Ives then owned a big Packard four-door convertible, and he was fond of taking his friends out for meals. On those occasions he always wanted to play the chauffeur, putting his friends in the backseat and driving them to a restaurant. He himself provided the entertainment, for a meal with Ives always included music. One day Ives came by and invited Leonard, Adele, and Jimmy out to dinner. He had arrived with his bagpipes, and he took them to Don the Beachcomber, a popular Chinese restaurant, for a meal and music. Another day, Ives dropped by around three in the afternoon and invited Jimmy and Lew off for a little entertainment at the Smoke House, the restaurant across the street from Warner. For all that afternoon and into the early evening, they sat in the bar where Ives entertained them with stories of his days rambling around the country as a folk singer.

Although Jimmy and Davalos did not get along well off screen, they worked well together before the cameras. The only member of the *Eden* cast who did not get along with Jimmy was Raymond Massey. Massey was then fifty-eight and had performed in more than thirty-five films in the United States and England, along the way serving—and getting wounded—in both world wars. He was closely identified with the role of Abraham Lincoln, having played him in both the stage and screen versions of *Abe Lincoln in Illinois*. Aloof, dignified, and educated at Oxford, he was an actor of the old school and believed actors should learn their lines and follow the script. Not surprisingly, he considered Jimmy unprofessional and rude. Massey couldn't stand the sight of Jimmy and dreaded every moment of working with him. "You never know what he's going to say or do," Massey complained to Kazan. "Make him read the lines the way they are written." For his part, Jimmy knew Massey disliked him and responded with unmasked hostility.

All the members of the cast of *Eden* had to put up with Jimmy's personal approach to acting. He had his own ways of preparing for a scene, and most often his preparations took a long time. He would go off alone and exercise, stretch out, shake his wrists, bounce up and down, kick the ground, and seem to pout. Or he'd disappear into his dressing room to meditate. Julie Harris was understanding and patient; Massey was outraged.

Kazan was not one to waste the friction between two actors and instead encouraged it. After all, Massey was playing Jimmy's puritanical father, and their personal conflicts off camera were an ideal match to the conflicts dictated by the script. Kazan aggravated the antagonism by never concealing from either actor what the other thought. Thus, when Jimmy and Massey were in a scene together, the screen was alive with precisely the tension Kazan wanted.

Kazan also used the personal situation between Jimmy and Massey to elicit better performances in certain specific scenes. One of the film's crucial scenes involves Adam having Cal read verses from the Bible as a form of punishment. Cal reads the verses, but does so defiantly, refusing to follow his father's directions. The script called for Massey to explode in rage, but the dignified actor remained composed.

Leonard Rosenman happened to be on the set that day and saw how Kazan solved the problem. After they had done six takes and Kazan still wasn't satisfied, Kazan took Jimmy aside and whispered something to him. Jimmy then sat back down at the table. When they started rolling the cameras, Jimmy looked down at the Bible and began saying, "The Lord is my shepherd, I shall not suck cock, up your ass, fuck you, shit, piss." And so on.

It was too much for Massey, who jumped up from the table and started to yell. "Gadge, I will not play with such a person! You'd better call my lawyers and—"

"Cut! Cut!" yelled Kazan. Then he turned to Massey. "I told Jimmy to say that," he explained. By having Jimmy infuriate Massey he'd got the reaction he wanted on camera, and later they dubbed in the dialogue.

Nor was Kazan averse to manipulating Jimmy's pride when it served the needs of the film. In one scene, Jimmy had to rush into his father's ice house and push out several of the large, and very heavy, blocks of ice. But try as he might, Jimmy couldn't budge the ice. Then—just loud enough so that Jimmy was sure to hear him—Kazan made a derogatory remark about Jimmy's acting ability. During the next take, Jimmy was close to a fit of rage as he hurled the ice to the ground below.

Jimmy had bought an expensive new Leica, which he took everywhere on the set with him, photographing everyone and everything and having the studio lab do his developing. Kazan thought Jimmy was being a nuisance and told him not to bring his camera on the stage when they were shooting. Because of the reprimand Jimmy sulked for a few days.

When he was not on call, Jimmy had a lot of free time, which he spent wandering around with his camera hoping to get good candid photos. And he was looking for companionship.

Chapter Nine

PIER

Fuel rom the outside, a soundstage looks like nothing but a square block of a building with no windows and only a few doors, each bearing a stenciled number. Soundstages are designed to be soundproof, and when a director and cast are in the course of shooting a scene, the doors are closed and, usually, locked from the inside. On any given day, at any one of Hollywood's major studios—assuming the studio is financially healthy—most of the soundstages are in use, and for most of the day the streets running between the blocks of soundstages are quiet and relatively empty.

But at lunchtime and between takes the doors open and actors in costume spill out into the sunshine. They go to the commissary for a meal, walk around the lot to see what friends are up to, sit on the grass to relax. I learned early on that those breaks were good times for impromptu interviews and good times in general just to watch what was going on. What actors do in their free time, when they're not on a set in front of the camera, does not go unnoticed. If a leading man gives a leading lady a public kiss, however chaste or quick, or if they retire to his or her private trailer with the door closed, someone will be there to spot it, and the next morning's trade papers will report it and ponder its significance.

In his free time, with or without his camera, Jimmy wandered through the Warner Bros. lot. He came to know the layout, learned which soundstages had both front doors and back, and enjoyed looking in on what other actors were doing. The people he met viewed him with curiosity: no one had seen any film of *Eden* yet, but the word was out that he was going to be a hot new star.

Although unimpressive from the outside, soundstages are other worlds within. For example, the soundstage for *East of Eden* re-created early 20th-century America. As Jimmy soon discovered, just down the block on the Warner lot was a soundstage re-creating the Roman world around A.D. 3: the actors inside were dressed in togas and sandals. The film was *The Silver Chalice*, the story of a Greek sculptor making a silver chalice to hold the cup Christ drank from at the Last Supper. Standard fare during the mid-1950s: that spring I counted twelve Bible stories in production. In fact, this project had two factors in its favor: it was based on a popular historical novel (by Thomas Costain), and it dealt with the Bible, always a safe subject—it was considered the most important biblical epic since *The Robe*.

Doing the casting for *The Silver Chalice* was its director-producer, Victor Saville. Like Kazan, and like many Hollywood filmmakers, Saville had raided Broadway in search of new talent for the film. For the central role of Basil, the Greek sculptor, he had chosen Paul Newman. So Newman, rejected by Kazan and taking the role Jane Deacy had turned down for Jimmy, made it out to Hollywood only a few months after his rival Jimmy.

This was Newman's first film, as it was also the first film for the actor Saville chose to play the Apostle Peter: Lorne Greene. Greene had been Canada's top newscaster before moving to the United States, where he had done well in television shows and on Broadway before being chosen by Saville. Virginia Mayo was the female lead in *The Silver Chalice*, playing the role of Helena; Natalie Wood played Helena as a young girl. Then sixteen, Natalie had begun her film career at age five and by the time of *The Silver Chalice* had acted in nearly twenty films, including *Miracle on 34th Street*. Also in the cast of *The Silver Chalice* was a young Italian actress named Pier Angeli.

I knew very little about Pier Angeli until I was assigned to write an article about her for *This Week*, a magazine syndicated in hundreds of Sunday newspapers. Before the interview I found out what I could from studio releases and press agents. She had been born

Anna Maria Pierangeli on June 19, 1932, in Cagliari, Sardinia, twenty minutes before her twin sister, Marisa. The two girls had grown up in an Italy devastated by war and had experienced postwar deprivations. (Years later I was told that Pier had been raped by an American GI when she was fifteen.)

Discovered by director Leonide Moguy, she had starred in two Italian films, both dealing with the pains of adolescence, and then screenwriter Stewart Stern had recommended her to director Fred Zinnemann for the starring role in the film *Teresa*, for which Stern was writing the screenplay. In the film she played a young Italian girl who leaves her family in war-ravaged Italy to marry an American soldier. At the time Pier spoke only a few words of English. And she was shy: the story in Hollywood was that she had passed out after her first screen kiss.

Anna Maria Pierangeli, given the screen name Pier Angeli, became an actress. Perhaps because of her gentle bearing, perhaps because of her elegant beauty, she was usually cast in roles of fragile, innocent women. Following *Teresa* she had acted in several films, including a role opposite Kirk Douglas in *The Story of Three Loves*.

For a while after the death of her father, Pier had been the sole support of her family: her mother, twin sister, and another sister, three years younger, named Patrizia. In Hollywood, her twin, Marisa, had been discovered and, under the name Marisa Pavan, had begun her own screen career. While Pier was working on *The Silver Chalice*, Marisa was getting ready to play Anna Magnani's daughter in *The Rose Tattoo*.

I arranged to meet Pier in the studio commissary during her lunch break. I remember being struck by Pier's lunch meal: raw hamburger, raw eggs, and a glass of water. "It's what I always eat when working," she explained. I was impressed by her diet but even more by her beauty. She had the face of a Madonna, pure and full of grace, more than a little like a Botticelli, with striking green eyes and auburn hair. She was tiny, barely an inch over five feet, and I doubt she weighed more than a hundred pounds.

She was eager to talk about her dog, a poodle named Oscar. Hoping for something more newsworthy, I asked her about Kirk Douglas.

PIER

In almost faultless but sweetly Italian-accented English, she said, "Oh, he was very nice, but he was not the marrying kind." She thought about that awhile and then added, "I pray that when I do marry I won't make a mistake."

When I complimented her on her English, she told me her best friend in Hollywood was Debbie Reynolds—then one of MGM's hottest young actresses—"and Debbie helps me with my English and also keeps me from being square. I want to be hep."

Pier Angeli, the embodiment of European beauty and charm, wanted to be hep. And with his Bach and Kierkegaard, photography and bullfighting, James Dean—the original hep cat—wanted most of all to be sophisticated and worldly. Thus what happened may have been inevitable, at least the way tragedies always seem at the end.

One night Jimmy was out with Paul Newman and actor Joseph Wiseman, and they introduced him to Pier. Following that first meeting, Jimmy began making frequent visits to the set of *The Silver Chalice*, and Pier began stopping by the set of *Eden*. No one paid much attention at first. Kazan put up with Pier's visits because he preferred having Jimmy hanging around the studio when not before the cameras, rather than driving around the city in his MG.

During the early part of their relationship, Jimmy sometimes dropped by Pier's home, and it was there that Arthur Loew, Jr. first saw him. At twenty-eight, Loew was then the youngest producer in Hollywood. His paternal grandfather was MGM founder Marcus Loew, his maternal grandfather was Adolph Zukor, founder of Paramount, and his father was a vice-president at MGM. During the period of *Eden* he was dating Marisa. He had never heard of Jimmy and had no idea he even existed until he dropped by the Angeli residence one evening to pick up Marisa for a date. As he came in the door she rushed up to him saying, "Shh, shh." He assumed someone in the house was deathly ill. But as he went inside he spotted a kid pacing up and down in the yard, flailing his arms with a script in his hands; sitting in front of the wildly gesturing kid—and staring at him mesmerized—was Pier.

"What's going on?" asked Loew.

"It's Jimmy Dean," loudly hissed Marisa. "He's rehearsing!"

"Who is Jimmy Dean?" he asked.

Marisa was astonished. "Oh!" was all she could say.

Loew thought it was all a lot of nonsense and laughed.

Such happy family moments were not to last, however, for Hollywood's gossip columnists soon reported that Pier and Jimmy had been spotted holding hands in the studio commissary at lunchtime.

They were in love, and it was out in the open. Before long, pictures were taken of them visiting each other on the set, kissing and holding hands. When Julie Harris saw them on the set of *Eden*, she thought they were like children. That sweet and that innocent: children.

The trouble began when the gossip came to the attention of Pier's mother. To her, there was something—among several things—very wrong with Jimmy: aside from the way he dressed and spoke and behaved, he wasn't Catholic. The thought of her daughter seriously dating a non-Catholic was anathema to her, and she did everything in her power to end the relationship.

And she was a powerful woman. I met Mrs. Pierangeli two or three times. Small, dark, and as beautifully elegant as her three daughters, she impressed me as the kind of woman who would fight fiercely to protect her family from any threat.

Jimmy and Pier responded with subterfuge. They took to meeting in out-of-the-way places and went for rides to the beach, where they would take long walks, holding hands and talking or just silently enjoying each other's company. They saw their love as pure and innocent; years later Pier said they were "like Romeo and Juliet."

When they went out in the evening, they were usually accompanied by a small circle of friends so that Pier could tell her mother she was going out with friends. A small lie of omission: she wouldn't mention that Jimmy was to be among those present.

The Rosenmans were among the first of Jimmy's friends to meet Pier. Jimmy brought her over to their apartment. Adele was pleased with Pier, thought she was nice and very pretty, and idly mused to herself that Pier and Jimmy were indeed a potential match.

Leonard saw another side of the couple. Although Leonard was a parental figure to Jimmy, Pier and Jimmy enjoyed acting like he was their baby. More than once, Pier said to Jimmy, "When we get married, we're going to have to buy Lenny a grand piano."

Although Leonard did not enjoy playing house, he would dutifully exclaim, "No shit? You really mean it?"

Not long after my interview with Pier, I met her again when Lew Bracker invited me to drop by his folks' home for dinner. At around 9:30 Jimmy and Pier arrived, holding hands and beaming. With obvious pride, Jimmy introduced Pier as "My best friend, the only girl I ever loved."

The effect of the romance on Jimmy was strong and visible. He became neater, exchanging his habitual torn jeans and leather for a jacket, slacks, and sometimes even a tie. His friends took notice and were mildly amused. And he began to worry about what the press was saying, for he knew only too well that anything in print would sooner or later get back to Mrs. Pierangeli.

Although I sometimes thought Jimmy immature—and I wasn't wrong; that was a large part of his charm—the acuity of his perceptions of himself and other people often astounded me. I noticed this particularly when watching him operate with the press. Before an interview Jimmy would research the interviewer, getting a run-down on who he or she was and what special interests he or she might have from press agents—or from me. Then he would charm the interviewer, win him or her over, by transforming himself into whatever he thought might appeal to that person.

However, if he didn't like someone, he could turn off the charm, which is what happened the first time he met Hedda Hopper, one of Hollywood's best known and most powerful gossip columnists. Born Elda Furry, Hopper was a former actress famous for her penchant for hats—on one occasion she wore two, one on top of the other—and for her ongoing feuds, particularly with her rival, Louella Parsons. Hopper worked with one secretary, one assistant, and one typist to whom she dictated her column.

She was originally thoroughly uncharmed by Jimmy. Used to studio publicity people calling her and announcing the arrival of some new acting genius, she responded with cool amusement when the chief of public relations at Warner Bros. called her one day and said she had to meet Jimmy Dean. "We think he's a genius, more or less," the man declared. "You've just got to come take a look." So she had gone to the Warner Bros. commissary with a press agent to meet Jimmy. As she reported:

"The latest genius sauntered in, dressed like a bum, and slouched down in silence at a table away from mine. He hooked another chair with his toe, dragged it close enough to put his feet up, while he watched me from the corner of his eye. Then he stood up to inspect the framed photographs of Warner stars that covered the wall by his head. He chose one of them, spat in its eye, wiped off his spittle with a handkerchief, then like a ravenous hyena, started to gulp the food that had been served him.

" 'Would you like to meet him?' asked the studio press agent who was my escort.

" 'No thank you, I've seen enough. If that's your prize package, you can take him. I don't want him.'

" 'He doesn't always behave like this,' said the agent apologetically.

" 'Why now?' I asked.

" 'I don't know. To be frank, he never acted this way before.' "

Hopper went back to her office and wrote a story about Jimmy, calling him "a member of the Dirty Shirttail group of actors from New York." She even mentioned that he'd had to borrow a tuxedo to take Pier out. "If this is the kind of talent they're importing, they can send it right back, as far as I'm concerned."

Such reports about Jimmy caused the Warner publicity department some anxious moments. It was their responsibility to present Jimmy to the public in the best possible light. Max Bercutt, head of the publicity department, soon discovered that Jimmy didn't care about his problems, nor did he care about the producers, directors, or even J. L. Warner: "He didn't give a shit about anybody." Max did, however, have a good fix on Jimmy. "He didn't have anybody who loved him and he didn't have anybody he could love. He had no faith in anybody other than the people around him, which is why he had them around. He was really a little boy lost."

Bercutt's perception was accurate in many ways, but Pier filled a gap in Jimmy's life by giving him the attention and coddling he seemed to crave, and their relationship continued to grow. He called her "Maw"—to his friends he referred to her affectionately as "Miss Pizza"—and she called him "Baby." They exchanged gifts. One night she gave him a gold St. Christopher medal, the patron saint of travelers, and he wore it on a gold chain around his neck. She also gave him a small gold frame with her picture, inscribed, "I love you, Maw." He kept the framed picture on his bureau along with a stack of pictures he had taken of Pier himself.

One afternoon on the set of *Eden* Jimmy told Julie Harris he had something he wanted to show her and pulled out of a pocket a gold and enamel charm. He opened it to reveal a small lock of hair. "It's Pier's hair," he said. Harris could see he was delighted.

From time to time they went to Kazan's office, where most of the New York cast gathered after shooting. Rhea Burakoff recalls that when the director walked in he'd look around at all the kids sprawled on his office floor and say gruffly, "What the hell is this, the Club Kazan?" But she believes Kazan was secretly delighted, for the members of the cast were truly like a family to him.

One day Jimmy and Pier bought gold friendship rings at a Beverly Hills jewelry store and showed them off to Rhea, giggling and gently touching each other. They were obviously proud of the rings, and it was clear to Rhea that they wanted to get married. As she and everyone else knew, the only thing standing in their way was Mrs. Pierangeli.

Opposed more than ever to the romance, Mrs. Pierangeli began taking steps of her own. To keep Jimmy from calling Pier at home, she had the phone company change the telephone number constantly, sometimes as often as twice a week. One day, when Jimmy was yet again unable to reach Pier, he sought out Dick Clayton and pleaded with him to get the new number, he just had to talk to her.

Clayton could see that Jimmy was seriously upset, and although it was difficult, he got the number from the studio front office. Later that same day he was standing on the lot with Jack Warner and Steve Trilling, Warner's executive assistant, when Jimmy came by. Without saying a word, Clayton reached into his pocket, took out the slip of paper with the number, and handed it to Jimmy. After glancing at the small piece of paper, Jimmy stepped up to Clayton and—to the absolute astonishment of Warner and Trilling—gave him a kiss on the cheek. Clayton offered no explanation to the two older men.

I knew where and when Jimmy and Pier met, and not infrequently I was with them; very often Lew Bracker was there, too. I didn't talk to anyone about what I knew, for both Lew and I were sworn to secrecy about the romance. For the second time in my Hollywood career—the first was Bogie—I became the trusted confidant of a star. I liked knowing that I was privy to information that could make a big story, and it pleased me to have the lovers beholden to me. There was also a practical side to my discretion, since betraying such a confidence would have destroyed my friendship with Jimmy, and by then I liked him very much.

Pier introduced Jimmy to the Villa Capri, her favorite Hollywood restaurant and at the time also very in, largely because Frank Sinatra and his pals could be found there nearly every night. It was also the preferred hangout of Mickey Cohen, then the West Coast's most celebrated gangster and a former friend of the late Benjamin "Bugsy" Siegel. Celebrities liked the Villa because photographers and autograph hunters were not allowed except on special occasions. It was one place where stars could let their hair down and be themselves. Personal eccentricities were permitted, if not encouraged. Each time Johnny Weissmuller—famous as the original Tarzan—came into the restaurant he let out an ear-splitting jungle yell and maniacally thumped his chest.

The Villa Capri, which soon became Jimmy's favorite hangout as well, was a Hollywood version of a Roman trattoria. Located on North McCadden Place half a block north of Hollywood Boulevard, it was a nondescript adobe building attached to a sleazy old residential hotel. The entrance was from the sidewalk, and the restaurant itself was just one large room with a seating capacity of fifty-two.

The Villa was owned and run by Italian-born Patsy D'Amore. The waiters were an international group, friendly and efficient, so good at their jobs, in fact, that today most of them own their own popular and posh restaurants.

Although no one at the Villa had seen Jimmy in a film, his confidence and presence convinced everyone that he was someone—he had that kind of charisma—and he and Pier were given the run of the place. They usually came in from the parking lot directly into the kitchen, and if their booth, number 6, was occupied, Patsy himself would make room for them at a table in his office just off the kitchen. Carmen, the chef, took their orders personally: usually a vegetable plate for Pier and Mostaccioli à la Mark Stevens—a pasta dish named for a popular actor—for Jimmy. Pier's wineglass almost always held water; Jimmy usually drank a white wine spritzer.

Lew and I ran into Jimmy and Pier at the Villa Capri quite often. On some evenings, Jimmy made it clear he wanted us to leave him and Pier alone, but sometimes he signaled us over and invited us to join them for dinner. Pier would spoon-feed Jimmy his meal, and when he'd had enough he would lay down with his head on Pier's lap and fall asleep. Pier would smile. Lew and I would smile at each other, quietly stand up from the table, wave goodbye to Pier, and leave.

Lew and I talked often about the relationship because the sweet virginal Pier was so unlike the other girls that Jimmy had dated. And that, we finally agreed, was what attracted Jimmy so much to her. We soon learned of another important element when Jimmy told us that when he and Pier made love, it was like nothing else he had ever experienced. I laughed and said it was all in his head. "There, too," Jimmy giggled.

Marriage to Pier was constantly on Jimmy's mind, and one day he told me that he intended to marry her, despite her mother's objections, but as a concession to Mrs. Pierangeli he was willing to have their children raised Catholic. He and Pier, he said, had spent hours discussing names for their future children. They'd even chosen the church for the wedding: St. Timothy's.

Jimmy even called Jane Deacy in New York to ask her what she thought about the marriage. She suggested he wait until he became better established. "Since *Eden* is not even completed, you'll be Mr. Pier Angeli if you marry her now," she warned. Jimmy made no comment and hung up. Later, he told Lew and me that he was going to marry Pier anyway, despite the objections of Deacy and MGM, where Pier was testing for her next film.

Early in July I drove Jimmy to the Department of Motor Vehicles to get his California driver's license; he had been driving both in Los Angeles and New York with his Indiana one. On the way, he told me again that he wanted to marry Pier, but said that although she loved him, she was afraid marriage to him would break her mother's heart. Then he told me he had taken Pier home to meet his father and stepmother.

"They liked her a lot," he said. "But I didn't say anything to them about our getting married."

We were both quiet for a while. The hot summer air seemed without oxygen, and I had the sense that we were driving in that car underwater: no air to breathe.

"I'm lonely, Joe," Jimmy suddenly blurted out. "I want to be married. Goddamn it, I'm going to study and become baptized as a Catholic. Then I'll join the Church so we can have the wedding that Pier and her old lady want."

That was all he said, and I didn't ask him any questions because I felt it incumbent on our relationship for me not to pry.

Meanwhile, Jimmy and Kazan were still living in adjoining dressing rooms on the Warner Bros. lot, and through the thin wall between the rooms Kazan could hear more than he wanted of Jimmy's private life. He could hear Jimmy and Pier making love, but far more often he heard them arguing.

Jimmy often got drunk after his arguments with Pier—he was not a heavy drinker, and it took only a few glasses of wine—and on one such occasion he had a falling out with Leonard Rosenman. He showed up at the Rosenmans' home one night, came in the door uninvited while they were having a party, staggering and disheveled and dirty drunk. Swaying on his feet, he announced in front of everyone—to all the guests but most of all to Adele—that Leonard was having an affair with the actress Lois Smith. Having delivered that homewrecking bomb, Jimmy staggered back out.

Leonard had indeed been having an affair with Lois as Adele probably already knew, but it was news to most everyone else. The Rosenmans' marriage, already shaken, would ultimately hold, but Leonard was justifiably furious with Jimmy.

The next morning he stormed across the street to the Warner lot and Jimmy's dressing room. He banged on the door, woke Jimmy up, and demanded in a barely controlled yell, "Do you remember what happened last night? Do you?" Jimmy acted guilty but said nothing. "Well, in case you don't remember, let me tell you what

you did." Leonard recounted the previous evening's painful episode, told Jimmy he was an absolute idiot, and said he didn't want
to see him around or speak to him. Jimmy started to cry as Leonard
left, slamming the door. Nearly a year was to pass before the two
spoke again.

A few weeks before *Eden* was completed, the Hollywood press
began touting Jimmy as the next big star. Evidently, some of this
went to Jimmy's head and affected his behavior. Kazan saw the
changes. When he found Jimmy being rude to the wardrobe man—
something he had never done before—he put a stop to it at once.
But he also noticed that Jimmy had fallen into a form of narcissism.
He would stand in front of the mirror in his dressing room and take
roll after roll of close-up pictures of his face, each with only the
slightest variation of expression. He'd show the contact sheets to
Kazan and ask him which shots he preferred. To Kazan, they were
all the same picture, but he said nothing. Jimmy, he knew, would
have to find himself on his own.

When filming of *Eden* ended on August 13, Jimmy traded in his
Triumph T-110 motorcycle and bought a new and more powerful
model, a Triumph 500. Kazan could no longer prohibit him from
riding motorcycles, and Jimmy, as always, wanted only to go faster.

Although the picture was completed, Jimmy was still living on
the Warner lot, and when Jack L. Warner learned about it, he
wasn't pleased. He was opposed to anyone living on the lot because
Warner had no insurance to cover people actually living in the
studio, and there had recently been a fire after a party that had
caused a lot of damage. He'd allowed Jimmy to stay on the lot
while working on *Eden* because Kazan had felt it important, but
with the film completed J.L. wanted Jimmy gone. The brunt of
his complaints fell on William T. Orr, J.L.'s son-in-law as well as
the studio manager.

J.L. called Orr and announced that he had to get Jimmy off the
lot: "Give him a week to find another place to live."

Orr called Dick Clayton. "J.L. says you have to get Jimmy off
the lot within a week."

"We're already looking for a place," replied Clayton.

"Do it before the deadline," said Orr.

For the next few days J.L. would call Orr and ask if "that kid" was off the lot.

"Not yet, Chief," Orr would answer. "They're looking for a place." Orr was stalling because he had been talking with Dick Clayton about extending Jimmy's contract and didn't want to antagonize either Jimmy or Clayton.

As Jimmy's stay dragged on, he became increasingly undesirable to J.L., progressing from being a "no good," to a "bastard," to an out-and-out "SOB." Once J.L. got absorbed in something he wanted, he wanted it done right away.

One day he called Orr while Jimmy was in his office. Orr had a squawk box, and Jimmy heard the conversation. J.L. said, "Get that little SOB off the lot! I gave you an order, now get it done!"

Orr said, "He's here now, and we're discussing it."

Jimmy listened with glee to both sides of the conversation, then enlisted Clayton's help in a frantic search for an apartment. Clayton heard of one in a nice neighborhood, and he and Jimmy went to visit the landlady together.

Wearing jeans, boots, and several days' growth of beard, Jimmy made a poor first impression on the landlady, but Clayton did his best to convince her that he was preparing for a film role and was in character.

Aware of the landlady's feelings toward him, Jimmy decided he didn't want the apartment anyway, so he said to Clayton, "You know, this living room would be ideal for my piano."

"Oh, you play the piano?" asked the landlady.

"I do," said Jimmy, "and I also have a wonderful hi-fi set that will go well here. You don't mind hi-fi, do you?"

"No, not as long as you don't have it on late at night."

"Well, then, it's settled," Jimmy said to Clayton. "Let's go get the bongo drums out of the car."

"Bongo drums?" repeated the landlady.

"Yes, ma'am," said Jimmy. "When I can't sleep at night I like to get up and beat the skins. It drives away the blues."

On the way out the door Jimmy giggled, and Clayton couldn't help joining in with laughter.

Clayton finally arranged for Jimmy to take over his apartment on

Sunset Plaza Drive, but Clayton wasn't prepared to move out for a week, and Jimmy was supposed to be out within three days.

The day inevitably came when the studio security chief came by Orr's office and stated, "I have orders to move Dean off the lot now." Orr bought more time with a fib, claiming he'd spoken with the boss (J.L.), who had okayed it for Jimmy to remain just a few more days.

When J.L. found out what had happened he subjected Orr to a terrific bawling out. Orr explained that he was trying to make a deal with Jimmy for future pictures.

When Jimmy showed up on the lot the following day he found all his luggage and clothes piled up and waiting for him at the gate. He asked permission to go into his dressing room for a moment. The room was nearly bare, but he went over to a vase on a shelf, reached into it, and pulled out a wad of bills, several thousand dollars. He'd been keeping his money in the vase because he still hadn't opened a bank account in Los Angeles and still relied on Jane Deacy for his allowance.

Jimmy never willingly spoke to Orr again. For his part, J.L. never said another word about the matter. His attitude was that he was the guy who had fired Clark Gable, and if that wasn't enough to make his position clear, he'd point up at the water tower, on which was stenciled WARNER STUDIOS, and ask whose name was on it.

With his books and bongos, bullfight paraphernalia, and stacks of photographs of Pier—and of himself—Jimmy moved into Dick Clayton's small apartment on Sunset Plaza Drive. He wasn't pleased with the place, however, and was soon calling it his "waste-basket with walls." It was an accurate description.

Dick Clayton arranged for Jimmy to take Terry Moore, a bosomy young starlet, to the premiere of Bogie's new movie, *Sabrina*, co-starring Audrey Hepburn. I attended the premiere with the Bogarts, and I waved when I saw Jimmy, but he gave me only a wrathful look.

Jimmy later described his date with Terry to Lew and me as "a fucking bore. She just went with me for the publicity, and I don't know why in hell I let Dick talk me into it."

Among the tourists in the bleachers set up outside the theater for the premiere was Maila Nurmi. Born in Finland and thirty-two years old, Nurmi was then at the height of her career as Vampira. Dressed like a character from a Charles Addams cartoon, Maila, who had long black hair and a voluptuous figure, introduced late-night horror movies on television. She was married—to a television writer named Dean Reisner—but she was eager to explore Hollywood, to get to know its denizens. At home in her small apartment over a garage, the phone rarely rang, so she took to the streets. On this evening she sat in the bleachers, a camera around her neck, and watched the important people arrive. And she spotted Jimmy and Terry Moore. She thought Jimmy—who looked sullen and angry—one of the most interesting men she had ever seen.

The next morning she was in Googie's, a coffee shop on the Sunset Strip near Schwab's, with a bit player named Jonathon Haze, and Jack Simmons, a young man she had met at the premiere who seemed enthralled with her and was something of a local character: he drove around Hollywood in a hearse. Looking out the window, Maila was thrilled to see Jimmy coming into the coffee shop.

"Jesus Christ," she said to Haze, "there's the only guy in Hollywood I want to meet."

Haze knew Jimmy and made the introductions. Jimmy was fascinated by Maila and her iconoclastic attitude. They became friendly. She was interested in the occult, and Jimmy—always intrigued by unusual characters—enjoyed spending time with her. She introduced him to some of her friends in the Maleficarum Coven, one of the oldest witch covens in Hollywood. For a short while, he was impressed. "It's all a bunch of cow pies," he told me, "but it's weird and kind of fascinating."

At about this time, director Nicholas Ray showed up at Warner Bros. with an idea for a film. Since his last picture had been a big box office success—the western *Johnny Guitar*—Warner was happy to have him and set him up in an office on the lot. Ray wanted to do a film about juvenile delinquency, and he wanted it to be romantic, similar to *Romeo and Juliet*, which he often cited as "the best play ever written about juvenile delinquency."

Warner just happened to own the rights to a book called *Rebel Without a Cause*, a psychological study of teenagers written by Dr. Robert M. Lindner. Warner had bought the rights in 1946, and in 1947, while a screenplay was being prepared, Bill Orr had gone to

New York City to cast the lead parts. He had ended up choosing Marlon Brando. But the finished screenplay was unusable, the picture was never made, and the screenplay was filed away in a corner.

Ray took only the title from that screenplay; he had arrived at Warner with an outline of his own, which he called *The Blind Run*. Warner sent over writer Leon Uris to work with him. Having just completed work on the screenplay for *Battle Cry*, Uris was considered a hot writer, and the two men began work on Ray's project. They soon encountered disagreements, however, and Ray took on Irving Shulman as screenwriter. For the next three months, Ray and Shulman struggled with the project.

There was never any doubt as to who would get the lead in the planned film: both Ray and Warner wanted it to be a vehicle for Warner's hottest new property, James Dean. Although four months would pass before he was officially signed for the film, Jimmy's next film was set.

Meanwhile, Jane Deacy had got him a role in a television show in New York, which meant he had to leave Los Angeles within a few days. On the night before Jimmy was to leave, Lew and I had dinner with him at the Villa Capri. Sullen and moody, Jimmy refused to eat.

"What's with you?" Lew asked.

"Pier missed her period and thinks she may be pregnant. I asked her to go to New York with me and get married there, but she said it would break her mother's heart if we eloped."

"So?"

"So, it's off. I put it to her: if she loves me and wants to marry me, she comes to New York; if not, I'm going alone to think it all over."

The TV show Jane Deacy had arranged for Jimmy was "Run Like a Thief," a 1954 episode of the NBC television program *Philco TV Playhouse*. The cast included two Austrians in the roles of his adopted parents: Gusti Huber, who had starred on Broadway in *The Diary of Anne Frank* (and later acted in the film based on the play), and Kurt Kasznar, a prominent Broadway actor who had been a friend of Jimmy's in New York.

Jimmy talked about Pier to Gusti and Kurt—both were convinced he was very much in love. Gusti had four children, including a set of young twins, and Jimmy took her aside one day to ask her where she bought clothes for her babies.

She told him, "Stand in front of St. Patrick's Cathedral, facing it, and the store is right there on the left in the side street."

The next day Kurt told Gusti, "Do you know what Jimmy did yesterday? He went to the store you told him about and bought several little outfits for a boy and girl and sent them to Pier as his declaration of love for her."

Pier was foremost in Jimmy's mind. He talked about her to everyone, and called her on the phone whenever he could. One night Jimmy telephoned Roy Schatt. In a dark voice—a voice that Schatt recognized as the voice of drama and tragedy—Jimmy asked, "May I come over?"

"Is something wrong?" Schatt asked.

In the same dark voice, Jimmy repeated his plea: "May I come over?"

"Sure," said Schatt.

Schatt was astonished when Jimmy arrived at his studio wearing a jacket and tie, his shoes shined, and his hair combed back neatly. As unusual as his dress was his behavior: he stalked up and down the apartment delivering a long tirade. Schatt couldn't understand what Jimmy was raving about, but he heard him mention the name Pier several times. Schatt had never heard of Pier and didn't know whether the name referred to a man or a woman, although he suspected the latter. He noticed that Jimmy kept glancing over at the clock. Finally Jimmy asked if he could use the telephone to call Hollywood.

"It'll be collect," he explained. "Pier's expecting it."

Schatt offered Jimmy the use of his desk phone.

"No," said Jimmy, "I'd like to make it in the darkroom." He went into the darkroom and closed the door.

After a few minutes, Jimmy called out to Schatt, "Hey, Roy! Come here!"

Schatt found Jimmy standing in the darkroom and blushing. "Here," he said, handing the phone to Schatt, "Tell her. Tell her where I am." He closed his eyes. Then he opened them and said, "Oh, yes, Roy, this is Pier Angeli."

PIER

"Hello, Pier," said Schatt.

"Hello, Roy," said Pier. Then, "Roy, please tell Jimmy not to get so excited."

"Yes, I'll do that," said Schatt, handing the phone back to Jimmy. "She said not to get excited," he told Jimmy and then left him to finish his conversation.

Jimmy said very little when he finally emerged from the darkroom. He asked for a glass of water, drank it down, and then left.

A few days after Jimmy left for New York, I was dumbfounded to hear on the radio that Pier had announced to her co-workers on an MGM set that she was engaged to marry Vic Damone.

I telephoned Lew, who had also heard the news and was trying to reach Jimmy at his apartment in Manhattan. Neither of us could understand the announcement, for we were both certain that Pier was as much in love with Jimmy as he was with her. The only theory we could come up with was that Pier really was pregnant and, thinking that Jimmy had run out on her, she had reacted in haste by getting engaged. But Vic Damone?

To Jimmy—to everyone who knew him—it was a bolt from the sky, absolutely unexpected and inexplicable. The truth, which Jimmy never learned, was quite different.

Pier had had a brief romance with Damone long before she met Jimmy. She had met him in Munich, Germany, in 1951. She was there to make a film, *The Devil Makes Three*, the story of an American soldier who returns to Germany to thank the family that helped him during World War II. Gene Kelly played the soldier; Pier had the role of the daughter with whom the soldier becomes involved.

Damone was in Germany because he had been drafted into the army: a serious blow to his career. Born on June 12, 1928, as Vito Farinola—he took his mother's maiden name when he became a performer—he had come to prominence at the age of seventeen, a kid from Brooklyn who imitated Frank Sinatra. In 1945 he tied for first place on *Arthur Godfrey's Talent Scouts*, a popular radio show; backstage was Milton Berle, who then arranged Damone's first nightclub engagement. His career moved quickly, and in 1947 he had a top ten hit with his first single, "I Have but One Heart."

Then, in 1951, the middle of the Korean War, he was drafted. He was sent not to Korea, but to Germany, where he was put to work in a warehouse stocked with USO costumes. Feeling lonely while on leave in Munich, he had heard that MGM had a film crew in town making a picture. Hoping to see a familiar face, he had gone to take a look—and met Pier. The two had begun dating, seeing each other whenever possible. He had invited her to make an appearance on a show he was putting together for the servicemen. At one point during the performance he had held her in his arms and sung "September Song." It became their song.

While in Germany he had proposed to Pier, but she had thought he was only being impetuous and turned him down. Then the army transferred him to Texas, breaking off their romantic involvement, but not ending their relationship.

After his discharge from the army in 1953, Damone's career had taken off quickly again. He had come out to Hollywood to work in films, and he hadn't forgotten Pier. Damone had many things going for him that Jimmy lacked; in particular, as a Catholic Italian-American, he had the open support of Pier's mother. In fact, when he got out of the army Pier's mother had helped him decorate his apartment. For a short time he had also dated Pier's twin, Marisa.

Damone was then co-starring with Debbie Reynolds and Tony Martin in *Hit the Deck* on the MGM lot. One evening he joined Pier for dinner at the Retake Room. He played their song—"September Song"—on the jukebox, and before leaving the café they were engaged. But no one in Hollywood knew any of this at the time.

So Pier was to marry Vic Damone, and on such short notice! When I finally reached Jimmy by phone and asked him if he'd heard the news, he snapped, "Yeah, man, I read about it, and she won't come to the phone." Since learning of the engagement he had been calling Pier constantly, but she refused to take the calls, which was driving him crazy. He was doing another TV show, but his mind was constantly on Pier.

The show he was then doing was "Padlocks," an episode of *Danger*, directed by John Frankenheimer, the boy wonder of television. Miserable and lonely, Jimmy called Chris White's telephone exchange leaving a terse message, "Where is everybody? J.D." He finally reached Chris and asked her to "come and sit in the weeds" (be in the audience). "He told me he didn't know his lines, didn't know what he was doing, and asked me to have dinner with him during the break," recalls Chris. "At the break we made a beeline to the Blue Danube, a Hungarian restaurant about eight blocks away. There, we talked about the show as though it was a tremendous treaty that would save the nation, and then he got on the subject of Pier. He was furious that she was going with Vic Damone, who he called all kinds of names. Then we got on the subject of a new Porsche he wanted to buy, which he described to me in minute detail, and then he jumped back to Pier. It was obvious to me that he really loved her."

After dinner, they returned to the studio where Jimmy finished the show, and then Chris went with Jimmy to a party at Jane Deacy's apartment. Jimmy was due to catch the red-eye to Hollywood, and Frankenheimer had volunteered to drive him to the airport. Jimmy lay on the backseat of the car with his head in Chris's lap. Suddenly he remembered he had forgotten his suitcase. He gave Chris his keys and asked her to go to his apartment and send him his sweater, boots, and records. "And don't forget the suitcase," he said. "I love it because it's all leather and it has my initials on it."

At the airport they all went to a snack bar and Jimmy told Chris about "this terrific picture coming up that I have to go back and do."

It was the last time Chris would see Jimmy and the event is still etched in her memory. "The plane was waiting like a big bird, and Jimmy said, 'Hey, I'll see you soon.' He walked backward toward the plane and waved to me, hand about chest height with fingers cupped. He ran back and kissed me, which I thought strange. Then he turned around again and ran up the stairs into the plane. I stood there and watched the plane take off until it was swallowed up into the stars, and I thought that Jimmy was a big star, and he was going to join the others in the sky."

Immediately after he returned to Los Angeles, Jimmy starred in an episode of CBS's *General Electric Theater* called "I'm a Fool." Eddie Albert and Natalie Wood were his co-stars.

Jimmy and Natalie had met briefly at the studio when he was making *Eden*, but this was the first time they were to work together. Jimmy arrived late on the set—everyone was just standing around waiting for him—and he came on his motorcycle. To the people involved in the production he seemed withdrawn and moody. Although he and Natalie were to play lovers, Jimmy paid no attention to her and, instead, sat off alone in a corner, grunting and mumbling. Finally, the producer, Mort Abrahams, called over to Jimmy, "Come on, Jimmy, sit next to Natalie. You're going to have to make love to this girl." But Jimmy just grunted again and stared down at his script.

Even so, Natalie was drawn to Jimmy, and during the rehearsals for the teleplay they often ate lunch together, with Jimmy invariably carrying a portable radio tuned to classical music.

I spoke to Jimmy on the phone one afternoon while he was making the TV show and asked him how things were going with Pier. He told me only that he had seen her secretly and that the wedding to Damone was planned for the last week of the month. He cut the conversation short.

On November 17 Jimmy kept a date he had made with Pier months earlier: he escorted her to the premiere of A Star Is Born. When Lew asked him about the evening, Jimmy's only comment was "She's going ahead with the wedding."

A day or so later I drove by Jimmy's house to see how he was. As I pulled into the driveway, Pier passed me, coming out in her car. I waved and honked, but she only nodded to me, and her face looked tear-stained.

Jimmy, too, looked distraught when I went in, and I felt it was best to leave him alone. Before going out I asked if there was anything I could do.

He looked down at his hands; he was balling his fingers into fists, over and over.

"It's already done," he said in a choked voice. He looked at me, and what I saw in his face shocked me.

"Pier thinks she's going to have a baby," he blurted out finally.

I was stunned by the news. I knew he had seen her from time to time since the announcement of her engagement, and I had been hoping that somehow they might get back together. I stood there silently, not knowing what to say.

Then Jimmy started to cry, and for the first time since the war I took a man in my arms and I rocked him.

The night before Pier's wedding, Lew and Jimmy went to the

Villa Capri for dinner. Jimmy was despondent, staring into space and barely speaking. Also in the restaurant that evening was Vic Damone, being toasted by friends. When Damone spotted Jimmy and Lew, he came over to their table. He wanted to shake hands with Jimmy.

Jimmy looked up at him. "You may be marrying Pier," he snapped, "but she isn't yours, never was, and never will be." That was too much for Damone, who took a swing at him. Waiters rushed over and pulled them apart.

Without eating, Jimmy and Lew left the restaurant.

Pier Angeli and Vic Damone were married on the morning of November 23, 1954, at St. Timothy's in Hollywood—the same church where she and Jimmy had planned to marry. Father William O'Shea officiated at the double-ring ceremony, which featured a forty-voice children's choir.

The rites were attended by more than six hundred people, including Jack Benny, Danny Thomas, Ann Blyth, Cyd Charisse, Ann Miller, and, of course, Debbie Reynolds (who had advised Pier not to marry Vic).

Pier came down the aisle clinging to the arm of E.J. Mannix, MGM vice-president, who gave the bride away. I covered the wedding for the *Tribune* and noted for the fashion conscious that Pier wore a modern Juliet gown of billowing white chiffon over white crepe.

Jimmy told Lew and me that Pier had specifically requested he not attend, but he was there on the day of the wedding, sitting on his motorcycle across the street from the church and watching. I saw him there, after the ceremony, wearing his jeans and motorcycle jacket. When the newlyweds came out of the church and paused on the steps to kiss for the photographers, Jimmy gunned the motorcycle loudly and then sped off. A few heads turned at the noise; I didn't look back in time to see Pier's reaction.

That evening I dropped by Jimmy's apartment on Sunset Plaza Drive to see what I could do to cheer him up. His motorcycle was in the garage, but there was no answer to my knock. I tried the door, found it unlocked, and went inside. It was dark, with all the curtains drawn. Gradually I made out Jimmy, huddled on the living room floor rocking back and forth like a mother with a child, cradling

Pier's framed picture in his hands. He was unshaven, his hair looked as if he had cut it himself, and his eyes, though open, were unseeing. If he was aware of me he gave no sign of it. I quietly backed out of the door and drove away.

Jimmy's love affair with Pier—perhaps the only true love affair of his life—was over. But that posed kiss on the steps of St. Timothy's was not the end of their relationship. Neither of them would ever be completely free of the other.

Chapter Ten

THE NIGHT WATCH

The next day was Thanksgiving, and although he might have preferred to spend the day alone, Jimmy had been invited to the home of Keenan and Sharley Wynn for Thanksgiving dinner.

The son of actor Ed Wynn, Keenan had made a career of his own in films, becoming one of Hollywood's most dependable, versatile, and prolific supporting actors. His real passion, however, was motorcycles. He had taught me to ride, but I was a novice compared to Jimmy and the others who went cycling with Keenan as their leader, hill-climbing in Hollywood and racing across the desert in Palm Springs.

Keenan and his wife had invited a small group of friends over for the Thanksgiving meal, most of them bachelors with nowhere else to go. The group included Ralph Meeker, whose film-acting career had taken off after he had assumed Marlon Brando's role of Stanley Kowalski in the Broadway production of *A Streetcar Named Desire*; Jim Backus—already famous as the voice of Mr. Magoo—whose wife, Henny, was out of town; and Arthur Loew, Jr. Also present that evening was Rod Steiger.

Jimmy and Steiger had both come a long way since the days when they shared cups of coffee and bitter jokes in Cromwell's Pharmacy. Like Jimmy, Steiger had finally been discovered and had made his way into films. His first role had been as a psychiatrist in *Teresa*, Pier's first American-made production, and he had then worked with Kazan in *On the Waterfront*, playing Marlon Brando's older brother.

So the two young actors could have talked about Kazan or Brando or even Pier. But Jimmy was keeping to himself that day and avoided conversation. He and Steiger exchanged very few words. Dressed for the occasion in a navy blue suit, black shirt, black boots, and new horn-rimmed glasses, Jimmy seemed ill at ease and did not take part in the industry talk. (Some of his discomfort was caused by his dental plate, which he somehow broke while chewing a mouthful of turkey.) He came to life only briefly, when the conversation—directed by Keenan—turned to racing and motorcycles. For a few moments Jimmy had a great deal to say, and charmed everyone present. But then he turned back into himself and his own thoughts.

Jimmy excused himself and left as soon as the meal was over. Backus was the last of the guests to leave, and on his way out he remarked to Keenan, "It was sweet of you and Sharley to have all of us lost souls for dinner, but don't you think that the kid who works in a garage was uncomfortable with all us hams?"

He was referring to Jimmy, of course, but he had no way of knowing that he would soon come to know Jimmy very well.

From the Wynns', Jimmy went back to his apartment and changed clothes, taking off the blue suit and putting on a shirt and white sailor pants. He then went to see who he might find to talk to at Googie's.

He found Maila Nurmi. When he spotted her at the counter, he smiled. She was delighted. She, too, was wearing white sailor pants, and Jimmy's smile had revealed the gap in his upper teeth. Nurmi smiled back to reveal her own missing teeth—for she, too, wore a dental plate and she, too, had broken it on that day's turkey. These coincidences were not enough to prove Nurmi's supernatural powers, but enough to give them something to talk about. For Jimmy, that Thanksgiving ended in the evening light in front of Googie's, talking to Nurmi and any other odd character who happened by.

After his breakup with Pier, Jimmy spent a great deal of time in the company of Nurmi and various other oddball types who appeared on Sunset Strip only after dark. *Eden* had not yet been released, and Jimmy was not yet a star; after midnight, he could pretend to be whoever he wished. The group he hung out with came to call itself "The Night Watch." When not at Googie's, they were at Schwab's or Barney's Beanery, the only places open after midnight, and they traveled from one to the other in Jack Simmons's Cadillac hearse. Their conversations were philosophical, which is to say they dwelt on death.

Always the insomniac, easily bored, and forever in search of new experiences, Jimmy was rarely alone and rarely at home. He used his apartment as a way station, stopping there to make phone calls and change clothes. He seemed to always be staying in someone else's home or guest house.

He had many friends, and some became quite close. One of the closest was the nightclub performer, actress, and dancer Eartha Kitt, who affectionately called him Jamie. Their relationship was like that of a brother and sister—intimate but platonic: she was Arthur Loew, Jr.'s girlfriend. When in New York he always spent time with her, but most of their relationship took place by phone—when Jimmy sat down to call friends, usually around three in the morning, hers was most often the first number he dialed—and when they saw each other it was usually in Los Angeles.

In the middle of the night Eartha's phone would ring, invariably awakening her. She'd grope around in the darkness to find the phone, struggle to hold it to her ear, and ask, "Yes?"

"Hi," Jimmy would yell.

"Oh, Jamie."

"How about going for a ride?" he'd ask.

She'd pull her alarm clock up close to her face to make out the time or switch on a light and squint over at the clock on her nightstand.

"Jamie, do you know what time it is? It's four in the morning."

"Yeah," he'd say. "So, you want to come?"

"Okay."

"Pick you up in ten minutes."

Jimmy never brought Eartha to visit the haunts of the Night Watch. Instead, they'd cruise along Sunset Boulevard, stopping in coffee shops along the way and talking to whomever they encountered.

Eartha remembers one night when a drunk came weaving and stumbling down the street past where she and Jimmy were sitting. Jimmy laughed and watched the drunk's movements closely, and when the drunk had passed out of view he stood up and performed an imitation of him. At times like those, bursting with laughter, Eartha felt convinced that Jimmy could have made his living as a stand-up comedian. He could imitate the movements of anyone he saw, and he often related conversations to her, imitating the voices perfectly.

Sometimes Jimmy and Eartha went to what they called drum parties: they'd take a set of drums and drop by someone's house for an evening of music and drumming.

Jimmy also dated. He followed a pattern with most of his dates—invariably young starlets—starting with dinner at the Villa Capri and then a movie. He was tremendously fond of movies, any kind and in any language. After dropping his date at home, he would go back to the Capri, sometimes staying until closing time, 2:00 A.M. Then he would go off in search of the Night Watch, catching up to them at one of the hangouts and talking with anyone he knew until four or five in the morning.

He occasionally disappeared over a weekend, and we would learn that he had driven to Tijuana, either alone or with a date, to attend a bullfight. He came to be on first-name terms with several *toreros*, and his little apartment was cluttered with autographed capes draped over chairs and *banderillas* stuck into the walls.

Lew Bracker and I both saw a lot of Jimmy. Sometimes we'd go to his apartment or to the home of Lew's parents where we'd sit on the floor to talk, Jimmy and Lew sipping red wine while I drank Coke. We'd talk into the early hours of the morning about life and what we wanted from it. Jimmy's desires were like those of any young man: changing and vague, but nonetheless desperately important. He wanted to get married and raise a family; he wanted enough money to trade in his MG for a new Porsche so he could become a professional racing driver; he wanted to just take off and travel alone through Europe. Or maybe not. Sometimes he and Lew talked about girls—a conversation I, married man that I was, stayed out of, though I often envied their activities—and sometimes Jimmy and I left Lew out and talked about photography. Or tape recorders or gadgets of any kind. On that subject, Jimmy and I had much in common.

We didn't talk about work, and since Jimmy could still walk down streets or sit in restaurants without being instantly recognized, the subject was easy to avoid. We all spoke more freely on those evenings because we were talking as our personal selves, as three friends, and not as an actor, a writer, and an insurance salesman.

Or perhaps Jimmy was always an actor. Just as he adapted himself to please interviewers, he enjoyed hanging around with bizarre characters—perhaps just for the opportunity to try on new masks. Such friendships were usually brief.

Jimmy planned to visit Fairmount and the East Coast for Christmas that year. Before leaving, he had a short relationship with a singer named Tony Lee, who had lost a leg in a motorcycle accident and wore a prosthetic leg and long, floor-length dresses. She had an apartment in Hollywood that she shared with six young men, all good-looking would-be actors. Tony prided herself on being able to hop on her one leg while holding a cup of hot chocolate all the way from the kitchen to the bedroom without spilling as much as a single drop. She did this hopping naked. Her six cohorts rewarded her efforts by rubbing her stump, and she claimed that the rubbing was her greatest joy in life.

Jimmy met her late on one Sunset Strip night and was fascinated by her. When she lifted her long dress and asked him if he'd like to fondle her stump, he said, "I'd love to."

The next day he took her for a drive. He had spotted something interesting in the window of a shop on Melrose Avenue—a bust of Marlon Brando. Jimmy wanted to find out about that bust, and thus he and one-legged Tony Lee walked through the door of sculptor Kenneth Kendall's studio.

Kendall was both surprised and vaguely disturbed by the odd couple that entered. It wasn't Tony; it was something about Jimmy. After brief introductions, Jimmy asked Kendall if Brando had seen the bust in the window, and if he had what he thought about it.

"Evidently not very much," replied Kendall. "It's still out there in the window."

"I can give you two reasons, one why he would like it and one why he wouldn't like it," said Jimmy. He had sat down in a chair; Lee was hopping around the studio. "First of all, sculpting is an intellectual pursuit, and Marlon likes to think he's an intellectual, which he's never going to be. But he wouldn't like it because you show him screaming, and he looks like he's about to suck cock."

Kendall had no time to respond, for Tony had suddenly begun talking about her amputated leg and how she'd kept it for quite a while after the accident.

"When they took the cast off," she said, "and I saw how ugly it looked, I just said, 'I don't want it. Cut if off.' And they did."

Jimmy clasped the arms of the chair and said, over and over, "Oh, shit, oh shit." Then Tony talked about the actress Suzan Ball and how she'd lost her right leg to cancer.

As Tony and Jimmy chatted on, Kendall found himself feeling increasingly anxious. He couldn't understand why, but he felt like a gibbering idiot. When Jimmy had come in, it had been for Kendall like Brando entering. Jimmy gave off some sort of energy that Kendall picked up on, and Kendall felt convinced that something important was happening. He opened the doors to his workroom to show Jimmy a head he was working on of Steve Reeves, an American actor who had played Hercules in an Italian film.

"Boy, that's great," said Jimmy.

While Kendall got out his portfolio on Brando, Jimmy stood up from the chair, slowly peeled off his jacket, and then held it out and let it drop to the floor. He glanced over at Kendall to see how the movement might have affected him. Then he went through the entire portfolio of Brando material.

When he'd looked through it all, Jimmy shyly stammered, "Would you be interested in sculpting me?"

"He's going to be the greatest actor in the world," chimed in Lee.

Kendall was taken aback. He wondered if Jimmy really imagined himself in the same class as Brando.

His silence lasted too long. "You have to give me a chance to finish what I'm working on," he finally said, but he could see that Jimmy saw through that excuse and was upset.

But Jimmy wasn't about to give up and asked Kendall how he worked.

"From life," Kendall said, "when possible. If not, from still shots."

"I have my portfolio in New York," said Jimmy. "I'm going to Fairmount first, for Christmas, and then I'll be back." He asked how much the work would cost.

"One hundred twenty-five for expenses," Kendall said, offering his services for free. "An original head would be more."

They agreed on the price, and Jimmy said he'd bring in the photographs. When Jimmy stepped out the door he turned, made a half bow, looked up into Kendall's eyes, and smiled. Kendall thought that smile the most beautiful thing he had ever seen.

That night Jimmy showed up at Googie's, sat down next to Maila, and announced, "There's a man in this town named Kendall, an artist."

"I know him," replied Maila. "He's got a studio with a bust of Brando in the window."

Jimmy told her that he'd gone by Kendall's studio that afternoon, hoping to be done by the same man who had done Marlon. "But I don't think he wants to do me," he said. Maila could sense his disappointment.

"His loss," she said.

For the next few days Jimmy continued to drive around with Tony, sometimes in his MG, sometimes with her riding on the back of his motorcycle. One night he called his friend Jonathan Gilmore and asked him to come up to the apartment. "I have a girl I want you to meet," Jimmy said. When Jonathan arrived, he found Jimmy in his shorts with a towel wrapped around his head like a turban and makeup on his face. Tony was putting lipstick on him with heavy eye shadow and dark liner around his eyelids. Jonathan sat down and watched as Jimmy, laughing, patted the stump of Tony's leg while she drank ale from a quart bottle. "You want to fuck her?" Jimmy asked. "Why don't you do it? I'm just sitting here being the sheik—being Valentino." Jimmy watched them make love with a curious bemused expression.

Later, while Tony started to pass out, Jimmy, as always, made phone calls. Jimmy finally asked Jonathan to take Tony home on his bike.

On another night Jimmy and Jonathan went on their motorcycles with Tony riding behind Jimmy to the home of Samson DeBrier, a film fan who kept an open house for young actors. Kenneth Anger's film *Inauguration of the Pleasure Dome* had been filmed at DeBrier's—one of the stars was Anaïs Nin—and Jimmy wanted to meet DeBrier, who was a friend of Jonathan's. Among the guests was Jack Nicholson, who was six years younger than Jimmy and a struggling actor looking forward to meeting the heralded star of *East of Eden*. Jonathan introduced them but Jimmy barely acknowledged the introduction and snubbed Nicholson. Jonathan tried to apologize for Jimmy by explaining that they had come to the party on their motorcycles and the wind had affected Jimmy's hearing and eyes.

Soon after that Tony Lee disappeared from Jimmy's life. When Maila Nurmi asked Jimmy what had happened to her, he said he didn't know, but added, "The next time I see that bitch, I'm going to trip her." That chapter was over.

Before going east for the holidays, Jimmy performed in another televison drama, "The Dark, Dark Hour," another episode of *General Electric Theater*. The production was directed by Don Medford, who did more work with Jimmy than any other television director, and had become his friend. Medford even hired Maila and Jack Simmons for small roles. Ronald Reagan, who was host of the series, opted to star in the show.

Jimmy then went home to spend Christmas with the Winslows. From Indiana he went to New York, arriving there during the last days of December.

On December 29, Jimmy went over to Schatt's studio. Jimmy had been hoping to get pictures of himself published in *Life*, at that time the nation's most important magazine, and he had asked Schatt to submit some of the pictures he had taken. An editor at *Life*, Frank D. Campion, thought the pictures were good but asked Schatt to provide something more "manly." Jimmy and Schatt were eager to meet the request, and the two of them went to work. The session went well: by then Jimmy knew a lot about photography, knew what he wanted, and Schatt let him direct some of the shots. At one point Jimmy suddenly stopped and looked over at Schatt. In his typical narcissistic fashion, he asked, "Don't I remind you of Michelangelo's *David*?"

Jimmy had shown up for the session wearing an old turtleneck sweater, and while making the prints of the shots Schatt noticed a tear in one of the sweater's shoulders that he hadn't spotted while taking the pictures.

The pictures were never published in *Life*. But the series of pictures of Jimmy wearing the sweater later became famous as the "Torn Sweater" series, perhaps the best known and most popular photographs ever taken of Jimmy.

Jimmy had not called Barbara Glenn but one afternoon he went to Cromwell's for a cup of coffee and saw her sitting at the counter with Joyce Van Patten. Barbara recalls that she and Jimmy looked at each other. "He came by to say a few words to Joyce and said nothing to me, but he took my hand and led me out of the drugstore to his apartment. We hadn't said a word to each other but we made love. Then we spoke a few words. I told him I wasn't going to get married, he nodded, and that was that. I left and it was like a sequence out of a very bad grade B movie. But that was the nature of our relationship."

Jimmy celebrated New Year's in Roy Schatt's studio. Among the other people present were Billy Gunn, Marty Landau, Bob Heller, and Tony Ray, Nick Ray's son. Jimmy had invited Barbara, who suffered through the long evening: it was clear to her that everyone in the room was trying desperately to please Jimmy, which included going along with his refusal to celebrate the New Year. At midnight sounds of merrymaking could be heard from the street outside— horns honking and people calling out—but the only sound in Schatt's studio was Jimmy playing his bongos. The other would-be celebrants watched him in silence.

A few days later, on January 4, 1955, Jimmy appeared in an episode of ABC's *The U.S. Steel Hour* called "The Thief." The stars of the production were Mary Astor and Paul Lukas. Both were experienced, well-known actors, and they both found working with Jimmy exasperating. Astor complained bitterly that Jimmy mumbled all of his lines and that she couldn't understand what he was saying. Lukas supported her, claiming they had no idea of what Jimmy was saying, when he was going to say it, or even where he would be when he said it. The director's response came over the loudspeaker, "I'm sorry, people. That's the way Jimmy has to work. Do the best you can. It's marvelous in here." Jimmy's style had made its mark.

On the day of the telecast Warner announced that he had been signed for the leading role in *Rebel Without a Cause*.

On one of his last nights in New York Jimmy had dinner in a backroom at the Capri Restaurant with Frank Corsaro. He had given Corsaro a 78 rpm recording of the Russian operatic bass Feodor Chaliapin as a Christmas present. The selection was proof that Jimmy had learned his music lessons well, and Corsaro was delighted with the gift. But Jimmy seemed nervous that night and sat silently swirling his brandy glass and sniffing it. Corsaro couldn't determine what was making Jimmy so edgy, but he sensed that his young friend was moving aggressively toward something important, and imagined that it was his career.

On Jimmy's return to Hollywood, he immediately resumed his old routine: up all night looking for action and sleeping most of the day. One night in mid-January he was sitting alone at a corner table near the jukebox at Googie's when an attractive, elegantly dressed blond woman showing her age—she was forty-three—nearly tripped over his legs. Jimmy apologized and asked her to join him for a hamburger. He introduced himself as a working actor, a former student of theater arts at UCLA, and modestly said his first film was in the can.

She introduced herself as Barbara Hutton. Barbara was the celebrated heiress to the Woolworth fortune, as Jimmy well knew: her son Lance Reventlow, who was a few years younger than Jimmy, was a well-known car buff and race driver. "So you're the lady who gets a little richer every time the cash register rings at Woolworth's," he quipped.

Jimmy poured on the charm as he told Barbara a series of self-deprecating stories, most of them not true, about how he spent a week at a five-and-dime in Los Angeles demonstrating can openers, and how during another dry spell he had sold encyclopedias door-to-door in South Bend, Indiana. Most of the housewives had slammed doors in his face, he said, and did an imitation: "Madame, will you kindly open the door so I can get my tie back."

He also flattered Barbara by asking questions about her past, her travels, her poetry, her friends, and what it was like to be so rich that you could buy anything you wanted. She was flattered by his interest, and readily answered his questions. She also admitted that she was alone at her hotel and bored, which was why she had come to Googie's. After a couple of hours of animated conversation, Barbara said she was going to call a taxi to take her back to her hotel. Jimmy volunteered to give her a lift on the back of his motorcycle. She accepted without hesitation.

She sat on the motorcycle in back of Jimmy with her hands around his waist, and they took off with her dress billowing behind. "If you pass this test, you can pass any test," Jimmy shouted into the wind as they raced along the Sunset Strip toward the Beverly Hills Hotel. When they reached it, Jimmy parked the bike on a side street and volunteered to see Barbara to her bungalow— number 6. When they got to the door, Jimmy simply walked inside with her.

Once inside, they polished off a chilled bottle of pouilly-fuissé and continued their conversation. Barbara asked Jimmy why he risked his neck on a motorcycle, and he told her that he was exhilarated by taking chances, the pursuit of the heightened moment, intensity for its own sake, "something men only find when they're with each other. Real life is experience, experiencing everything without restrictions or moral restraints."

Jimmy shucked off his boots and cradled his head in Barbara's lap, one of his favorite seduction techniques.

Barbara's notebook for the day contains the rest of the story: "It was late and he was drunk and I was drunk, so I asked him to stay. He removed his shirt and pants and climbed into bed, and I snuggled in next to him. We made love then and then we made love again. It seemed the right and natural thing to do, although I couldn't help but wonder about his sexuality. He talked so fervently about men and adventure and masculinity. We talked and dozed and made love until long after the sun rose. In the morning he ordered black coffee and scrambled eggs and the waiter served it in the dining room. Then I watched as he climbed on his motorcycle and disappeared around the bend. Forever."

Meanwhile, *Eden* was being shown to select people, including top columnists. Not surprisingly, when Hedda Hopper received her invitation to see a preview of the film, she declined. But her good friend Clifton Webb, whose opinion she trusted, went and reported back to her, "Last night I saw one of the most extraordinary performances of my life. Get the studio to run that movie over for you. You'll be crazy about this boy Jimmy Dean."

"I've already seen him," Hopper snapped.

"Forget it," said Webb. "I read your piece. Just watch him in the picture."

Hopper got in touch with Kazan. "I'm sorry I missed the preview," she said. "I hear Jimmy Dean is electrifying as Cal Trask—"

Kazan cut her off. "When would you like to see it?" he asked.

"Today."

"Name the time, and I'll have it run for you," said Kazan.

Like so many other people, Hopper was spellbound by Jimmy's performance. She immediately called Jack Warner.

"I'd like to talk with your Mr. Dean," she said. "He may not want to do an interview with me after what I wrote about him, and if he doesn't, I won't hold it against him. But I'd love to have him come over to my house."

A few days later Jimmy showed up at her doorstep, neat and clean in black pants and a black leather jacket.

"You misbehaved terribly," began Hopper, referring to their first encounter.

"I know," admitted Jimmy. "I wanted to see if anybody in this town had guts enough to tell the truth."

From that beginning the two talked on for several hours. As Jimmy finally left, Hopper told him, "If you get into any kind of trouble, I'd like to be your friend."

"I'd like you to be," replied Jimmy politely. He had just made an important ally.

I knew Jimmy didn't like Hopper, and when I heard about the interview I accused him of being a phony.

"If you don't like her, why did you go to such pains to win her over?"

After a long pause, Jimmy—who, like Bogie, usually had only unkind things to say about obsequious actors—slowly nodded.

"You're right," he said, "but look at it as protective coloration. If I conform to myself, the only one I'm hurting with the press is myself. So, instead, I'm a nice, polite, well-raised young boy full of respect—which is what Hedda likes. Instead of being on my back, she'll be on my side, and she'll defend me against the other press, the ones who say I'm just an irresponsible no-good rebel. She's my friend in court."

Jimmy was being smart. Hedda could be a powerful friend or a dangerous enemy. Jimmy made her his confidante. She came to see him as a misunderstood boy whom only she understood.

Despite Jimmy's stony silence during Keenan's Thanksgiving dinner, Arthur Loew, Jr. had been impressed with him and had invited him to come to dinner at his house on Miller Drive when he returned from the East Coast.

One of the other guests that night was Arthur's cousin, Stewart Stern, who had come out to spend Christmas in Los Angeles from his home in New York, where he had been writing live television shows for *Philco TV Playhouse*: he had also written the movie *Teresa*, starring Pier and Steiger.

His meeting with Jimmy began poorly. Jimmy was in the living room, rotating in a swivel chair. When introduced to Stern he gave a curt hello and continued spinning. Arthur went upstairs to attend to some business, and Stern looked around the room once and then sat down in another swivel chair opposite Jimmy's. When he did so, Jimmy turned in his chair so that his back was to Stern; Stern did the same. They sat there like two bookends, back-to-back, for about ten minutes. Then Jimmy mooed: he bent back his head and gave his loudest imitation of a cow. Whatever else he was to become, Jimmy had once been a good farmboy and knew what a cow sounded like. After a moment's silence, Stern—although a true cityboy—surprised Jimmy by replying with an equally convincing moo of his own. The mooing contest went on for a few minutes until Jimmy, his back still to Stern, asked, "Can you do a bull?" Stern imitated a bull, and Jimmy then asked him if he could imitate a calf. Stern could and asked Jimmy if he could do a *roped* calf. Jimmy couldn't, but Stern could. At this the two of them broke down in laughter and swiveled their chairs around to face each other. A friendship had begun.

Two days later, Gene Kelly invited Arthur Loew, Jr., to a Saturday night dinner followed by charades, a popular game in Hollywood at the time, and Arthur invited Stewart to come along. Among the other guests was Nicholas Ray, accompanied by Marilyn Monroe.

When Stewart was introduced to Ray, the director told him he had seen *Teresa* and liked it. He also mentioned that they had some friends in common: Leonard Rosenman and Jimmy Dean.

"From what I know about you and from what I've heard, I think you and I should have a talk at the studio," said Ray.

During that meeting, Ray recounted the problems he'd been having with the screenplay for *Rebel Without a Cause*. He had just had a falling out with Irving Shulman, the second writer on the project, and he wasn't happy. He believed Stewart was the right man, and said he'd talked it over with Jimmy and Leonard, who concurred. Would he consider it?

Challenged by the idea, Stern agreed. A deal was made, Stern was hired to write a draft, and *Rebel Without a Cause* went ahead. On January 18, Ray began production meetings with Jimmy. In the beginning, the two got along effortlessly. If anything, Ray was even more indulgent with Jimmy than Kazan had been. He listened to all his opinions, allowed him to contribute to every aspect of the project. Ray had about him the aura of a powerfully creative man, and he was truly brilliant, full of ideas, and forever open to new ways of looking at life.

Like many creative people, he was also desperately unhappy and beset by personal demons. In an effort to exorcise them, he resorted to alcohol.

Ray staged regular Sunday afternoon soirees in his bungalow on the grounds of the Chateau Marmont, a hotel on the Sunset Strip favored by show biz folk. (Years later, comedian John Belushi died in the same bungalow.) All day each Sunday, Nick's small white bungalow was crowded with people from the film industry along with a heady mix of New Yorkers and other Easterners, who viewed themselves as the intellectual elite. People came and went—a stop at Ray's bungalow was part of every Sunday for many people.

The sole refreshment served was wine, poured from jugs, and the participants drank as much as they wanted and quite often a tad more than they needed.

One of Ray's occasional guests was Dennis Stock, a young New York–based freelance photographer who had already acquired a reputation as an up-and-coming photojournalist: at the age of twenty-three he had been awarded *Life* magazine's first prize for Young Professional Photographers. Ray, who had met Dennis through Humphrey Bogart, was impressed by talented, brassy Easterners who were unimpressed with Hollywood hype, so he immediately struck up a friendship with him.

Dennis was never happy in Los Angeles, which he saw as artificial and superficial. His only purpose for being in Hollywood was to find assignments, and he mixed with the crowd, looking and listening, trying to piece out something that might make a good story. Ray did his best to introduce him around, get him involved.

One Sunday near the end of January, Ray took Dennis by the arm and led him up a small flight of stairs to a far corner where a young man was slouched in a chair. Dennis thought the young man looked as uncomfortable as he himself felt: he recognized the mood and sensed something between attraction and identification.

"Dennis," Ray said, "I want you to meet James Dean. He's an actor. Jimmy," he said, turning to Jimmy, "this is Dennis Stock. He's a photographer, someone you should really get to know." Having made the introductions, Ray walked off.

Dennis and Jimmy exchanged a few words. Jimmy looked up only when necessary to follow a line of thought, and, as usual with strangers, limited himself to monosyllabic responses. As he held up his end of the conversation, Dennis wondered what Ray saw in the moody, bespectacled young boy. But as they drank more wine their conversation became more lively. Dennis, after all, was a photographer. Jimmy asked questions about equipment and technique, and Dennis did his best to respond. They found they had someone in common: Gjon Mili, the eminent *Life* photographer. Mili had directed Jimmy's screen test for Kazan in New York, and Dennis had worked as Mili's apprentice for four years and was also his good friend.

When the conversation got around to Jimmy's line of work,

Jimmy mentioned that he had just finished a film with Kazan. Dennis had never heard of *East of Eden*, so the subject was soon dropped, but as they said their goodbyes at the end of the evening, Dean invited Dennis to attend a sneak preview of the film the following Wednesday at a Santa Monica theater. Dennis thanked him and said he'd see him there.

Meanwhile Jimmy had himself seen a sneak preview of the film at a theater out in the San Fernando Valley. He took with him both Stewart Stern and Arthur Loew, Jr. By then, the three were good friends, but neither Stern nor Loew had any sense of Jimmy's acting ability. No one turned to look at Jimmy when the three friends walked into the theater—before the house lights went out that evening, he was still nobody—and even the Warner Bros. executives in the theater paid no attention to him. But when the film was over and the lights came up again, Jimmy was a star. To Loew it was like an opening-night success story on Broadway—and there it was, happening right before his eyes, in a small movie house in the Valley.

On the way home, the three friends stopped at a bar. While they were having their drinks, Warner representatives came in the door: the Warner people had been looking everywhere for Jimmy, checking every possible bar and restaurant, and they had finally found the right place. For those executives, too, the screening of the film had been a revelation. Until then Jimmy had been just another kid, but now he was an actor, and not only an actor, but one with that special magic that is so rarely seen. Once again, there in the bar, Loew found himself witnessing what he could describe only as "a star is born."

I'd been invited to a studio premiere of *Eden* and went with Lew. Like so many people—like almost everyone who knew Jimmy—I was astonished by what I saw. After Jimmy's first few scenes I stopped keeping my distance, found myself thoroughly involved with him on the screen, unable to take my eyes off him even when there were other people in the scene. As I watched Jimmy, I recalled episodes and moments from my own youth. Never before had I identified with a screen personality in that way, and I was amazed and a little unnerved by my response. When the film ended

I was both drained and exhilarated. There was no doubt in my mind then that James Dean was going to be Hollywood's next big star.

Later, Lew and I drove into Hollywood to meet Jimmy at the Villa Capri. He was sitting alone at a table, carefully building a house out of breadsticks.

"Well, what did you think of it?"

I was embarrassed to admit how impressed I had been. "Pretty good for a first film," I said lightly.

Jimmy gave a little laugh, and I was immediately sorry my praise had been so faint. But before I could amend my answer, Lew spoke up. "In the car coming over here, Joe told me he thought you were the most dynamic new personality he'd seen on the screen."

"What I said was I thought you were great. Really great," I chimed in.

Apparently we'd overcompensated, because at this Jimmy scrunched down in his seat and readdressed himself to his breadsticks.

"Well, then," he said. "Now that you've seen the picture, let's get on with the business of life."

Dennis Stock, who went to a different screening, was also unprepared for what he saw. Jimmy's casual description of his work had led Dennis to believe his was only a small part. Instead, Dennis found himself watching a brilliant and profound performance. He, too, knew he was witnessing the birth of a star, and he felt that Dean's appeal was immediate and unconditional. When the lights came up at the end, the audience burst into applause. Dennis, too, clapped his hands, and as he did so he realized he wanted to do a story on James Dean, whom he visualized as representative of the new style of actors, people like Marlon Brando and Montgomery Clift, who were revolutionizing acting in films.

When he left the theater, Dennis looked for Jimmy out front, expecting he would have exited with everybody else and would probably be surrounded by admirers. But Jimmy was nowhere in sight. Dennis walked a little way down the street. He passed an alley alongside the theater, looked down it, and recognized Jimmy wearing a leather jacket hunched on his motorcycle. He was alone, watching the crowd from that safe distance, trying to get a sense of the reaction. He grinned when he saw Dennis coming toward him and asked what he thought of the film.

"You are an outstanding actor!" was all Dennis could find to say and immediately felt embarrassed by both the formality and the inadequacy of the phrase. He had no time to go on, however, for Jimmy was soon surrounded by friends voicing their congratulations. In the midst of this shower of praise, Dennis and Jimmy managed to set a date to meet the next day for breakfast at Googie's.

They met at nine, sat down together in a booth, and began to talk, but their conversation was cut short by the arrival of a crowd of admirers. News of the previous night's showing of *Eden* was the only topic in Googie's that morning—Jimmy had become a sensation overnight—and as more and more fans arrived and pushed their way in to be near Jimmy, Dennis found himself forced into a corner. From there, he watched Jimmy enjoy his new status. And he was enjoying it thoroughly. Like a little boy bursting with pleasure, he was giggling and laughing and basking in the thick praise being poured on him. Dennis saw no reason why he should interrupt and deprive Jimmy of that moment, although it did seem artificial to him. But when two hours had gone by and Jimmy had done nothing to indicate he was sated and his fans had not diminished in number, Dennis had had enough.

"Listen," he called across the table to Jimmy, "if we don't get out of here right now I'm going to leave by myself." He got up. To his surprise, Jimmy leaped up from the booth, paid the bill, and led Dennis to his motorcycle in the parking lot.

"Get on the back," he said. "Let's go up into the hills. My agent's got a vacant lot up there with a beautiful view, and we can talk." Dennis had never been on a motorcycle and got on with more than a little trepidation. He sensed that he was being tested. He wrapped his arms around Jimmy's waist, and they took off.

Jimmy took Laurel Canyon Boulevard, a narrow road that makes its way up the hills in tight curves. On the inside of each curve, Jimmy leaned deeply, and Dennis held on tighter, certain Jimmy was trying to kill him, his only consolation being that Jimmy, too, was taking the risks. Above the roar of the bike he shouted toward Jimmy's ears, over and over, "If I go, you go! If I go, you go!"

When the curves finally came to an end and the roar of the bike diminished, Dennis loosened his grasp on Jimmy's jacket. They had reached Dick Clayton's lot, the place where Dick would later build his home. Jimmy stopped the bike. When Dennis swung his leg off the backseat and stood up he found himself looking down on a broad stretch of the city, with further off the dark blue of the Pacific. He and Jimmy walked a short distance toward the view and then sat down together on the ground.

In a nostalgic mood, Jimmy talked about his childhood in Indiana with such feeling that Dennis had an idea. Dennis was an admirer of the great photo essayist Eugene Smith, who stayed with his subjects long enough to reveal their inner character. Dennis told Jimmy that he would like to create a photo essay of him that would reveal the environment and background that had formed his unique persona. He wanted to go home to Fairmount with Jimmy.

What the two young men were outlining was unique: few photographers have ever asked to visit the childhood home of an actor, and few actors have ever been willing to expose their roots, to admit that the seeds of their talent grew from quite ordinary soil. What Dennis was proposing fit his personal philosophy of photography, and it also suited Jimmy's sense of himself. They talked on and on, and only when they got up to leave did they realize they'd been talking for five hours.

Dennis occasionally worked for *Life*, and he felt it would be the ideal buyer for the photo essay he wanted to do. Again they were not enthusiastic about assigning a layout on an unknown actor— one of the reasons they had passed on Schatt's photos—but there were already positive reports in the press about Jimmy's performance. Dennis carried the day when he said he could deliver photographs that would be exclusive to the magazine. He was given a $100-a-day three-day guarantee.

The next time Jimmy saw Stewart Stern at the studio he told him of Dennis's idea and asked him to go along with them and write the story for *Life*. Stewart thought the idea splendid and told Jimmy that if he was acceptable to *Life*, he'd take time off and write the story. However, *Life* didn't feel a writer was necessary on the project. It was agreed that Jimmy and Dennis would leave almost at once, before shooting on *Rebel* was to begin. Dennis suggested they visit New York first because he wanted to film Jimmy at the Actors Studio and in his New York environment.

Early in February, a few days before he was to leave for the East, Jimmy called me to ask a favor. "I'd like to borrow your Minifon," he said. "Maybe I can record my grandfather, Cal, and some of my other relatives and get them talking about the old times."

The Minifon he wanted to borrow was a small wire recorder that I sometimes used on interviews. It had originally been designed in Germany as a spy tool, and as far as I know I was among the first reporters to use such a device, but on long interviews it helped me get accurate quotes. I wore the recorder in a small holster inside my jacket, with a wire extending down my sleeve to a microphone disguised as a wristwatch. I was careful to tell interviewees I had it. Although cumbersome by today's standards, it was easy to operate, with one push-pull knob for off and on. The sound quality coming from the thin strand of wire was only fair, but I could record an hour on each side.

Jimmy dropped by my house the day before he was to leave. I showed him how to knot the wire in the event it broke, which was often.

"When you get back, I'll transfer the recordings you've made onto a record," I promised.

Delighted, Jimmy immediately tucked the recorder into the white holster under his coat. He left the house giggling.

Chapter Eleven

THE LAST VISIT

J immy and Dennis flew to New York together and parted company at the midtown bus terminal, making plans to meet the following morning at Jimmy's apartment on West Sixty-eighth.

In his apartment Jimmy found a stack of mail, most of it unopened, on the seat of the one chair in the room. One of the letters was from Dr. Carel Van der Heide, a psychoanalyst Jimmy had been seeing in Beverly Hills. Jimmy had chosen the doctor, a highly respected Freudian analyst, because, he told me, the dreams were finally getting to him and Freudians were the experts in dream analysis. Dr. Van der Heide wrote that he was enclosing a bill for past sessions with a request for payment, and added, "I am glad to hear from you that you are able to continue work without much difficulty. Meanwhile—my suggestion that you allow time for a prolonged period of treatment when you are in New York still stands."

Jimmy and Dennis began the day with Dennis taking photographs at Cromwell's, where many of Roy Schatt's photos, including several of Jimmy, were on display. Then Dennis photographed Jimmy, wearing a sailor shirt and jeans, playing bongos with Cyril Jackson in a rental studio off Times Square. They then went to Katherine Dunham's School of Dance studio. Jimmy's tastes—his instincts—veered away from the mainstream. When he took dance lessons, he didn't attend a standard ballet school, but chose instead Dunham, then famous as the best choreographer of Afro-American dance. While in Dunham's studio Jimmy met up with Eartha Kitt. She had performed with Dunham's troupe and gone with them on a European tour. Kitt had scored a personal triumph of sorts on Broadway in 1952's *New Faces* at the Royale Theatre. She was then performing in *House of Flowers* at the Alvin Theatre with Pearl Bailey and Diahann Carroll and gave Jimmy tickets for that evening's performance.

In the afternoon Jimmy and Dennis went backstage to visit Geraldine Page at the Cort Theatre, where she was performing in *The Rainmaker*, another play written by N. Richard Nash. They met Chris White at Jerry's Bar for dinner. Jimmy introduced Dennis to his friends diffidently as a *Life* photographer who was covering him, and then did his best to ignore Dennis, who unobtrusively snapped photos that he felt were revelatory of Jimmy's character and his interaction with friends. When they parted company around eight that night, Jimmy said he was going home to get some sleep.

Instead, he went to the theater to see Eartha's performance, but he was so tired he fell asleep during the first act. At intermission he met Bill Gunn and admitted he had dozed off and asked him to tell him what had happened during the first act. Gunn filled him in and then scouted around until he found a friend who gave him a benny, which he gave to Jimmy to help him stay awake. During the next intermission Jimmy called Marty Landau. "I heard this voice yell, 'HELLO,' " Landau recalls. "I said, 'Who the hell is this?' 'It's Jimmy. I feel just like you.' I never heard him talk so fast and loud before with his voice up two octaves. He shouted, 'I feel terrific! Jesus, is this the way you feel all the time?' I said, 'Holy Christ, you're not going to miss the last half of the show, are you?' He said, 'I'LL SEE YA,' and I said, 'Okay, man,' and I heard him laughing like hell, and then he hung up. Later, I found out that he'd taken the benny, probably the first one he'd ever had, and I understood what he meant when he said he felt just like me. My energy level was always much higher than his—I could jump right into a scene with minimal preparation while he was laconic, but more intense. Because of the benny, he suddenly felt full of energy."

When Jimmy met Dennis the following morning he had circles under his eyes, and as Dennis recalls, "He looked like hell. Jimmy was an insomniac, the worst I've ever met, and he would simply pass out, for a few minutes or a few hours, then wake up and start out again."

It was drizzling when they went out on the streets, with Jimmy wearing an old black chief petty officer's coat that he had bought at an army surplus store. As they were walking down Broadway, Jimmy stopped outside a furniture display window near Rockefeller Center. "Performers are always being looked at," he told Dennis. "I wonder what it feels like to be inside and look out. Why don't you stay outside and photograph people's reaction to me sitting inside and staring out."

Jimmy went into the display window facing the street and sat down in a chair. What would have been unusual in Fairmount was of little interest to busy New Yorkers but a few people stopped and stared. Jimmy sat motionless and didn't move for about ten minutes as Dennis shot pictures of him. When Jimmy felt he had created the desired effect, he got up.

The next day it was still raining. Dennis took pictures of Jimmy walking alone in Times Square with billboards in the background. As they ambled aimlessly along, Jimmy would occasionally pause and Dennis would take a photograph. The classic picture of Jimmy walking along Broadway in the rain with his hands in his coat pockets is a perfect example of their collaboration.

"Everything I do is fifty percent improvisation and fifty percent preconception," Dennis says. "It is the preconception that gets me into the spot, and then it's the improvisation that moves me further on. I think both are necessary to all creativity. To me, Times Square was Jimmy's ultimate goal: in many ways he wanted to be like the king of the square.

"He was very playful, and I was very playful. What we had in common was the sense of the surreal, and when I saw that I grabbed the opportunity and photographed it. I think he perceived me as his Boswell.

"I wasn't interested in the poses he would take, they were artificial, and I had to let him go through a lot of nonsense until he relaxed and became spontaneous. Then I took photos which I thought were revealing of his true character.

"He was a bastard sometimes in the sense that he was not reliable and didn't show up for many appointments, but I hung in because I liked him enough so that when he got into one of his moods, I would pull away and not get near him for a while. I was able to relate to him because he often expressed different parts of me."

One night Jimmy called Dizzy Sheridan, who was staying at a friend's apartment where a party was in progress. She invited Jimmy to come over. Jimmy explained that he was with Leonard, who was in New York visiting his parents, and Jane Deacy, his agent. "The more the merrier," said Dizzy.

When Jimmy arrived and Dizzy let him in she was astounded to see him wearing a yellow turtleneck sweater. "My God, you've gone Hollywood," said Dizzy.

"I was only teasing him. The words just leapt out my mouth, but I don't think he liked it at all because as the party started getting to be fun, he started to get nasty. Not that he said 'fuck you' to anybody or anything, but he just didn't want to play games. I don't think he was in a party mood. Mostly he just hung on to this long braid I had hanging down my back and wanted to get in a corner and talk. Finally, he managed to clear the room. I don't know how he did it, but we were the only ones left."

He then took her to Grand Central Station and kissed her goodbye. Both of them knew they would never see each other again.

Jimmy also went to Arlene's apartment, where she was entertaining her friend Don Miele, a volatile Italian in his thirties who was a brilliant actor and a genuine rebel. Miele had quit the Actors Studio after a memorable exchange with Kazan, who asked why he was leaving.

"You're all a bunch of prostitutes," said Miele.

"But you're a genius," protested Kazan.

"Yeah, I am, but you're not," retorted Miele.

Miele still had a sharp tongue, as demonstrated by his greeting to Jimmy, whom he had known for some time. "So, kid, you're now a movie star. They say you gave head to get ahead."

THE LAST VISIT

Arlene gasped as Jimmy forced a laugh and tried to take the comment as a joke.

Arlene left the room, fearful that Miele, who was in love with her and jealous of Jimmy, was trying to start a fight. When she returned, however, the two men were sitting next to each other on a couch having a heated discussion of *Romeo and Juliet*.

Jimmy telephoned Barbara Glenn, who told him that she had met a director friend of Marty Landau's named Mark Gordon whom she was madly in love with and was going to marry.

"All right," said Jimmy. "I want to meet him."

Barbara thought such a meeting was sure to be awkward: she knew Jimmy's "cutesies" and was aware of how offensive and perverse he could be if he didn't like somebody. But Jimmy insisted, so dinner was arranged at a local restaurant. According to Barbara Jimmy was open and warm and he and Mark got along famously with both men liking each other on sight.

The next day Jimmy called Barbara and said, "You know, I wanted to hate Mark, but I don't. He's good for you. But I can't leave without saying goodbye. Please meet me today and we'll just talk."

At first Barbara refused, but Jimmy begged her to see him. Begging was not his style, so she ultimately gave in.

Barbara went to Jimmy's apartment that afternoon. When she came in the door he pointed to a suitcase full of money opened up on the bed. "Take it. Go ahead, take it," he said.

Barbara was shocked. During the two years she and Jimmy had gone together, Barbara had loaned him a lot of money, so she said, "What are you trying to do, pay me back?"

"You can't leave me, Barbara," Jimmy said. "You can't go. We can't end like this."

"I'm going to marry Mark and that's that," Barbara said. "I hope we can be friends sometime in the future."

Barbara put on her coat, went to the door, and said goodbye. As she headed down the stairs, Jimmy suddenly appeared at the landing and began screaming epithets at her as he hurled fistfuls of money down the stairs shouting, "And when I die, it'll be your fault." They were the last words he ever said to her.

Having severed ties with old girlfriends, Jimmy also ended his relationship with Rogers Brackett, his onetime friend and former lover. Brackett had been fired from his job and was short of money: he wanted to borrow a few hundred dollars from Jimmy to make an overdue rent payment. Jimmy refused, claiming that he now had a business manager and that any such loan would have to be done in a businesslike manner. When Brackett protested, reminding Jimmy of the times he had helped him out without a written promise of repayment let alone a demand for collateral, Jimmy retorted that he had outgrown Brackett and his "fairy" friends.

After he had tied up some of the loose ends in his life, Jimmy flew with Dennis to Indianapolis and they then went by bus to Fairmount, where they were met at the bus station by the Winslows and young Markie. They all hugged Jimmy and then Dennis, who was touched by the genuine warmth of their greeting.

When they drove through Marion Jimmy pointed to Park Cemetery and told Dennis, "My mom's buried there."

Within minutes of their arrival at the farm, even before Dennis had unpacked his bag in the spare room, Jimmy appeared in his doorway grinning and giggling. He had changed into his old work clothes—bib overalls, chino jacket, worn boots, and an old camel-hair cap tilted over his eyes at a rakish angle.

Dennis realized that he had been right, that one of the major influences in Jimmy's life was his rural upbringing, and he found the farm and the area surrounding it plus the small town of Fairmount to be everything, perhaps even more, that he had hoped for. Most of the photos he took of Jimmy were within a one-mile radius of the farm. Dennis's photo reportage included pictures of Jimmy playing his bongo drums in the pasture surrounded by Herefords and Poland China hogs; posing for a family picture à la Grant Wood with a giant seven-hundred-pound sow; standing alongside his great-grandfather Cal Dean's headstone in Fairmount's Park Cemetery where generations of Deans, Winslows, Woolens, and Wilsons are buried; and wearing his high school graduation suit while reading a book of poetry in the cobwebbed attic of the Winslow barn.

Almost everywhere they went, young Markie tagged along, his worship of his older "brother" reflected in his eyes every time he looked at Jimmy.

THE LAST VISIT

Most evenings were spent with the entire Winslow-Dean clan gathered around the big dining table in the Winslow home; three generations of a tightknit and proud, typical American Midwestern family. Only Dennis knew that Jimmy was surreptitiously recording much of the conversation with the Minifon he had borrowed from me. The microphone was there on his wrist.

On one of the wire recordings Jimmy asked his grandparents to trace their ancestry. Jimmy found out that his great-great-grandfather was related to the scion of country singer Jimmy Dean's family.

A giggling Jimmy can be heard on one of the scratchy recordings saying to Grandpa Charlie Dean, "You know, Grandpa, in the movie *East of Eden* it was so funny because I played a character named Cal . . . and Cal Dean, he was your father, right? Markie and I went to the cemetery today and saw where great-granddaddy Cal Dean is buried. What was he like? Did he have any interest in art or anything? Was he an arty kind of kid? Or what kind of kid was he?"

"He was one of the best auctioneers I reckon I ever did hear."

"Well, what does it take to be a good auctioneer?"

"You got to be a good judge of stock, you got to be a good judge of human nature, and you've got to have a talent at it."

"How do you do it?"

Charlie Dean demonstrated with a singsong rush of words delivered in typical auctioneer cadence: "Hey, I have three dollars, will you go, will you make it four, will you buy four, I gotta three, now four, wouldya go a five, who make it five, I gotta five howany nowso leds gititup there do I hearasix now I gotta six . . ."

Later, on the recording, Grandpa Dean says, "I'll tell you what kills auctioneers. You take a man who talks to the public every day, he'll eventually get too much confidence in himself. He fools himself by thinkin' he's gettin' by with it, and as soon as the people finds out, they quit him. And that's what kills 'em off."

Grandpa Dean recited a poem Cal's brother had written so people could remember the names of the six Dean brothers: "Joe Bennel, Kil Cal, while Harry, Pat, and John stood off and looked on."

When his grandfather finished the poem, Jimmy's delighted laughter can be heard over that of the rest of the family.

Late on another night, Jimmy and Dennis went into the kitchen where Jimmy wanted to read aloud some of James Whitcomb Riley's famous Hoosier poems. They started searching in the kitchen for some alcoholic refreshment and found a bottle of Manischewitz Concord wine tucked away in the back of a cabinet. They laughed uproariously because the Winslows were Quakers and did not drink: the wine was probably for mixing with sauces or gravies. Jimmy read aloud Riley's poem "We Must Get Home."

"I could feel Jimmy's love of Riley's poems coming through with every word he spoke," Dennis recalls.

Bob Pulley, who went from the seventh to twelfth grade with Jimmy, heard his old friend was in town and wanted to call him but was hesitant, fearing that Jimmy had gotten bigheaded and was too good for him now that he had gone to Hollywood. But his mother insisted he call.

"He came on the phone and asked me what I wanted to do," recalls Bob. "I said, 'I reckon we should go out and get drunk.' And he said, 'Let's go.' And that's just what we did."

Jimmy also spent time talking with his cousin Markie, now twelve years old, in whom he saw much of himself as a child. He repaired Markie's bicycle, bought him a speedometer for it, and played with him in his improvised Soap Box Derby racer. The resentment he had felt toward Markie as a baby was forgotten.

One cold day while Dennis and Jimmy were walking around the town, they passed by Hunt's Furniture Store on Main Street. Jimmy, who was wearing a white scarf with his CPO coat (formal attire for him), told Dennis, "I'm going to take you somewhere," and walked into the store. Dennis was puzzled but followed him into a closed and windowless back room where there were dozens of coffins.

To Stock's horror, Jimmy took off his boots and climbed into a big bronze casket. He crossed his arms and shouted, "Shoot."

Dennis refused, arguing that it was in bad taste and Jimmy had better get out of the casket before someone came in. But Jimmy insisted. To humor him, Dennis snapped a picture. Then Jimmy reached up and grasped the coffin lid. He pulled it down over himself and then jack-in-the-boxed up from the coffin, giggling.

"It was not funny, and he was not funny," recalls Stock. "I had no idea he was going to do that, and I would never have asked him to do such a thing. It frightened me, and I know it frightened him, too. He was afraid, but his way of dealing with that fear was to make fun of it, to taunt it. When he did things like that I just wanted to take him by the shoulders and shake him and say, 'How dare you?' "

Dennis took a sequence of pictures: Jimmy lying down with his eyes closed, hands clasped over his chest; Jimmy smiling and making infantile expressions; Jimmy sitting up and laughing as he flashed a V for victory.

Dennis recalls feeling distaste at what he considered to be Jimmy's black humor, but he realized that in some perverse way Jimmy was trying to express the image of a lost person.

"In the one photo where he sits up and looks directly at the camera, everything has gone out of him, all the showmanship, all the cuteness," Stock says. "There is nothing there other than a lost person who really doesn't quite understand why he is doing what he's doing. That's not a moment to underestimate. Implicit in that series of photos was Jimmy's dark side coupled with his desire to be close to his mother. He missed her."

On the way out of the furniture store, Stock asked, "Why did you want pictures of yourself in the coffin, Jimmy?"

"I dunno," Jimmy answered. "Sarah Bernhardt had pictures taken of herself in a coffin while she was still alive, and it seemed like a good idea. And I always wondered what it was like to be in a coffin, and this seemed like as good a time as any to find out."

"Well," asked Dennis, "what was it like?"

"When the lid's shut, it squashes your nose," said Jimmy, and both of them laughed.

The door hadn't closed behind them at Hunt's before somebody in Fairmount told someone else, "You'll never guess what happened in there." The story of Jimmy in the coffin stood the town on its ear for weeks. Jerry Lee Payne, whose parents were friends of Mildred and Winton Dean, recalls that "some people in town thought Jimmy was deep-ended, because that was unacceptable behavior. You just didn't put on jeans and a white shirt in Fairmount and climb into a coffin."

When the story reached Marcus's ears he shrugged philosophically. "You never do know what Jimmy's going to do next," he said.

On February 14, Jimmy and Dennis were invited to the Fairmount High School Valentine's Day Dance. Jimmy brought his bongo drums and went up on the stage to play with the band. Many of the school's seniors remembered him, and he relished signing their yearbooks. Oddly, he refused to wear his glasses for many of the pictures that Dennis took that night.

One of the last photographs Dennis took, and the one of which he is personally most proud, is of Jimmy in the foreground with the house and barn in the background and, off to the side, his dog, Tuck, turning away from him. "We were both saddened by the end of the week, and I think that we both knew that Jimmy would never come back home again. We both recognized that life would never be the same for him there, and that the trip was really a nostalgic farewell to his origins."

Thinking back on it now, I believe that the trip to Fairmount, like the New York trip, seemed to be Jimmy's way of saying goodbye to the past. I don't mean to imply that he felt he was going to die, but I believe that Jimmy felt that he was truly on the way to stardom.

From Fairmount, Jimmy went back to New York, and Dennis returned to Los Angeles. He withheld the coffin pictures and submitted the rest to *Life*. The editors were initially reluctant to publish the layout: they were accustomed to more glamorous coverage of upcoming young stars. But movie editor Mary Leatherbee carried the day by insisting that Jimmy was going to be an important young star, and the layout was prepared for publication.

Jimmy was not alone in New York for long. Nick Ray decided to visit him there, to see how he lived, and to try to get a fix on his real character. Also, Jimmy had suggested Marty Landau for the role of Buzz in *Rebel* and Nick wanted to surreptitiously observe him. An elaborate plot was hatched. Jimmy would give Nick a fictitious name, and not tell anyone that he was really a film director.

Marty Landau recalls being introduced to an older man with a strange name that Jimmy mumbled. "There was something mysterious about him and his relationship with Jimmy," says Landau, "but we figured that maybe because he was so old [Ray was in his forties] he was a friend of Jimmy's dad."

Nick hung out with Jimmy's friends, including Bobby Heller, Leonard Rosenman, Arlene Sachs, and Tony Ray, who was in on the gag.

One night the group went to Arlene's brownstone for a party. Some young men in leather jackets crashed the party and started to quietly terrorize the guests. Jimmy and Marty went into the kitchen and decided to do something drastic that would frighten the unwanted guests into leaving. They flipped coins to decide who would be the victim and who would be the killer, and then they started a loud argument in the kitchen that spilled out into the living room where Marty, with ketchup on his chest, fell onto the floor as Jimmy stood over him with a kitchen knife in hand. "It was an impromptu scene, but it worked," recalls Marty. "The guys split. They figured the cops would be on the way any minute."

Before Nick left for the Coast, Jimmy introduced him to his friends with his real name and identity. Nick thought Marty looked too old to play a high schooler, even though he and Jimmy were the same age, but he offered Marty a job as dialogue director on *Rebel*. Although Marty was dead broke at the time, he refused the job. "I didn't want to be known as Jimmy's friend."

Marty asked Jimmy if he thought the deception was really necessary. "Did you really think I would act any differently if I thought a director was watching me?"

"Maybe," said Jimmy.

As a parting gesture, Nick arranged a screening of *Eden* for Jimmy, Mark Gordon, and Marty. They were all impressed with Jimmy's performance and sensed that their friend was on his way to stardom.

Chapter Twelve

DANGEROUS SKILL

Dennis Stock's photo essay, along with some stills from *East of Eden*, was published in *Life* on March 7, 1955, under the heading of "Moody New Star." The subtitle was "Hoosier James Dean Excites Hollywood." On March 8, exactly one year from the day Jimmy had gone to Hollywood with Elia Kazan, a star-studded celebrity preview of *Eden* was held at the Astor Theatre in New York. One of the largest crowds ever recorded in Times Square gathered in front and continued around the block. Premiere tickets, which included a swank post-premiere dinner at the Sheraton Astor Roof, went for $150 to benefit the Actors Studio. Marilyn Monroe and Marlene Dietrich headed the honorary usherette brigade, which also included Eva Marie Saint, Anita Loos, Celeste Holm, and Terry Moore. One celebrity who was not there, and very conspicuous by his absence, was James Dean. Jimmy had left New York just the day before, explaining to Jane Deacy, "I'm sorry, but I can't handle that scene."

Jimmy spent that night in Los Angeles with Lilli Kardell, a young Swedish girl he had met at one of Arthur Loew, Jr.'s parties in February. Lilli had been discovered at RKO's Stockholm office where she worked as a secretary, and sent to Hollywood to become an actress. The quintessential starlet, Lilli was a pretty brunette with almond-shaped eyes and a big bosom. She was good-natured, forgiving, and generous with her favors. She was also dedicated to improving her craft: before seeing Jimmy that night she had taken singing, dancing, and diction lessons. But Jimmy was her big passion. She kept a diary, writing down each day's events—even the most intimate—in Swedish. Her entry for March 8 reads, "Had dinner at his [Jimmy's] place. He left me around 3 o'clock."

The next morning I woke Jimmy to tell him about the *Eden* review by William Zinsser, the critic for my paper, the conservative *New York Herald Tribune*. He answered the phone sleepily.

"You awake?" I asked him.

"Barely," he said, and started coughing. "I was on the phone with Pier in Palm Springs. She's in the hospital."

I knew that earlier in the week Pier, who was pregnant, had been on a plane to Palm Springs and was thrown violently against a partition when it struck an air pocket; she suffered a double fracture of the pelvis. "She okay?" I asked.

"Yeah, but she's going to be hospitalized for the month." He paused, and I could sense he was lighting a cigarette. "I still miss her." I heard him take a drag on the cigarette before asking, "What's with you?"

"I just got my *Trib*, and I thought you'd like to hear the review of *Eden*."

"Was it good?" Jimmy asked.

"A rave," I said.

"What did they write about me?"

I read a portion of the review aloud: "Everything about Dean suggests the lonely misunderstood nineteen-year-old. Even from a distance you know a lot about him by the way he walks, with his hands in his pockets and his head down, slinking like a dog waiting for a home. When he talks, he stammers and pauses, uncertain of what he is trying to say. When he listens, he is full of restless energy and stretches, he rolls on the ground, he chins himself on the porch railing, like a small boy impatient of his elder's chatter. . . . He has all the awkwardness of an adolescent who must ask a few tremendous questions and can only blurt them out crudely. Occasionally he smiles unaccountably as if at some dark joke known only to him. . . . You sense the badness in him, but you also like him."

I heard Jimmy giggle on the other end of the line. "Is this guy Zinsser on your paper considered a good critic?"

"One of the best," I said. "He's tough, but fair."

"And what did the *New York Times* critic write?" he asked.

"Bosley Crowther said that you were a mess of histrionic gingerbread and a carbon copy Brando."

"The stupid cunt," snapped Jimmy.

There was a long pause, and for a moment I thought he had hung up. Then I heard his voice again. "On the other hand that's not the worst thing he could say, is it? But I wish he'd compared me to Monty [Clift] instead."

When I saw Jimmy a day or so later, I asked him why he didn't attend the New York premiere. His answer was vehement. "Fuck them! They didn't do anything for me so why should I do anything for them?"

While Jimmy was on his trip east with Dennis, *Rebel Without a Cause* had been scheduled to go before the cameras around the end of March. Stewart Stern was still at Warner fine-tuning his screenplay when Jimmy returned.

Stewart lived in a basement apartment in the Hollywood Hills, and Jimmy would come by to chauffeur him over the hills to the studio in his new Porsche or, more often, on his motorcycle. "He would just tootle up to where I lived, and lead me over the tortuous roads holding his hands straight out—no hands on the bars—speeding through the S curves and hairpin turns, and my heart would stop," recalls Stewart. "He loved to scare me because I was a great fall guy for him. When I rode with him on the back of his bike I'd hide inside my leather jacket and zip it up over my head so I wouldn't have to look."

Stewart had condensed all the action of the film into a twenty-four-hour time frame because he believed that one day is an eternity to teenagers. It was his intention to tell the story of a generation coming of age in one night.

The story begins in the predawn darkness and ends precisely at dawn the following day. The mood of the film is established in the opening scene with Jim Stark, a happily drunk teenager wearing a suit and tie, lying in a street with a clockwork animal, which he puts to sleep under a newspaper in a manner at once childlike and paternal. Over the scene is heard the ominous approach of an unseen police car.

Some of the principal characters are in the police station: Ray, a detective who is the only really responsible adult in the film; the Juliet-to-be aptly named Judy; a psychotic and alienated adolescent named Plato; and Jim Stark's ineffectual father, who takes Jim home.

The following morning is Jim Stark's first day at his new high school. Still wearing a suit and tie, he immediately engages the hostility of a local gang, led by the leather-jacketed Buzz, who is Judy's boyfriend. The antagonism peaks later in the school day during a field trip to the Griffith Park Planetarium. A knife fight between Jim and Buzz evolves into a chickie run challenge: they will drive two stolen cars at high speed toward a cliff with the winner being the last to jump from his vehicle. Jim, who is seeking self-definition, returns home and changes into jeans, boots, and a red windbreaker.

The events that take place during that night are the crux of the film. Buzz accidentally dies during the chickie run; Jim and Judy are drawn together; Plato comes to view Jim and Judy as substitutes for his own apparently uncaring parents.

Buzz's gang are determined to avenge his death, and Plato gets a gun to help protect his new friends. Jim, Judy, and Plato leave their homes after bitter arguments with their respective parents and hide out in a deserted mansion near the planetarium. Plato, who is fleeing both the gang and the police, hides in the planetarium itself, where Jim finds and vainly attempts to disarm him.

At dawn, Plato, wearing Jim's red jacket, is killed by the police. The film ends with the sound of an ambulance siren, and Jim again wearing adult clothes, having borrowed his father's sport coat.

Stewart wrote a brief description of each of the major characters to aid Nick Ray with casting. Jim Stark was based on Stewart's own relationship with his parents. His notes for the character read: "The angry victim and the result. At seventeen, he is filled with confusion about his role in life. Because of his 'nowhere' father he does not know how to be a man. Because of his wounding mother, he anticipates destruction in all women. And yet he wants to find a girl who will be willing to receive his tenderness."

Judy was described by Stewart: "At sixteen, she is in a panic of frustration regarding her father—needing his love and suffering when it is denied. This forces her to invite the attention of other men in order to punish him."

Plato: "The son of a divided family. . . . He feels himself the target of desertion. At fifteen, he wants to find a substitute family for himself so that he need no longer feel cold, and especially a friend who will supply the fatherly protection and warmth he needs."

Buzz: "A sadomasochistic boy of seventeen who acts out aggressively his idea of what a man should be in order to hide his real sensitivities and needs."

The various kids in the gang were "all searching for recognition in the only way available to them; all suffering from unfulfilled hungers at home; all creating an outside world of chaos in order to bear the chaos they feel inside. They are soldiers in search of an enemy."

The studio's initial casting call produced almost five hundred young California teenagers, and they were auditioned by Nick and producer David Weisbart on a stage set that had been used for *A Streetcar Named Desire*. The group was narrowed down to around fifty that Nick wanted to test with Jimmy. Nick was determined that they look like real teenagers, not stereotypes from central casting, and he was careful to avoid youngsters taller than Jimmy's five feet eight.

Nick broke his height rule with one of the first actors he signed, Corey Allen to play Buzz Gunderson, Jimmy's principal antagonist in the film. Corey, who was just twenty years old, had appeared in one film and bore some resemblance to Marlon Brando. Nick first spotted him in a Los Angeles stage play, *The Pick-up Girl*. Frank Mazzola was chosen to play Crunch, Buzz's second lieutenant, not because of any particular acting talent, but because he was the real-life leader of a gang at Hollywood High known as the Athenians. Nick wanted to have him around to keep the gang scenes realistic. Dennis Hopper was signed as Goon, one of the gang members. Barely twenty, he was under contract to Warner, and the studio—to use the cliché popular at the time—was "grooming him for stardom." Dennis was also to be Jimmy's stand-in on some of the tests with other actors. Nick Adams, who had worked with Jimmy five years earlier in the Pepsi-Cola commercial and who also just happened to be Dennis Hopper's roommate, was signed for the role of Cookie. Jack Grinnage and Tom Bernard rounded out the male members of the gang.

Jimmy wanted his friend Jack Simmons to play Plato, but Nick didn't think he was right. Jimmy persisted and finally persuaded Nick to do a test.

A scene between Jimmy and Jack was scheduled on a soundstage set up for a feature film with a crane and lights. While Nick and the camera crew prepared for the test, Jimmy and Jack disappeared. A few moments later hysterical giggling could be heard coming from somewhere behind the set, and then Nick and the cameramen were surprised to see a single stream of bright liquid—obviously urine—come in through one of the flat's windows. Jimmy and Jack were out behind the flat having a peeing contest to see who could make it through the window. One of them was successful, a feat they both found uproarious.

Suddenly Jimmy yanked Jack through the door onto the set and began the scene. Nick, ready for anything, already had the camera rolling. The purpose of Jimmy's peeing contest had been to get Jack so relaxed that the spirit of the scene would be there before they got on the set. Thus, to Jimmy's way of thinking, Jack was tested under the best possible circumstances. Even so, he didn't get the role of Plato and was signed instead for the smaller part of Moose, one of the gang members.

Nick spotted Sal Mineo during a casting call. Slight and almost pretty, with large, sad eyes, Mineo was an unlikely candidate for a gang member, but Nick thought he resembled his own son and asked him about his acting experience. Although only fifteen, Sal was a veteran of two Broadway shows and had acted in two films.

Nick had Sal do an improvisation with Corey Allen, which went well, and the next step was to see how Jimmy and Sal related. They read through a key scene but failed to establish any real contact. Nick suggested the two sit and talk for a while, hoping it would relax Sal. Jimmy was delighted to learn that Sal was from the Bronx and soon had him talking about New York. Then they moved on to the subject of cars. They soon established a rapport, and Sal got the role of Plato.

The female members of the gang included pretty Beverly Long, who also had been in the Pepsi commercial with Jimmy and Nick Adams and whom Nick Ray had spotted in the same Hollywood stage play with Corey Allen. After an audition she was signed to play a tough, pony-tailed blonde. Among the young actresses Nick considered for the lead female role of Judy was Steffi Skolsky, actress daughter of columnist Sidney Skolsky (one of my favorite Hollywood characters, he had his office on the mezzanine of Schwab's, the better to interview young talent). Nick eventually turned Steffi down for the role of Judy, and she became instead a gang member named Millie.

Among the other actresses auditioning for the role of Judy was Natalie Wood, the child star who had just finished a role in *The Silver Chalice*. Natalie had turned seventeen and needed a part in a more adult film to continue her screen career. Nick interviewed and tested Natalie but was undecided: he admitted to her that he didn't believe audiences would accept her in the role of a juvenile delinquent.

A few nights later, Nick got a telephone call at his hotel from Dennis Hopper. "Now, don't get excited, Nick," Hopper said, "but I was out driving with Natalie and Faye [Nuell, Natalie's girlfriend], and we've had an accident."

"Dennis, have you been drinking?" Nick asked.

"Yes."

"Where are you?"

"At the police station."

"For Christ's sake, get the hell out of there," Nick warned. "Chew some gum and run around the block a few times before you get yourself arrested."

"I can't leave," said Dennis. "There's been some trouble. Natalie's hurt. I think she has a concussion."

"Call her doctor right away."

"Nat doesn't want to call her family, and she doesn't know if they have a doctor."

"I'll be there as soon as I can," said Nick and hung up. He then called his doctor and notified Natalie's parents.

When Nick arrived at the police station he found Natalie lying on a stretcher. She reached up and pulled him close to her, pointed to the precinct doctor, and whispered in his ear, "You see that son of a bitch over there? Well, he called me a juvenile delinquent. Now do I get the part?"

Signing Sal and Natalie presented Nick with certain problems: because both were minors, California law required they have a special tutor on the set so they would not fall behind in their schoolwork. They could be at the studio only eight hours a day, four hours in school and four hours on the set, and they absolutely could not work after midnight. Because of all these problems, the Warner Bros. front office had given Nick strict instructions not to hire any minors, but Nick was a willful man, and Sal and Natalie got the roles. Faye Nuell, a pretty brunette dancer, was taken on as an extra but then promoted to serve as Natalie's double.

Many of the teenage cast members had worked together in local plays or on television shows, and a few had gone to Hollywood High together. Nick wanted the gang to be a cohesive group, "a family" is the way he put it to me, and that's what he got.

Jim Backus was surprised when Nick cast him as the father. It was, in fact, an odd choice—Backus was then best known as the voice of Mr. Magoo—and Nick encountered studio pressure to select another actor, but in the end he had his way. Nick was more conventional in his choice of the mother, selecting Ann Doran, an established thirty-five-year-old actress who usually played mothers in films.

Jimmy developed a close relationship with Doran: his mother in the film, she ultimately came to play a similar role in his life during work on the film and even later. He began their relationship the way he began so many others. Having spotted her on the lot, he drove up beside her on his motorcycle and called out, "Let me take you for a ride."

"No way," she replied and tried to walk away. But he begged her until finally she climbed onto the seat behind him.

By the time of *Rebel*, Jimmy knew his way around the Warner lot, knew which soundstages had both front and back doors—and which were usually open—and he took Doran for a hair-raising ride up and down the studio streets and into and out of the many soundstages. From the bright sunlight they would suddenly enter the cool darkness of a set only to suddenly burst with a roar out into the light again.

At the end of the ride Doran was a nervous wreck. Jimmy was delighted.

Because the film budget was low (less than $1 million) Nick didn't think he could afford a still photographer on the set. He hired Dennis Stock to be Jimmy's dialogue coach with the understanding that Dennis would also take occasional photographs. He also reasoned that Dennis had a good rapport with Jimmy and might be of help in keeping Jimmy in line. Nick also hired another of Jimmy's friends, Leonard Rosenman, to write the score.

While he was in New York, Jimmy had been signed by Warner to play the role of Jett Rink in *Giant*, a film version of Edna Ferber's sprawling saga of Texas, which had been a best-seller in 1952. The character of Jett Rink was described in the script as "a violent young ranch hand, half juvenile delinquent, half genius, who wants to make a million (He makes a hundred million). . . . Tough, always angry, restless, bewildered and reckless with animal charm and a tycoon's magnetism." The script called for Jimmy to age from nineteen to forty-six. The film was to be directed by George Stevens with an all-star cast, including Elizabeth Taylor and Rock Hudson.

A press conference was held on Jimmy's return at the studio commissary to announce the start of production. Rock Hudson, Liz Taylor, Mercedes McCambridge, and Chill Wills were on a dais with George Stevens when Jimmy arrived wearing blue jeans, an old red-flannel shirt, battered cowboy hat, scuffed boots, and an old silver-buckled cowboy belt. The usual cigarette was drooping from his mouth, and he wore sunglasses, which he refused to take off for a group photo. Unlike the others who stood up when introduced, Jimmy just sat in his chair, studying his boots.

After the conference, Jimmy, Lew, and I went to the Smoke House for coffee. When Jimmy took off the sunglasses he had big black bags under his eyes. Lew asked him what he had been doing with himself at night.

"Just can't get any goddamned sleep," he said. "I still have the same dreams about my mother and they're driving me crazy."

"What's your shrink think about them?" I asked.

"All he does is have me write them down, and then he has me try and interpret him. Shit, I pay him to do the interpreting."

I asked Jimmy what he was going to do after *Rebel*.

"It all depends," he said.

"Depends on what?"

"On my draft board," he said. "I've asked for a deferment but haven't heard yet."

Two weeks before *Rebel* was scheduled to begin, Jimmy disappeared. No one knew where he was, and Warner told Jane Deacy that they were planning to suspend him.

Late one night Stewart Stern got a telephone call from Jimmy. "He started this mooing business on the phone with me," Stewart recalls. "Of course, I knew it was Jimmy so I asked him where he was. He said he was in New York, and he wanted to know if he was in trouble. I said, 'Yeah, they're going to put you on suspension unless you come back.' He said he just didn't know if he wanted to come back. I asked what was going on. He said, 'I'm scared. I just don't trust Nick.' "

"Why not?" Stewart asked.

"It's just that I really don't trust anyone but Kazan. I had that experience in *Eden*, and I totally trust that man. I don't know if I can trust Nick, and I've got to, and I don't know whether I'm coming back. What should I do?"

"I can't tell you that," Stewart said. "I'm in a very funny position, because I don't want to influence you."

"Do you want me to come back?" Jimmy asked.

"Jimmy, I'm not going to say that."

"Well, if I come back, it'll be for you."

"Don't put that on me," replied Stewart.

"Well, do you want me to do your picture?" Jimmy asked.

Stewart had to search his soul before answering. "I would be a liar and an idiot if I said I didn't want you to do my script, but I'm not going to tell you to come back. If you do the picture and you're miserable in it or it turns out badly, then it'll be on my head, and I don't want that responsibility."

The conversation ended there. Ten days later Stewart was at the studio sitting at his typewriter when Jimmy walked in and looked at the blank green office wall. "Jesus, God," Jimmy said. "He was talented. I never realized it was this big."

"What are you talking about?" Stewart asked.

"Look at the bull, the screaming bull, the screaming horse," said Jimmy.

Stewart finally realized that Jimmy was visualizing Picasso's huge mural of *Guernica* on the wall, and when Jimmy asked him if it was real or a reproduction, Stewart, who had gotten into the game, answered, "It's real, of course."

Jimmy left without saying a word about the film. He was present the next day, however, when everyone in the cast got together at Nick's bungalow at the Chateau Marmont and read the script aloud for the first time. Nick encouraged his cast to improvise, change the dialogue, even suggest scenes. He was quick to admit to his teenage cast that he as an adult was far removed from adolescence, and he wanted the picture to be real.

Nick even held juvenile delinquency classes for the actors play-ing gang members. He had the police arrange for the principals to meet with real gang members so the actors could see for themselves just how they talked and acted. The actors were warned not to play games or get smart with them. Jimmy was enchanted with the youngsters in the gang and kept in touch with them.

Nick encouraged his teenage cast to hang out together as much as possible. "He wanted the movie to come from us, rather than from his direction," recalls Steffi Skolsky. "We were really not together as a gang when we started rehearsing. Nick told us we were playing individually instead of together. So we all went out together, except for Jimmy. We went to the beach, and climbed around a deserted warehouse one night, to get the feeling of being a group. By the time we were ready to start shooting, we were really thinking as one."

Meanwhile, Jimmy had entered the eighth annual Palm Springs Road Races, a two-day event and an ideal excuse for a holiday before starting the film. He planned to drive his new Porsche Super Speedster. When he excitedly told Nick about his plans, the director said, "Just take it easy. I don't want you to get hurt."

"I encouraged the racing," Ray told me sometime later. "It was good for Jimmy to do something on his own with clarity and precision."

That Friday afternoon Jimmy rented a car for Dennis Stock, Lilli Kardell, and a friend of hers, and they followed him in his Porsche to Palm Springs where they all stayed overnight at Dick Clayton's home in nearby Palm Desert. I drove down by myself the next day to see the race.

In his black coveralls with black-and-white checkered hat, Jimmy was a dramatic figure in the pits. The other drivers silently weighed him as a possible threat, with most of them believing he was just there for publicity. Nobody figured he had much of a chance.

Before the race, Jimmy disappeared from the pits and went off by himself. I watched him as he dropped his head and shook it vigorously as though it were on a swivel. Then he kicked the ground. When I asked him what that was all about, he explained, "I've got to loosen up before I get in there and drive the car. I've got to unlimber to be right."

Jimmy easily qualified for one of the two main events in which he would compete against veteran drivers. He won his first race, leading a field of veteran drivers by three hundred yards, and thus earned the right to go against the best in his class the following day. The other drivers and mechanics began to look at him with respect. He was accepted not as James Dean, actor, but as James Dean, race driver, which delighted him.

After the race, however, Jimmy was in a foul mood. Lilli had gone for a drink with Bob Evans, an actor who would one day become a producer, and returned to the cottage late. In her diary for the day Lilli wrote: "Jimmy and I were angry at one another and also others. Idiotic evening. Finished with myself drunk and sleeping in the rented car."

The following day Jimmy surprised everyone again and placed second. I remember him pulling into the pits after the race, taking off his helmet, lighting a cigarette, and grinning. Ken Miles, a professional driver competing against Jimmy in that race, claims he had never before seen such latent skill in any driver. "But it was dangerous skill, the kind that comes as a desperate desire to win," he said. "Jimmy was a menace to himself and other drivers. He wanted to win too much and would take any kind of chance to be first."

That night Jimmy went with Lilli to the Shadow Mountain Club to celebrate, but as Lilli noted in her diary, "Jimmy and I did not talk with one another. Terrible atmosphere between us. He behaved in a ridiculous fashion and ignored me completely and flirted with other girls . . . [finally] we got reconciled. Came home here and Jimmy slept a little and we made love. Everything is well between us now, I hope."

On his return to Los Angeles on Sunday night, Jimmy dropped Lilli off at her apartment and went to Arthur Loew, Jr.'s home where he and Stewart started horsing around. Jimmy playfully hit Stewart lightly. Stewart responded with a tap on Jimmy's chest. The game got out of hand, and Stewart accidentally put his fist through Jimmy's glasses.

Stewart remembers that his first thought was "Here's my star who starts tomorrow and I've blinded him. I started pulling shards of glass out of Jimmy's hair, and then we had to start calling around to get somebody to make up a new set of glasses for the next day because Jimmy had to go over his lines." Instead of being upset, however, Jimmy considered the episode hilarious. The evening ended with the two combatants throwing their arms around each other.

Although Stewart broke through the initial barrier to friendship with Jimmy, he never felt he got past all the barriers. "We talked once about the defenses people use to keep people out and bring people in," Stewart told me. "I don't think that inside Jimmy thought he was interesting, and that's why he tried to fill his life up with so much—to make himself more interesting.

"Part of his strangeness was deliberate, part mischief. He wanted reassurance the same way as a child who hits. He wanted to see if you loved him at his worst and then you must surely love him. This made friendship almost impossible because you could never get really close to him."

Chapter Thirteen

REBEL

Filming of *Rebel* began on Monday, March 28, 1955. After it had been in front of the cameras for less than a week, Nick Ray was called into Jack Warner's office. Some of the studio's production executives had seen the dailies and didn't understand what he was doing. He was ordered to halt production.

"Fine," said Nick. "Take me off salary and sell me all the rights to the film."

The executives hesitated and said they'd get back to him. Steve Trilling, Jack Warner's executive assistant overseeing the production, asked the projectionist what he thought of the film he had seen to date. "Frankly, I think it's the only picture worth anything on the lot," the projectionist answered. Trilling reported that opinion back to Jack Warner at another meeting, and the studio head agreed to let Nick continue.

Two days later, Nick was told that the film, originally shot in black-and-white CinemaScope, had to be filmed in color. This meant that everything done to date had to be done over again. Ray was delighted. He far preferred working in color, which he had always been able to use to advantage. The first thing he did was pull a red nylon windbreaker off a Red Cross man, have it dipped in black paint to remove some of the sheen, and gave it to Jimmy to wear. The red jacket became a symbol of defiance.

Reshooting some of the scenes led to changes in the original film, particularly in the opening scenes. The black-and-white opening to the film showed a man walking home with his arms full of packages of Christmas gifts. He is attacked by a gang of kids who knock away his packages and set fire to them. A toy monkey falls out of one of the packages. The gang runs off when they hear a police car approaching: the toy monkey is left on the street. Then Jimmy appears, sees the monkey, and picks it up.

With the change to color, Stewart Stern also changed the time of the film from Christmas to Easter, and Nick decided to cut the scene of the man being roughed up by the gang. The Christmas-present monkey thus lost its reason for appearing in the film, but Jimmy was unwilling to see it go.

Jimmy's first scene—and the opening scene of the movie—had to be filmed at dawn, and the cast and crew were exhausted because they had been working for twenty-three hours straight that day so that they could get the dawn light. No special bit of business had been planned for Jimmy, and everyone was curious to see what he would do, particularly with the monkey.

Jimmy told the director, "Please let me do something here, you know, play with it. Just keep the cameras rolling."

Nick hadn't a clue what Jimmy had in mind, but he went along and gave the order to roll the cameras.

The entire scene was a classic of improvisation. The camera closed in on Jimmy lying drunk on the sidewalk, curled up next to the toy monkey, which he was trying to blanket with a piece of paper. In that one bit, Jimmy involved the audience in the character he was playing: an isolated and defenseless teenager in a world of his own creation.

The next scene called for Jimmy to be searched in the police station, and here again he proved his ability to improvise. As the police officer searches him, he suddenly begins to giggle: he is ticklish. Dennis Hopper was astonished by this display of Jimmy's skill. "Where did that come from? It came from genius, that's where it came from. And that was all him. Nobody directed him to do that. James Dean directed James Dean."

Leonard Rosenman agrees. "Jimmy stepped all over Nick, who catered to him and allowed him to prepare as long as he wanted.

Jimmy told him what to do, what not to do, and where to put the camera."

That perception about Nick's direction of Jimmy was at variance with mine. As a frequent visitor to the sets and locations, I was fascinated by Nick's style of directing. He never gave instructions to an actor out loud. Instead he would go over and put an arm around the actor and have him or her walk with him a few paces while he talked quietly and earnestly. It seemed to me that most of the cast adored their director, whom they considered a guru: much of the time he walked around in Levi's and bare feet.

After much cutting and recutting, *East of Eden* finally opened in Los Angeles. That day, Lew, Jimmy, and I drove down Hollywood Boulevard in my car to check out the business the picture was doing at the Egyptian Theater. As we passed a line of people extending around the block, Jimmy jumped excitedly up and down in the backseat and shouted, "Hey, man, look at that. I'm a star."

Most of the youngsters in *Rebel* went to see the film. Beverly Long, who went with Jack Grinnage, recalls, "We were nailed to the back of our seats. We had done the tests with Jimmy but we had no inkling of what a great actor he was. We were stunned, and came out of the theater dazed."

By the time *Rebel* was in its second week of production, *Eden* was the number one grossing film in the country, and even Elia Kazan admitted he was totally unprepared for Jimmy's success.

Jimmy began to get the first of thousands of fan letters requesting autographs or photographs. Most of the letters were from teenagers who had seen *Eden* two or three times and who identified with him. Never before in the history of Warner Bros.—and of motion pictures—had young filmgoers so completely identified with a young actor. The fact that Jimmy was playing a role was unimportant: they recognized something of themselves in him. The mail and the critics' praise amazed Jimmy. He knew he was good in *Eden*, but he had no idea he was that good.

Jimmy was completely unprepared for success and its by-product—fame. Fame, of course, was exactly what he wanted; considering all the photographs he had taken of himself, he had always acted like he already was world famous, but now he truly was. At parties people would follow him from room to room. Dennis Hopper, who had become a friend of Jimmy's, claims that in his life he has seen that kind of thing happen only with two other individuals, Brando and Bob Dylan. The attention he received was overwhelming, and he wasn't equipped to handle it. If nothing else, he had no real family, no real love for anyone else, and thus no strong backup support—he could not withdraw anywhere to be himself.

He became nervous and edgy when people swarmed around him in the hope that some of his prominence or talent would rub off on them. He soon found that if he went to Googie's or Schwab's, his favorite breakfast hangouts, he was no longer "just there." Everyone came to his table, and more often than not he was left to pick up the check.

Fan magazine writers and photographers were after him continually. The girls he dated, including Lilli, were pestered by writers wanting to know what he was really like.

Suddenly everything he said was considered important, and he was misquoted or quoted out of context so often that he became wary of interviews.

I know he resumed his thrice weekly psychoanalysis sessions because once or twice when his car was being repaired I dropped him off at Dr. Van der Heide's office on Wilshire Boulevard in Beverly Hills and picked him up an hour later. Jimmy told me that he was afraid of what he would find out in analysis, but he was determined to go through with it if it would help him sleep at night. Sleep meant dreams, he said, and they frightened him. He began to think more and more about his mother, and on nights when he was unable to sleep he would call up friends. Nick Adams told me that Jimmy would call him late at night to ask questions about Nick's mother: Jimmy wanted to talk about a mother, anybody's mother.

Jimmy became even more of an insomniac during the filming of *Rebel*. I despaired of going out with him at night because I had to start preparing my column early in the morning for a noon deadline with my New York office. As a result I saw him only rarely in the evenings while *Rebel* was being filmed, usually only for a quick dinner with him and Lew Bracker at the Villa Capri.

Lilli Kardell's diary entries for the month of April record many of the evenings they spent together. Lilli had a code, an asterisk, which indicated that they made love. Her entries referring to Jimmy are full of asterisks. For example, her entry of April 6 reads: "My darling called and came here *." Ten days later she wrote, "had a dinner date with Jimmy at Villa Capri. Drove home to his place ** there."

In many ways Jimmy was still an adolescent. His interests were those of many twenty-three-year-olds. He liked sex; he drove his car and motorcycle too fast; he stayed out late; he dressed lazily and comfortably. He didn't want to be bothered with responsibilities: he felt there was time for them later.

Most every other actor working at Warner, such as Bogie and William Holden, usually came to the studio dressed in a sport coat and slacks, but Jimmy always wore pretty much the same outfit: jeans, a windbreaker over a T-shirt, and the inevitable cigarette drooping from his mouth. More often than not he was unshaven and his hair was a mess.

The Hollywood press was welcome on the sets and location shootings of *Rebel*, probably as a way Nick Ray could deal with his limited budget: any free publicity the film received would excite interest.

One of the key sequences, filmed over a period of weeks, took place at the Griffith Planetarium, high in the hills above the Hollywood Bowl. Jimmy had had me buy for him a Minifon wire recorder similar to the one I had lent to him for his trip to Fairmount, and he showed it to Nick, who was fascinated with it, especially the watch microphone, and he had Jimmy wear it so he could later check the dialogue.

I had a choice seat on a ledge with some other press spectators on one of the days that the knife fight between Jim and Buzz at the Planetarium was filmed. Neither Jimmy nor Corey Allen had ever been in a knife fight before, and they both wore chest protectors. Jimmy had the Minifon holster snugged tight under his left arm.

Nick, who had directed two musicals on Broadway, and Leonard Rosenman had determined that every move in the knife fight be choreographed like a ballet, combining elements of a bullfight and dance. Frank Mazzola and Mushy Callahan, an ex-boxer who was

Jimmy's stand-in, worked out the choreography in accordance with Nick's precise instructions.

Both boys were using real switchblades with the edges dulled, but the points were intact so there was the possibility of a real accident. Three CinemaScope cameras covered the action, and there was an aura of palpable tension on the set as they went at it.

The first few takes were disastrous. The boys circled each other gracefully and menacingly, but neither one wanted to close the distance enough to make the fight look real: each was fearful of hurting the other. If memory serves, it was on the eighth or ninth take before they started to get into the spirit of battle. Suddenly Nick shouted in a panicky voice, "Cut! Get a first aid man to Jimmy on the double."

A thin trickle of blood was coming down Jimmy's neck, but he was furious. "Goddamn it, Nick," he yelled. "What the fuck are you doing? Can't you see this is a real moment? Don't you ever cut a scene while I'm having a real moment. That's what I'm here for." The scene was finally filmed satisfactorily with Rod Amateau, a young stuntman, doubling for Jimmy in some of the action.

Another pivotal scene in the film was the chickie run, part of which was filmed one cold night in late April on location at the Warner Bros. ranch. Faye Nuell stood in for Natalie, who was supposed to be in the middle of the course as the cars raced around her. Stuntmen did the actual driving, with Rod Amateau doubling Jimmy in a raked '46 Ford.

Amateau recalls that after the chickie run was filmed, Jimmy wanted to know how it was done. "He was interested in anything and everything that had to do with cars and driving. He had me demonstrate a bootleg turn, a technique of making a complete 180-degree turn without losing speed. And he had me show him how to get out of a car so that he wasn't blocking the camera. Then he had me draw a diagram of all the camera lenses and what they encompassed. Until then I thought he was pretty standoffish, but then I realized he was curious about everything that had to do with films."

At the end of the chickie run Jimmy was supposed to look over a cliff at Buzz's body below. The scene was actually filmed on a soundstage with the camera shooting from above and behind. The ocean below was really a black velvet drape. Jimmy was unable to relate to the drape, so he took an apple core, dipped it in ketchup, threw it on the floor, and pretended it was Buzz.

Despite the love interest, the strongest personal relationship in the film is between Jimmy and Sal Mineo's Plato. Nick Ray was not adverse to using Jimmy's bisexuality to good purpose. The director knew that Sal was homosexual, and he encouraged him to explore that part of himself that would love Jimmy. At the same time, according to Ray, Jimmy fell in love with Sal. "He knew it and I knew it. I didn't stop it because it was helping the film. I heard him explaining things to Sal: 'You know how I am with Nat. Well, why don't you pretend I'm her and you're me. . . . Pretend you want to touch my hair, but you're shy.' Then Jimmy says, 'I'm not shy like you. I love you. I'll touch your hair.' I took one look at the kid's face . . . he was transcendent, the feeling coming out of him. You saw the film was something to cry about, so I tiptoed away. The next scene Sal broke the sound barrier."

Sometime later, Sal told me that he and Jimmy never became lovers. "But we could have—just like that." I took what Sal said with a grain of salt.

Most of Jimmy's friends, including Dennis Stock, Lew Bracker, Leonard Rosenman, and Marty Landau, believe that Jimmy's homosexual activities ceased when he came to Hollywood for *East of Eden*. He had broken off all relations with Rogers Brackett on one of his recent visits to New York, and the Jimmy we all knew in Hollywood was very much a swinging heterosexual. Nevertheless, Jimmy's sexuality seems to be central to who he was and to the fascination he still holds: he's one of the rare stars, like Rock Hudson and Montgomery Clift, who both men and women find sexy.

Although I was not privy to the homosexual part of Jimmy's early life until I had done research after his death, I do know something about some of his affairs in Hollywood, including the one with Lilli. One day when I visited the set the crew was setting up for the next shot, and Lilli arrived for a visit with Jimmy. We started chatting and she told me that she and Jimmy had been to Tijuana to see the bullfights. "You know what he did that night?" she asked me. "When I went to bed he climbed naked on top of a bureau with a cape in his hands. He asked if I was ready. 'Ready for what?' I said. He leaped on me and plunged his 'sword' in me just like I was the bull!''

Toward the end of April, Jimmy called Lew and invited him to lunch at the studio with me because he had news of great importance to tell us. When Lew asked what the news was, Jimmy would only say, "It can be done."

Over lunch Jimmy told us that the previous night he and Natalie had gone by Lew's house to take him to the Villa Capri for dinner. Since Lew wasn't home, they had gone up to Mulholland Drive, where Jimmy showed off some of his driving skill in the Porsche. Then they parked to look at the city lights and pretty soon they were involved. "We found a way to make love in the Speedster," Jimmy gleefully said. "We did the impossible." We broke up laughing, not at Natalie, but at the idea of making love in the cramped interior of the small sports car. We all swore by the Porsche and knew there were a lot of things you could do in one, but we never thought sex was a possibility.

I don't know if Jimmy and Natalie had a continuing relationship after that. She was, however, having simultaneous affairs with Nick Ray and Dennis Hopper.

Adele Rosenman recalls being shocked when she came in on Natalie and Nick while they were taking a shower together in a poolside cabana at the Chateau Marmont. Dennis Hopper was the next person to learn of the affair. One night he arrived in tears at Steffi Skolsky's house during a party of the movie's gang members. Beverly Long, who was there, says, "He was crazy about Natalie, and he felt it was horrible for the director to be fooling around with an underage girl. Everybody agreed with him, but it wasn't any of our business."

Meanwhile, Jimmy had met a new girl. Her name was Ursula Andress. She was from Switzerland and had made films in Italy and was under contract to Paramount. Dick Clayton had seen her at the studio one day and told her about Jimmy, and asked if she would like to meet him. A date was arranged and Jimmy was captivated with her European background and accent.

Over dinner at the Villa Capri with Lew and me, Jimmy told us about Ursula. "A real free spirit," he said. "She sleeps even less than I do so we party at night and I don't get any sleep. I need matchsticks to prop up my eyes if I want to keep them open."

On one of their first dates, he said, she told him she already had another date she couldn't break, so she suggested that Jimmy go along. When Jimmy went by her home, he noticed a man sitting in an old car outside the house. When Ursula came out she introduced the man to Jimmy as Howard Hughes.

The three of them sat in the front seat of Hughes's car with Ursula in the middle and Hughes driving toward the beach. They stopped at a traffic light on Santa Monica Boulevard. Hughes turned to Jimmy and said, "I'm out of cigarettes. Would you mind getting out and going into the store and getting me some?"

Jimmy got out of the car. The light changed, and Hughes drove off.

We all broke up laughing. "Are you sure it was Howard Hughes?" I asked.

"The son of a bitch was wearing sneakers is all I can tell you," said Jimmy.

What Jimmy didn't tell us was that Ursula was in love with John Derek, whose wife had threatened to have Ursula deported if he continued to see her: Ursula was in the country on a work visa and the deportation threat was very real. Ursula recently told me that she had warned Jimmy that she was in love with John, "but Jimmy wanted a relationship with someone and he chose me. He knew about John but he thought I would get over him. Jimmy started to come over to my house every day on his motorcycle, and then he asked me to visit him on the set, and then we started to go out, at first to places like Will Wright's for ice cream cones: he loved to mix coffee and raspberry together. We would sit on the curb eating our cones by his motorcycle.

"Sometimes we sat in my house with a tape recorder because I was trying to improve my English and my accent. But he didn't want me to change the accent, he loved it. We talked endlessly about everything: his childhood, his aunt Ortense, who he loved, and his father, who he didn't care for. He rarely mentioned Pier although I knew about her. We often talked about Europe. He wanted so much to go there with me: he wanted to marry me but I always told him that I was still in love with John. Jimmy said that he felt like a caged animal because of his contract with the studio, and he said he was willing to give up everything to go to Europe and feel free. He wanted life and love and not only a career. Although he was a very aggressive, ambitious actor he was very sensitive, with beautiful feelings.

"Sometimes he would pick me up on his motorcycle at Marlon Brando's. Marlon was engaged to Josianne [Berenger, a French fisherman's daughter] and I would visit her there, and we would practice English together. But Marlon was very strange toward Jimmy, and very upset when he would arrive. Marlon would ask me, 'What are you doing with this boy? Why do you go out with him?' "

Although Jimmy was spending a lot of time with Ursula, I got the impression from him that they were buddies rather than lovers, an impression Ursula confirmed during a recent interview.

Because I was on the set of *Rebel* so often, and accepted as Jimmy's friend, I was able to observe some of the fun and games that almost invariably take place when the actors are well fed and happy with their work. For example, there was a lot of down time on the planetarium set while the cameras were being set up or moved. Jimmy frequently drove his Porsche to the location, and during breaks he would race it around the parking lot, offering rides to anyone who dared go with him. One day he asked Bev Long if she wanted to go for a spin. She declined, saying he drove too fast. "I've got to," retorted Jim. "I'm not going to be around too long." Then he giggled and sped off. "It was a kind of romantic line," says Bev. "But he was an actor and I thought he was just being theatrical."

It was throwaway lines like this that later would prompt some people to believe that Jimmy had a death wish or a premonition of his death. I, however, tend to agree with Bev's interpretation—that Jimmy's innate sense of drama was at the heart of such comments.

The gang sometimes played charades to stave off the boredom on the set. Jimmy's imagination and creative ability to improvise was impressive. It seemed to me that he could mimic anything or anyone. He would also do impersonations, including a first-rate Charlie Chaplin. He had the walk and attitude down pat, and did first-rate with the click of the heels.

Once, during a game of charades, Nick Adams was up, and everyone had their eyes on him. Nick wasn't aware that Jimmy was standing behind him and doing everything he did. The group roared with laughter, and Nick thought they were laughing at him. Jimmy broke a doughnut in half and stuck a piece in each of his ears. Then he did a pirouette and sat in a trash can. Nick heard that, turned around, and said, "I don't think that's very funny." He pouted the rest of the afternoon.

Nick Ray was often the target of jokes. One day someone suggested that Natalie stuff big falsies in her brassiere. When she appeared on the set for a scene with Jimmy, Nick did a double take and then broke up laughing.

Jimmy was also the butt of a joke organized by producer David Weisbart, who was probably the best-liked person on the set. Somehow Weisbart had managed to obtain an official summons from a magistrate's court in New York. He arranged to have the summons served by a studio policeman while Jimmy was at lunch with the cast and crew. Jimmy read the summons and shouted, "What the hell is this, it's not possible!" Everyone broke up with laughter. The summons ordered Jimmy to appear in a Brooklyn court to answer a charge made against him by police officer Nick Ray. The charge was rape.

Jimmy was somewhat of an enigma to the actor gang members in the cast, all of whom were younger than him. Having seen *Eden*, most of them were impressed with his talent so they tolerated what they considered his eccentricities. "In the mornings you never knew whether he was going to speak to you," says Bev Long. "That made you extremely wary, because one morning you would say, 'Good morning, Jim,' and he would look through you as though you didn't exist. On another morning you would not say hello, and he would say, 'Well, good morning,' like his feelings were hurt, and then he would give out with that mischievous grin and giggle. You never could win."

He could also be a tease. One day he went over to Bev Long carrying a manila envelope and asked her if she wanted to see some pictures. "From the way he said it, I was sure they were dirty pictures," Beverly told me. "You never could know with him. So I was very cautious and said okay. Then he opened the envelope and took out some pictures. They were of him racing in Palm Springs. He proceeded to describe each picture in minute detail along with a running commentary of every minute in the race. He was really like a little boy, very shy and very unsophisticated. He was an enigma to all of us."

Because of his recent celebrity Jimmy was wary of most strangers: he told me once that everybody new he met seemed to want something from him. During the filming of *Rebel* he narrowed his circle of friends down to only a few people, plus one or two in the cast.

Faye Nuell, Natalie's double, was one of the few girls that Jimmy seemed to truly like, probably because he felt comfortable with her around. She sometimes met him for breakfast at Googie's, drove him on errands, and occasionally visited him in his dressing room. "There were times when I was in his dressing room and he'd tell me, 'I don't feel like talking, but stay anyway.' I would sit there and read while he listened to music and played his bongo drums."

Jimmy had told Nick Adams that I was studying kenpo karate. Karate was just coming into vogue then, and Nick asked me to take Jimmy and him to one of my classes. I arranged with my instructor, Ed Parker, to put on a private demonstration for just the two of them. Jimmy was not overly impressed: "I still think a finger in the eye and a kick in the balls is the most effective way to end a fight."

Nick Adams, who was far less secure in his ability to fight than Jimmy, started to take private lessons from Ed. Occasionally I would go by his house during a lesson to see how he was doing and to work out with him.

Saturday mornings I usually went horseback riding with Hank Fine, a publicist born in my hometown of Brookline, Massachusetts. Hank had gone out west and become a real cowboy before coming to Hollywood, and he enjoyed taking neophytes out riding on rented horses in Griffith Park. I invited Jimmy, Nick Adams, and Natalie to join me. Jimmy declined. "I'm really not that good a rider," he said, "and I don't want them [Nick and Nat] to know it. They think I'm good because I grew up on a farm."

"But you may have to ride in *Giant*," I said.

"I've already arranged for Monty to come up from Salinas and double for me," said Jimmy.

On May 1, without telling anyone at the studio, Jimmy entered another road race. This one was held in the rain at Bakersfield's Minter Field, and although he finished third in the main event, he was first in his class.

Five days later, Jimmy made his last television drama, playing the role of a hitchhiker who gets a job and innocently becomes involved with criminals in "The Unlighted Road," an episode of CBS's *Schlitz Playhouse of Stars*.

On Saturday, May 14, Jimmy had a night call for shooting. Faye Nuell's diary notes that she was on location to double Natalie, and had dinner with Jimmy on the set at 9:00 P.M. "Sat and talked with Jimmy in his dressing room until 3:30 A.M. Rode with him around the ranch [where the chicken run was shot]. 6:30 Jim drove me back to the studio. Then met him at Googie's for breakfast at 8 A.M."

Jimmy's own note pad for May 17 has some doodles of plants, ferns, and a five-pointed star on top of the page. Below it he had written a list of names and telephone numbers: "F. Worth— pictures to show me [Frank Worth, a Hollywood photographer], Carli and Kathleen, Marilyn Morrison [daughter of the owner of the Mocambo nightclub, whom he occasionally dated], Marla English [Paramount starlet], Van der Hiedi [Heide]—change date Judd Marmor."

Judd Marmor was a prominent psychoanalyst in Beverly Hills, less orthodox than most traditional Freudian analysts: he has since emerged as a renowned authority in the area of homosexuality. I don't know who recommended Dr. Marmor to Jimmy, but I do know he was in the process of switching analysts because, he said, "It's the dreams, man. I have to figure them out." Dr. Marmor saw Jimmy only twice.

At some point around the first week of June I saw Jimmy in the studio parking lot. "Have I got something to show you," he said and reached into the glove compartment of the Porsche. He took out a piece of paper and handed it to me. It was from his local draft board. Jimmy was found "not acceptable for induction."

"How'd you get so lucky?" I asked him.

"Flat feet, bad eyes, butt fucking, who knows? Your guess is as good as mine," Jimmy said and laughed. "What counts is the draft isn't hanging over my head anymore. I can do *Giant* after all. And I'm free to do anything else I want."

On Memorial Day weekend, the day after his scenes in *Rebel* were completed, Jimmy entered the third annual Santa Barbara Road Races in the under 1500 cc class. Starting eighteenth, he had worked his way up to fourth when another Porsche cut in front of him. To avoid a collision, Jimmy swerved and sideswiped some of the bales of hay that lined the course as a protective barrier. He resumed his pace, however, and was back in fourth place when the Speedster blew a piston, and he was forced to quit.

When he returned home, Jimmy mounted the piston on a board and gave it to Winton as a souvenir of the race.

While the engine of his Porsche was being rebuilt, he told Johnny Von Neumann, the owner of Competition Motors where he had bought the car, that the Speedster was too slow. He wanted something faster. Von Neumann was expecting a few Porsche 550s, called Spyders, early in September and promised that Jimmy could have one. But Jimmy was impatient: he contacted the local Lotus dealer and special ordered a Lotus Mk9, to be made to his specifications.

George Stevens was already in production on *Giant* in Virginia. When he heard that Jimmy had been in a race he telephoned him at home and made him promise that he would not race again until *Giant* was completed. Unlike Nick Ray, Stevens had no intention of pampering Jimmy.

From Virginia the *Giant* company moved to Marfa, Texas, a desert town fifty-nine miles from the Mexican border. Along with the rest of the cast, Jimmy was to travel by Southern Pacific railway to Marfa for six weeks of shooting.

Just as he had originally feared working with Nick Ray, Jimmy had many misgivings about his coming work with George Stevens. Unlike Kazan and Ray, Stevens was not known as an actor's director. He was, rather, a technician who shot thousands of feet of film—taking each scene from every conceivable angle—and then assembled it in the cutting room. For the first time, Jimmy was not going to be the star of the production and, perhaps even more importantly, for the first time he was going to be working among strangers—very famous strangers—far away from his home and friends.

Shortly after work ended on *Rebel*, Ann Doran was awakened at her home around three in the morning. Someone was standing out in her front yard yelling, "Mom! Mom!" She stuck her head out the window and called back, "Who's there? You're going to wake up all the neighbors."

From someplace out in the darkness below her she heard a drunken voice call out, "It's your son Jimmy." Doran went downstairs, opened the front door, and invited Jimmy in for some coffee. The two of them then sat on the floor of her kitchen, and he opened his heart to her, talking about his loneliness and his fears. When he finally left, the sun was just coming up. This was only the first of several such visits. It was clear to Doran that Jimmy needed someone to talk to.

It was true. He came by my house early one evening and said he didn't feel like being alone and wanted someone to talk with. He asked if I would go for a ride with him: we were to meet Lew on top of Mulholland Drive and go for a spin. Happily, Mulholland was rarely busy at that time of the evening. Lew was gunning his motor as we went by, and I could hear his Buick roaring behind us.

As we came to a ninety-degree curve the speedometer needle flickered between sixty and sixty-five and I was certain we would not safely make it. Jimmy hit the brakes hard, shifting from fourth to second, and went into the curve with the car drifting to the far edge of the road where there was a very steep drop-off. I was well aware that more than one amateur racer had gone off the road on that particular curve, and I braced himself. But Jimmy adroitly accelerated out of the curve into a series of S curves, which he drove through in a straight line.

On the next curve, I heard the squealing of Lew's Buick coming up fast on the outside. By the time we reached another curve the cars were almost abreast; quickly, Jimmy double declutched and down shifted, then roared into the curve with enough speed to keep him in front of Lew.

Right before we reached the Japanese home of *Los Angeles Times* food and wine expert Robert Baltzer (a home later bought by Marlon Brando), Jimmy abruptly turned off the road into a patch of dirt, flicked the gearshift into neutral, twisted the steering wheel, and grabbed the hand brake: the trick Rod Amateau had taught him. We did a complete 180-degree turn and came out of the spin almost face-to-face with Lew, who roared on by.

My stomach caught up with me as we drove back along Mulholland at a more sedate speed, waiting for Lew to catch up with us.

Suddenly, Jimmy broke the silence. "You studied psychology in college," he said, looking in his rear-view mirror for Lew.

"A little."

"Then tell me what you think of this. Last night I dreamed of my mother again. In the dream I was a child, and my mother was calling to me. We were in a desert and I tried to run to her but my feet kept plunging into the sand. With each step I took toward her she seemed to drift away so the distance between us was constant no matter how hard I ran. She was trying to say something to me—something I knew was important—but I was never able to get close enough to hear her words clearly. Then I awoke from the dream with the sensation of falling."

Jimmy put a hand on my arm just as we came into another curve. I watched nervously as he negotiated it with only one hand on the wheel. "Well, what do you think of it?" he asked. A shadow crossed his face. "Does it mean I am going to die soon?"

"Only if you insist on driving flat out on curves like these. And I'm not ready to die yet, so take it easy."

Jimmy didn't smile. "I'm serious."

I looked at him and tried to recall what little he had told me of his childhood. I knew about his mother and how she had died of cancer. I also knew about how he had gone with his mother's coffin on the train from California back to Fairmount. He had told me that he kept a lock of his mother's hair, cut from her forehead while she was in the coffin, in an envelope under his pillow for weeks. I knew all that but had no means of determining its effect on Jimmy.

I suspected that, perhaps through his analysis, he was finally beginning to come to grips with the loss of his mother and that perhaps she was finally trying to say goodbye to him. But I also knew just enough about dreams to realize that any interpretation I could offer would probably be wrong, and I sensed that what he was really asking for was reassurance. So I told him what I thought he probably wanted to hear. "I think it probably means that your mother didn't have a last chance to tell you she loved you and that's what she's trying to tell you in the dream."

Jimmy's hands relaxed a little on the steering wheel, and his face became more placid. He nodded. "I know she loved me. She loved me more than anything."

Chapter Fourteen

GIANT

Jimmy was especially nervous on June 3, his first day before the cameras in *Giant*. George Stevens had an open set, and most of the 2,500 residents of Marfa were standing behind a roped-off area on the Worth Evans Ranch watching the filming of a scene between Jimmy and Liz Taylor.

After several takes, Stevens was still not satisfied. Jimmy walked away from the set and faced the crowd. Standing squarely in front of everyone, he unzipped his pants, took out his penis, and calmly urinated before them. He then zipped his pants back up, returned to the set, and announced to the astonished director, "Okay, let's go. I'm ready."

Dennis Hopper, whom Jimmy had come to like while working on *Rebel*, was also cast in *Giant*, and he was flabbergasted by Jimmy's behavior and asked him why he did it. "I was nervous," Jimmy told him. "If you're nervous your senses can't reach your subconscious, and that's that—you just can't work. So I figured if I could piss in front of all those people, and be cool about it, I could go in front of the camera and do just about anything at all."

Stevens and Jimmy soon began to have conflicts. The fifty-one-year-old director, who had started his career in 1921 in silent movies as a cameraman, not only shot every scene from every possible angle but was determined that his actors hit their lines precisely so he could control the focus.

Stevens put marks where he wanted Jimmy to stand during a scene, and Jimmy said he didn't use marks. Stevens retorted that the cameraman used them.

"I wanted to nail him quick," Stevens told me during an on-set interview. "There's always a testing period in the beginning of a picture when an actor wants to find out who's boss. Jimmy was predisposed to do a scene as he saw it, and I had my way of doing it.

"Very seldom does an actor entirely favor the director's way. Some actors, and Jimmy was one of them, are too ready to debate the director's point of view, and I found myself imposing it."

Despite the conflict between them, Stevens was getting a good performance from Jimmy, and they both knew it. Also, Jimmy was secretly watching every movement Stevens made: he was taking notes and making sketches of camera angles in a little book. Before going to Marfa he had told Lew and me at dinner that he wanted to form his own company and make independent pictures as a director. "I want to direct because I can be a better director than actor," he said. He had even bought a 16mm Bolex movie camera with three lenses so he could start by shooting his own short films.

Marfa offered few distractions for Jimmy. The dusty little town—stricken by seven years of drought—had one small grocery store, a used-car lot, three cafés, two bars, a movie theater called the Palace—which had been closed for two years—two motels, and two hotels. Most of the cast were staying in one of the two hotels, but Stevens had Rock Hudson, Chill Wills, and Jimmy put up together in a private home. Like Elia Kazan before him, Stevens knew that rooming his stars together was certain to help them develop the friction and animosity they would need for their roles in the film. The trio drank Lone Star beer out of red Coca-Cola cups and had a running poker game, although Jimmy once confided to me that he didn't like Rock, but he never gave a specific reason.

Jimmy also spent time with former rodeo star Bob Hinkle, a Texan who had been hired to teach the non-native actors Texas dialects. Some nights they borrowed one of the film company's Jeeps and drove out onto the desert with Hinkle at the wheel and Jimmy sitting on a fender with a .22 rifle plinking at jackrabbits illuminated by the Jeep's headlights.

Jimmy and Dennis Hopper became close on the location and devised ways to entertain themselves. Joe Hamilton, a young student who was working as night clerk at the El Paisano Lodge, recalls a night when Jimmy and Dennis came bursting through the double doors from the patio, roaring with laughter and holding out a woman's skirt, blouse, bra, slip, and panties for him to see. Then they ran out onto the main street.

Hamilton followed them outside where the company parked the five black limousines that took the cast to work each morning. He saw a head bobbing up and down in one of the cars and recognized a young woman who worked as a waitress with the catering company from El Paso.

When he went to the car the girl whimpered, "Joe, they talked me out of my clothes and then ran off."

Hamilton went back into the hotel and removed a blanket from the linen closet. He gave it to the nude girl, who wrapped it around herself and disappeared into the night.

When Monty Roberts, Jimmy's old friend from Salinas, was not working as a wrangler on the film, he continued teaching Jimmy rope tricks. "He really kind of aspired to be a Will Rogers type," Monty recalls. "He wanted to be quiet and occasionally say something intellectually deep while he twirled the rope." One day Jimmy told Monty that everybody had told him he was going to make a lot of money in the future. "This may sound crazy, but I've got them fooled," Jimmy said. "I have managers now that are telling me I have to get my money in real estate, so be on the lookout for a good buy in a ranch around the Salinas area."

Jimmy also made friends with Sandy Roth, an ex–ad man who had become a popular photographer: his portraits of Picasso and Einstein had impressed Jimmy. Roth was on assignment from *Collier's* magazine to take photographs of the *Giant* cast.

As usual, Jimmy found mother surrogates on the location. His principal female allies were Mercedes McCambridge and Liz Taylor. Mercedes has been quoted often as saying of Jimmy, "I can't tell you how he wanted to be patted. He was the runt in a litter of thoroughbreds, and you could feel the loneliness beating out of him."

Jimmy was probably closest to Elizabeth Taylor, who saw many sides of his character. She recalls how she often sat up with Jimmy until 3.00 A.M. talking. "He would tell me about his past life, some of the grief and unhappiness he had experienced, and some of his loves and tragedies. Then, the next day on the set, I would say, 'Hi, Jimmy,' and he would give me a cursory nod of his head. It was almost as if he didn't want to recognize me, as if he was ashamed of having revealed so much of himself the night before. It would take maybe a day or two for him to become my friend again."

One of the first persons Jimmy saw when he returned from Marfa to Hollywood to continue filming at the studio was Lilli Kardell, who had forgiven him for not writing or calling while he was away. On July 12, Lilli wrote in her diary: "Was with Jimmy. Villa Capri with Jimmy. Made love first. Then Nick Ray's house. Came home. Claire [Kelly, a Paramount contract player] here. Jim stayed until 7 [A.M.]. Talked with Claire the whole time."

A few nights later Jimmy went to the Villa Capri for dinner with Ursula Andress and Lew. After dinner they drove up Sunset Boulevard and stopped to look in Ernie MacAfee's show window where several high-powered racers were on display. "A helluva way to spend a date on a nice summer evening," Lew wryly told me later.

Jimmy's dates with Ursula soon led to his arriving late on the set, something Stevens couldn't tolerate. In turn, Jimmy was furious when he did show up on time and had to sit around for hours waiting for his scenes.

Jimmy didn't show up at all on August 23, the day he moved into a log house on Sutton Street in Sherman Oaks that he had rented for $250 a month from Nikko Romanos, the maitre d' at the Villa Capri. Jimmy later told the studio that he was too tired to work but, as luck would have it, early that morning Mercedes fell out of bed and broke her arm. She arrived on the set on time, but with her broken arm in a sling.

Stevens waited in vain for Jimmy all day. The next day when Jimmy arrived Stevens berated him in front of the entire cast and crew using Mercedes as an example of professionalism, finally working himself into a caustic rage while Jimmy stood silently and took it.

Later that week Tom Pryor, correspondent for *The New York Times*, went into the projection room with Stevens to see some early rushes of *Giant*. When Dean came on the screen, Stevens turned to Pryor and said, "Just once, I'd like to fire the bastard." In recalling the incident, Pryor said, "Stevens wasn't really bitter. I think he was annoyed that a man of his stature was not catered to by a young man of almost no stature at all in his view."

Jimmy knew he was in trouble with the director, and as was his habit he took to calling his friends late at night to unburden his soul. The most frequent recipient of his calls was Eartha Kitt, then in New York. Jimmy called Eartha almost every night—usually waking her up—and she sensed that he was so upset that he dreaded going before the cameras each day. He vowed to Eartha that when the film was complete he would never go to see it.

Jimmy also called his old friend Rod Steiger and said he had to talk with him. Steiger asked what the problem was. "George Stevens doesn't know how to direct," said Jimmy. "Please, come have lunch with me at Warner."

The conversation continued over a steak at the studio where Jimmy told Steiger about his problems with Stevens. Steiger, an intelligent and thoughtful man, tried to quiet Jimmy down and give him some advice. "Maybe Stevens doesn't know how to help you because he doesn't know that much about acting, but when something is good he knows how to use it and put a picture together. Don't argue with him in front of the company. Do what I do, say, 'You gave me an idea,' or do it first and then let him say something, but don't get into a discussion or an argument and get emotional."

When they were almost through with lunch, Jimmy called to the waitress. "Sweetheart, come here," he said. "I don't like this steak."

The waitress protested, "But, Mr. Dean, you've eaten three-quarters of it."

"Honey, this is Hollywood," said Jimmy. "Take it back."

In recalling the incident, Steiger says, "This was the only time I heard Jimmy say something that bothered me. I looked at him, surrounded by a lot of people, and I thought, 'We're going to destroy him.' "

Although Jimmy was out with Ursula most evenings, he still

occasionally dropped by the Villa Capri for dinner alone. One night while he was there he spotted Arlene Sachs, his old girlfriend from New York, sitting at a table with another very pretty girl. Jimmy picked a strawberry out of a bowl of fruit, and holding it in his hand, walked over to their table. Ignoring Arlene, he turned to the other girl, dropped the strawberry onto her plate, and introduced himself. She was Janette Miller, a tall brunette who had been one of the most popular girls at Hollywood High when she graduated a few years earlier. Jimmy asked Janette if she would like to go to a karate class with him, and she accepted.

Although Jimmy had declined to study with Ed Parker, he sometimes showed up at a nighttime karate class to watch me work out, but I was surprised to see him with a date. He left, however, before the class was over. When I saw him later and asked about the girl he was with, he said only that she was a friend of Arlene's and he was showing her around town.

Janette, who is now a psychologist, liked Jimmy, although she found him strange, almost macabre. "He had a really hard time being straight with people. Always this masked man, and inside was this depressed child who would draw on napkins phallic pictures of any person he disliked. But his masks were so inventive and colorful that you couldn't help but be fascinated by them.

"I felt that Hollywood exploited his dark side, his eccentricities and his psychological hang-ups. And it worked really well for the studios. But he was angry at the people who were abusive or exploitative, and especially angry at those who challenged him."

There was always another side to Jimmy, however, a side few people were fortunate to see. But those who witnessed it never forgot it. Oscar Levant, one of my favorite people in Hollywood, experienced Jimmy's kinder side. Neurotic and hypochondriacal, Levant was also the most erudite man I had ever met, and I enjoyed every moment with him, although such moments could be trying.

One night I picked Oscar up at his Beverly Hills home to take him to dinner at Chasen's restaurant, a drive that would normally take under five minutes. But I was with Oscar, and there were many streets in Beverly Hills that Oscar absolutely refused to travel on. Each time I turned onto one such street he'd yell, "No, no, a bad thing happened to me on this street two years ago. We can't go down it." So I'd turn back and try to go down another. "No, no," Oscar would call out, saying that someone or other lived on the street—someone he didn't like—so we'd have to use another.

The short drive to the restaurant thus took more than half an hour, and during that time, going up and down back streets, Oscar told me a story about Jimmy.

Oscar's fifteen-year-old daughter, Marcia, had seen *Eden* and fallen completely and hopelessly in love with Jimmy. The walls of her bedroom were literally covered with his photos. On a recent night, Arthur Loew, Jr. had called Oscar from a restaurant saying he was with a group of people, and could they come over? Even though it was late, Oscar and his wife, June, were delighted to have company. Within a few minutes Arthur showed up at the door with Liz Taylor, her husband Michael Wilding, Joan Collins, Henry Ginsberg, producer of *Giant*, Jimmy, and a couple of girls he had picked up at the restaurant. Liz and Jimmy were still in makeup for their roles.

Joan knew that Marcia wanted nothing more than to meet Jimmy. With Joan leading the way and Elizabeth, Jimmy, and June in tow, they went up the stairs to Marcia's bedroom where she was asleep. Jimmy sat by the edge of the bed and touched Marcia lightly with the tip of his finger on her nose. She turned over and brushed the hand away. Jimmy giggled and Marcia woke up and saw Jimmy. She screeched and dove under the blankets.

Everyone laughed. Jimmy walked around the room looking at her collection of his pictures and finally said, "Come on out, and come downstairs with us, Marcia. I want to talk to you."

Marcia came downstairs wearing a robe. Jimmy spent half an hour in a corner talking with Marcia about school and her friends, and her life. She sat open-mouthed and hanging on to his every word until, finally, he said gently, "You'd better go back to bed. We're all tired." Marcia's eyes were still glazed with excitement as she went up the stairs.

After the others left, Oscar, who was also an insomniac, talked with Jimmy about Bach, Mozart, Arthur Honegger, Charles Ives, and Stan Getz. They hummed portions of scores together and listened to records. A piano virtuoso and composer himself, Oscar played bits of his own compositions. Jimmy left at 4:00 A.M. "An amazing young man," Oscar told me. "He knows so much about music, and he was so considerate of Marcia."

Hearing the story—while busy backing out of yet another street that Oscar simply could not drive down—I remembered Jimmy's story of his mother's wishing game. When he could, Jimmy always tried to make children's wishes come true.

Stewart Stern hadn't seen Jimmy since the end of work on *Rebel*. He was at Arthur Loew, Jr.'s home one night, standing alone at the bar, when someone came up behind him and put gloved hands over his eyes. He smelled leather and knew it was Jimmy before he turned around.

"I didn't know you were back," he said to Jimmy.

Jimmy smiled and said, "Let's go outside for a walk."

They went out into the garden by the pool where there was a nearby barbecue pit. The two felt close, it was a special moment in their friendship, one of the nicest they had together. They didn't speak, just stood there enjoying it. Then, all of a sudden, Jimmy said, "If my mother hadn't died when she did, I would have been queer." That was all he said, and Stewart made no comment although he at first thought it an odd, curious thing for Jimmy to say. After thinking about it some more, Stewart finally concluded that, somehow through his analysis, Jimmy had determined that if he had remained overconnected to his (seductive) mother and pampered by her he would have turned into a momma's boy. But Stewart, who was a relatively new friend of Jimmy's, knew nothing about Jimmy's sexual proclivities.

During one of the days *Giant* was filming at the studio, I went to visit Jimmy at his dressing room. He was in an unusually somber mood. I asked him if something was troubling him. Again, he talked about the dreams. "They don't stop," he said. "It's like my mother is trying to tell me something, but I don't know what it is."

"What's your new shrink say about the dreams?" I asked, this time trying to avoid offering an interpretation.

"He tells me I'm getting near some kind of breakthrough in my analysis. According to him, the fact that my mother is trying to say something to me means something big."

Toward the end of August I went to see Jimmy's new house. He showed it off to me proudly. As I recall, the house had no bedroom, just a second-floor alcove where he slept, reached by a wooden ladder. There was a seven-foot-tall stone fireplace in the large living room with a white bearskin rug on the hearth. An old-fashioned wheel lamp hung from the beamed ceiling. Nikko had left behind an enormous bronzed eagle, with wings and talons outstretched as though screaming in on its prey. As with most of the places where I had visited Jimmy, there was a clutter of dirty dishes, cameras, bongo drums, and clothes: it was obvious that Susan Bray, his weekly maid, had not been in to clean for some time. State-of-the-art James B. Lansing loudspeakers were stacked almost to the ceiling with two large horns suspended from the beams: Jimmy liked his music only one way—loud! Record albums were on every flat surface, and the walls were hung with the bullfight posters, bullfight paraphernalia, and Sidney Franklin's cape.

When I got through expressing admiration for his lucky find—it was indeed a perfect house for him—Jimmy sat cross-legged on the floor, picked up a wooden recorder, and began to play some discordant tune with a rapturous look on his face.

I applauded the noise he was making, and Jimmy put down the flute. "Would you do a favor for me?" he asked.

He had never asked for a favor before, and I was flattered. "Name it and you've got it," I said.

He picked up the recorder again and tootled a few notes. "You remember I told you about Ursula Andress?"

"After you told me about her I checked with Paramount. A publicist said she's only eighteen years old, and she's being groomed as a young Marlene Dietrich. He also said that she's being kept under wraps, and he wanted to know how I'd heard about her. I told him I'd seen her in the commissary and was just curious."

Jimmy grinned. "They'll never do anything with her unless she gets some publicity on her own, so I volunteered to be her press agent. She thinks I'm a hotshot Hollywood type, but the truth is you're the only newspaper friend I have. Will you write about her and make me a big man with my girl?"

"You have a deal," I said. "But in exchange I want to write about you. I never have, you know, and it's time I did. If we weren't friends I'd have written a column about you long ago."

"You're on," said Jimmy, who agreed to arrange the interview with Ursula since I couldn't ask any of my press contacts at Paramount to do it.

For my column the next day I wrote about Jimmy and described him as "the hottest young actor in Hollywood." A few days later, he called to say he had read my column and liked it, and the interview with Ursula was set for four o'clock that day. He gave me her address.

It was dusk when I arrived at a small guest house on a side street in a modest area of Hollywood. Ursula was on the lawn waiting for me, wearing an old blue sweatshirt, several sizes too large, and faded blue jeans. Her feet were bare. She was carrying a Siamese kitten in her arms, and by her side was a huge German shepherd that watched my every move so closely I didn't dare shake hands with her. A miniature French poodle, presumably Josianne's, was waiting inside, tail wagging, as we walked through the door of her house, which was a shambles with clothes and luggage everywhere.

Ursula put the cat down and picked up the poodle. "The studio tol' me I shouldn't talk to nobody," she said. "You a nice man and a friend of Jimmy so I talk with you. Jimmy a nice boy but he come by my house one hour late. I hate to wait. He come in room like animal in cage. Walk around and sniff of things like an animal. I don' like. We go hear jazz music and he leave table. Say he going play drums. He no play drums, no come back. I don' like be alone. I better go home.

"He come by here later with motorsickle. Say he sorry and ask if I want see motorsickle. We sit on walk in front of motorsickle and talk until five. He nice but only boy."

I sat down on a couch between the shepherd and the poodle and made some notes about Ursula. She had short blond hair in a boyish cut and almond-shaped dark eyes framed by black eyebrows. Her face was oval, and she had a generous, full mouth, strong, healthy teeth, and a straight nose. She also had a boy's figure except for a big bosom.

Physically, she was a total contrast with Pier, except that they were both Europeans. I thought Ursula one of the most attractive young actresses I had seen for some time, and it was obvious why the studio had such high hopes for her.

"Do you know anyone else in Hollywood besides Jimmy?" I asked her.

"I know Marlon Brando two-three-four years," Ursula said in very accented English. "My friends in Europe tell me I look like him, talk like him, act like him. I am female Marlon Brando, they say. They tell him about me, too. Finally we meet."

She smiled. I got the impression that Marlon was one of her boyfriends and made a mental note to interview him about her if she were to become well known. And, since she had mentioned it, I did see a resemblance between her and Marlon. While talking she used her arms, not just her hands, as he did. She also had his habit of lowering her head so she looked up at the person she was talking to.

"How did you get discovered?" I asked.

Ursula tucked her bare feet underneath her on the couch. "Paramount chase me all over Europe and test me in Rome. They say they have picture in Hollywood for me so I sign. Hollywood inters' me. Everything inters' me but only little while. Then I tire. I am learning English only four months. When I talk it good they put me in a picture. If they don', I go back to Italy.

"I am no beauty queen who not know feelings. I am actress. I act with eyes and heart. I shouldn't talk with press because I am under wraps. What that mean?"

"That means they don't want anyone to write a story about you," I said as I put away my notes.

My column in the *Tribune* two days later (on July 11) was head-lined: A FEMALE BRANDO.

The publicity department at Paramount was not happy that I had broken a story on their new discovery, the girl they had taken such pains to keep secret. Jimmy called me and complained about my description of Ursula as a female Brando. "There's no more resemblance between her and Marlon than there is between her and me." Other than that, he thought the story was great, "just what was needed to get the ball rolling." He was right. Within a few days Ursula was deluged with requests for interviews, and I was back in the studio's good graces.

Leonard Rosenman was at Lew's parents' home on a night when Jimmy arrived with Ursula. "Holy Christ, he's got a twin of himself there," he told me later. I realized that he was absolutely on target: she did resemble Jimmy more than Marlon—they even dressed alike in matching white T-shirts and Levi's, to emphasize their resemblance—and I was a fool not to have realized it.

Jimmy telephoned me on August 1 to say that he had just read my column on Cecil B. DeMille's chair boy, Justin Buehrlin, a former tank driver with Rommel in Africa. It was Justin's job on *The Ten Commandments* to anticipate Mr. DeMille by having one of three chairs or two padded stools ready and in place whenever the great director indicated that he wanted to sit. "Funniest column I ever read," said Jimmy. "That Justin is a real ass man." With that Jimmy burst into giggles and hung up.

I was busy for much of the following week writing about actress Suzan Ball, who had died of cancer on August 5: she had lost a leg to the disease two years earlier, but had bravely continued acting. Her death came only a few days after a plane crash in Burbank that claimed the life of Robert Francis, a promising young actor who had a starring role in *The Caine Mutiny*.

On the night of Suzan's death Jimmy went out with his old friends Maila Nurmi and Jack Simmons. While they were walking down a street they saw the newspaper headline. Jimmy turned to his friends and said, "Such deaths always happen in threes. Well, I'll be the next." Maila was to remember his words although at the time Jimmy was just putting a spin on the old show biz tradition.

On August 12, I went on the set of *Giant* looking for Jimmy only to find that he was at the dentist having a wisdom tooth pulled. However, the press agent introduced me to Edna Ferber, who was on the set watching the filming of her book. Ferber, who was then sixty-eight, was a tiny woman with white, freshly waved hair. She said she had seen Jimmy on Broadway in *The Immoralist* and thought him miscast, but she liked him in *East of Eden*. She described Jimmy's nonconformist attitude as "success poisoning," a disease she had when she had two hits on Broadway within a week of each other. For months, she said, she "didn't want to see or talk with anyone."

I lost touch with Jimmy for a few days. When I asked Lew what Jimmy was doing, he said that he had been at the studio almost every day and planned to spend the weekend with Lilli. Her diary for Sunday, August 14, confirms that. The entry reads: "Jimmy came over in the afternoon. Drove me to his house, were there a couple of hours. He went to Frank Sinatra's party at the Villa Capri with another girl. I was never invited. Was at home the whole day alone. Nobody called. Everything was so depressing and sad. I am not happy anymore."

The other girl was Ursula, and the gathering was a bon voyage party that Sinatra threw for owner Patsy D'Amore, who was soon to leave for a cruise with his wife, Rose. Sammy Davis, Jr., and other members of Sinatra's Rat Pack were on hand, along with comedian Milton Berle and columnist Sidney Skolsky. Jimmy joked with the other guests. He'd brought a camera along and took a few pictures.

On Sunday, August 21, 1955, Pier Angeli was rushed to the maternity ward of Cedars of Lebanon Hospital in Los Angeles where, by cesarian delivery, she gave birth to an eight-pound, thirteen-ounce son, who was named Perry, after Vic Damone's friend Perry Como.

That night Lew had dinner with Jimmy at the Villa Capri. Vic Damone came over to their table holding a bottle of champagne.

"Come on," he said to Jimmy. "Let's drink a toast to my son."

The three men raised their glasses and drank the champagne. Jimmy said nothing until Damone walked back to his table. Then he turned to Lew and said, "I'll drink a toast to *my* son anytime."

Two days later, at lunch with an old girlfriend, Damone confided, "Pier's a mother all right, but I'm not so certain I'm a father."

Early in September the California Highway Patrol contacted Warner to ask for Jimmy to do a public service announcement promoting safe driving that would appear on one of the studio's television shows. William Orr called Dick Clayton and told him about the request. Clayton said he'd talk with Jimmy. He telephoned Orr a few days later and reported, "I spoke to him, and Jimmy doesn't want to do it."

"What do you mean?" said Orr. "It's not for Warner, it's for public safety, for Christ's sake. Talk to him again." Clayton refused to take it up with Jimmy again.

"Well, then," said Orr, "where is the little SOB? I'll ask him myself." Orr learned that Jimmy was on a studio soundstage. He hung around on the stage for an hour until the scene was filmed and then followed Jimmy back to his dressing room. He found Jimmy sitting on the day bed.

"Listen," said Orr, "I've just been talking with Dick Clayton. You've got to do this highway safety thing. It's not for Warner, it's for the Highway Patrol."

"I'm not doing anyone any favors," snapped Jimmy.

When Orr repeated the request, Jimmy stood up and said, "I'm not going to do it."

"Sit down," said Orr, angrily pushing Jimmy down on the bed, an act so completely out of character for the usually mild-mannered studio executive that it amused Jimmy.

Jimmy grinned sheepishly and said, "All right, if it means that much to you, I'll do it."

The next day, John Veitch flagged down Jimmy, who was driving his Porsche too fast on one of the Warner studio streets. Veitch, the studio production executive on each of Jimmy's pictures, had cautioned Jimmy many times about the way he drove around the lot at double the posted speeds of five or ten miles an hour. On this day he gave Jimmy a short lecture.

"You're going to get yourself killed driving like that, or you may hurt somebody else."

"Okay," said Jimmy, "I'll take care."

Jimmy knew that once the picture was ended, however, his race driving was no longer the studio's business, and he told one of the press agents about his future race plans. On Friday, September 16, the Warner publicity department issued a press release, stating: "James Dean plans to go on a racing kick when *Giant* ends."

That night, Jimmy had dinner with Janette Miller at the Villa Capri. After a meal of pasta and wine they drove by Competition Motors on North Vine Street in Hollywood and looked at the cars in the showroom window. Earlier in the day Lew had told Jimmy there was a new silver Porsche 550 Spyder on display, and Jimmy wanted to see it. He and Janette went around to the garage in back, where he introduced her to Rolf Weutherich, a darkly handsome twenty-eight-year-old German mechanic who was working late. Jimmy told Weutherich, "I'm going to buy the Spyder on the condition that you personally check it before each race and that you go with me to the races." Weutherich, who spoke and understood only a limited amount of English, said that was fine with him if "The Chef" (Von Neumann) agreed.

The following morning Jimmy reported early to the studio to redo the "Last Supper" scene, a banquet in which he was to appear as a man forty-six years old. Jimmy had refused to wear a makeup department wig and, instead, had his hair shaved back to give him a receding hairline, and that's the way he appeared at the party. The scene required Jimmy—acting as though drunk—to recite a difficult twelve-minute monologue. In previous takes, he had done the scene badly, and he knew it, so he went to Stevens for help. On this morning everything was set up and waiting for him, and even Stevens was pleased with Jimmy's performance.

As Jimmy left the soundstage he saw David Weisbart, the producer of *Rebel*, and called to him. "Jimmy was terribly excited," Weisbart later told me. "He said that for the first time during the film he and Stevens had come to an understanding. 'I asked for help, and George gave it to me, and he was right. I feel like I'm nine feet tall. It was a perfect scene.' I had never seen Jimmy so excited. It must have been a wonderful experience for him."

That afternoon, Jimmy filmed the thirty-second commercial for the National Safety Council with Gig Young. The scene involved a short conversation between the two men about racing and highway safety. For his closing line, Jimmy was supposed to use the committee's standard motto: "Drive safely, because the life you save may be your own." But when Young gave him the lead-in to the line, asking him if he had any other advice to offer young drivers, Jimmy put his own personal spin on the motto. "And remember," he said, stepping out the door, "drive safely because the life you save may be mine."

The following Wednesday Jimmy went to Competition Motors and made the deal: he gave Von Neumann three thousand dollars and his old Speedster for a silver Spyder with dark blue tail stripes. Von Neumann also agreed that Weutherich would be available to Jimmy for each race. Jimmy could not take the car at once, however; it still had to be prepped for the road. What Von Neumann neglected to tell Jimmy was that one mechanic had his finger smashed when one of the doors accidentally shut; another had cut his finger on a hose ring. In retrospect, the car already seemed as ominous as its later history would confirm. Jimmy also bought a Ford station wagon, white with wood paneling on the sides, to haul the Spyder.

Jimmy and Lew Bracker met for dinner at the Villa that night. Jimmy had brought a brochure of the Porsche 550 with him, and they both went over the specs of the car in detail, agreeing that its only drawback was the high pivot swing axles, which aggravated the weight transfer during cornering, with resultant vicious oversteer.

As they were getting ready to leave, Jimmy started to talk about getting married. The idea of being married and having someone to share things with had begun to appeal more and more to him. Lew was pleased because for the first time Jimmy seemed willing to discuss insurance seriously.

Lew was Jimmy's insurance man as well as friend, so that Friday he drove to Jimmy's house to discuss an accidental death policy he had arranged with Lloyd's of London. He found Jimmy sitting at the wheel of the new car in the driveway. After some speculation on how fast the Spyder could really go, Lew handed Jimmy the application for a $100,000 policy and suggested he also select his beneficiary.

"I can fill out everything but the beneficiary for you," Lew explained. "How do you want me to make that out?"

"Tell you later," Jimmy said, accelerating the motor and listening carefully to be certain it was firing properly.

"Tell me now," Bracker insisted, "so we can start the application through the mill."

"Put yourself down," Jimmy said.

Bracker reached over and turned off the ignition key. "Come on, Jimmy, this is serious."

"Why can't you put yourself down?"

"Because I'm the agent issuing the insurance."

"It's for $100,000," Jimmy said, "so leave $5,000 to Grandma and Grampa Dean, $10,000 for Markie's education, and the rest to Ortense and Marcus."

"The way it's distributed is for your will, Jimmy," Lew explained. "Did you make that out yet?"

"No, I'll do it next week."

"Well, then, why don't I put down you want your estate to be a beneficiary, and you can change it when you make out the will."

"Yeah," said Jimmy, "that's good." He put the policy on the steering wheel and signed it with Bracker's pen.

Jimmy then put on his driving gloves, adjusted his cap at a rakish angle, and turned on the motor again. "Gotta get hopping and put more mileage on this thing. You put the insurance through as is, and we'll meet for dinner tonight. Usual place."

Jimmy drove to the studio lot to show off his new car. Although his work on *Giant* was finished, there was still a lot left to be done on the film. George Stevens was in the middle of a conference on the soundstage when he felt someone tap him on the shoulder. He turned around to see Jimmy, who motioned for him to come outside. Stevens excused himself from the group and followed Jimmy out to the studio street.

"Let me take you for a little ride," said Jimmy, indicating the Porsche. Stevens got in the car, and Jimmy took him for a fast trip up and down the studio's streets. When they got back to the soundstage they found a crowd waiting for them. Stevens realized that Jimmy hadn't asked him along for the ride only out of friendship—by stealing Stevens away from the meeting, Jimmy had effectively ended all activity on the soundstage so that everyone inside had been left with nothing else to do but go out and admire his car. It was the last time Stevens saw Jimmy.

Jimmy's little spin around the lot had also attracted the attention of the studio guards, one of whom admonished him, "You can never drive this car on the lot again; you're going to kill a carpenter or an actor or somebody."

That night Jimmy drove to the Villa Capri, where he showed the Spyder off to Patsy D'Amore, who was not impressed. "I didn't like it," Patsy recalls. "I tell him he die in that car."

Jimmy joined Lew at a front table at the Villa, one of the few times they had ever sat out front, but they had arrived early. As they were ordering their meal, Alec Guinness walked in with Thelma Moss, sister of Oscar-winning writer Charles Schnee, and a writer and parapsychologist. Guinness was in Hollywood for *The Swan* at MGM, in which he was acting with Grace Kelly. When

Guinness saw the crowd at the Villa, he turned around and walked out.

Jimmy got up from his table, ran after them, and invited Guinness and Thelma to look at his car and then join him for dinner.

They went to look at the car. Like D'Amore, Guinness was not impressed and was, instead, made uneasy by the low-slung automobile. It looked sinister to him. Jimmy's delighted explanations of the car, particularly his boasts of its potential speed, only increased Guinness's bizarre sense of unease.

"Please," he said, "never get in it." He then looked at his watch and continued, "It is now ten o'clock, Friday, the twenty-third of September 1955. If you get in that car you will be found dead in it by this time next week."

Jimmy only laughed, and they all went back into the restaurant.

With his work on *Giant* completed, Jimmy finally had some spare time. He had invited Marcus and Ortense to come visit him and stay in his new house. They came with his uncle Charles Nolan Dean, who had taught Jimmy to ride his first motorcycle. Not surprisingly, the Deans thought Jimmy's one-room apartment too small for all of them, and they opted to stay with Winton. On a visit with the family, Jimmy took Marcus for a ride in the new Porsche, but Ortense declined: she said it was too low for her.

During the afternoon of September 25, Jimmy attended a party in his honor given by Jane Deacy at the Chateau Marmont. She had flown out to Hollywood to negotiate a new contract for Jimmy with Warner Bros., and she and Jimmy had many plans for his future. He was already set to star in a television production of Ernest Hemingway's story "The Battler," scheduled to be broadcast live from New York on October 18 as part of the *Pontiac Presents Playwrights 56* series. And Jimmy had his other plans—to direct, to form his own production company. Among those present at the party was James Sheldon, and he was struck by Jimmy's obvious excitement for his future career.

Jimmy went to visit Arthur Loew, Jr., and while he was there the front doorbell rang. Jimmy opened the door and was surprised and delighted to see Eartha Kitt—just as she was surprised to find Jimmy answering Arthur's door. As they always did, they threw their arms around each other for a long embrace. Holding Jimmy in her arms, Eartha sensed something was wrong—Jimmy felt strangely empty to her.

"What's happened to you, Jamie?" she asked. "Something's wrong. You're not here."

"Come on now, Kitt," replied Jimmy. "You're running one of your spiritual numbers on me again."

But Eartha was convinced that something was wrong, and she was disturbed. She'd come out to Los Angeles for a few days of rest between engagements, and although she was pleased to see Jimmy, when he left she was still worried. She was never to see him again.

Not long after that, Arthur Loew, Jr., saw Jimmy for the last time. Jimmy had been sick, was just getting over a bout with the flu, and stopped by Arthur's house to find the usual small crowd of Hollywood people. Still feeling tired from his illness, Jimmy slumped down in a chair and promptly fell asleep. By the time all the other guests had left, it was late, so Arthur woke him up and told him what time it was. Still sleepy, and not feeling well, Jimmy sat up and pulled himself together, then got to his feet and picked up his coat. It was a dark blue coat that actually belonged to Arthur; Arthur had loaned it to Jimmy earlier for one of his many trips to New York.

When Jimmy reached the front door he stopped and turned. With an expansive, sweeping gesture, he threw the coat over his shoulder, looked at Arthur, and said, "Show business is in very bad shape."

"Why?" asked Arthur.

"Because Barrymore is dead, and I'm not feeling well." With that he swept out the door and into the night.

Chapter Fifteen

THE LAST RACE

On the morning of Monday, September 26, 1955, Jimmy drove the Spyder to the customizing shop of George Barris in Compton. Barris painted the racing number 130 in black on the doors and the front engine deck lid. At Jimmy's special request he painted the words LITTLE BASTARD in red across the rear cowling. This was the nickname Bill Hickman had given him. Hickman, who had been his dialogue coach on *Giant*, was a rugged thirty-five-year-old service veteran and a former stuntman. He had been teaching Jimmy some of the techniques of race driving, and he called Jimmy Little Bastard; in turn, Jimmy called him Big Bastard.

After leaving Barris, Jimmy spent the afternoon with Jane Deacy talking about the new contract the studio had offered him and plans for the future. "If I live to be one hundred there'll never be time enough for me to get in everything I want to do," Jimmy told Jane.

In the evening Jimmy picked up Janette at her apartment to take her for a ride. It was a chilly night and they sped out to the beach and then over Topanga Canyon to the San Fernando Valley on a winding narrow road with the icy wind in their faces. When Janette returned home she was already feeling ill. By morning she had a temperature of 103 and got into bed.

On Tuesday, Lilli Kardell noted in her diary: "My service said that Jimmy Dean had called me and tried to reach me."

Wednesday afternoon Jimmy had Lew join him at a meeting with Jane Deacy. Jimmy wanted to go into independent production with Lew as his producer and me as a writer: Jimmy thought it was about time that I graduated into "serious writing." After the meeting Lew and Jimmy went to the movies together and saw *Magnificent Obsession*, starring Jane Wyman and Rock Hudson.

Late that evening, Janette had a surprise visitor. Jimmy arrived without calling first as he generally did. Still rattled from her ride in the Porsche, Janette was in bed sweating out a fever and coughing. "Are you coming with me?" Jimmy asked her.

"What do you mean, am I coming with you? Where are you going?

"I'm going to Monterey."

"I can't go with you," Janette said. "I've got pneumonia. I've got the flu. I'm sick. I just want to be left alone."

"Oh," said Jimmy, who started pacing the floor in silence. He finally sat down on a couch bed. Janette noticed that his skin color was unnaturally white. Then Jimmy started twisting around, and Janette felt panicky: she wondered if there was something wrong with him. At the same time she wondered if he was just acting strange so she'd change her mind. Then he started to cry.

"I didn't mean to hurt your feelings," Janette said, "and I don't want you to feel rejected. I'm seriously ill. I'm not making excuses. What's wrong?"

"I can't talk about it," he said, "but I'm upset."

"I've never seen you cry before. Please tell me what's wrong."

"I can't talk about it."

Janette asked him again to tell her what was wrong, but Jimmy refused. He then walked to the telephone, dialed, and Janette heard him say, "I'll see you in a few minutes." Jimmy stayed a little while longer, and then he left, shutting the door very softly.

"It was clear to me that something very emotional was going on in Jimmy's life at the time," Janette says. "I had never before seen him so uptight."

At seven o'clock Thursday morning Jimmy awakened Janette. In his arms was his beige-and-brown Siamese cat, Marcus, a gift from Elizabeth Taylor. "I'm getting ready to leave and I hoped you would take care of Marcus while I'm gone," Jimmy explained.

Janette was delighted to do the favor: she loved cats. Jimmy gave her some feeding instructions scribbled on the back of an envelope: "1 teaspoon white Karo. 1 big can evaporated milk. Equal part boiled water or distilled water. 1 egg yolk. Mix and chill. Don't feed him meat or formula cold. 1 drop vitamin solution per day. If I'm not back take Marcus to Dr. Cooper for shots next week."

Before leaving, Jimmy took a medallion of the Virgin of Guadalupe from around his neck and gave it to Janette. "It was almost as though he was saying goodbye," Janette recalls, "although he said he would call me when he got back."

Jimmy then drove to Ursula Andress's house and asked her to go with him to Salinas. As luck would have it, while they were talking, John Derek arrived: the first time Ursula had seen him in months. Jimmy asked Derek if he would like to go for a ride in his new car. When they returned, Jimmy, who apparently realized that John was upset because he was visiting Ursula, said he had to leave, but would call her after the race was over.

In the afternoon Jimmy called his father and asked him to go to Salinas. Winton was unable to make it because Jimmy's uncle Charles Nolan was leaving for Mexico the next day. But Winton said that he and Charles would meet Jimmy at Competition Motors for lunch.

Jimmy called a few other friends, asking them to go to the race. Dennis Stock's first reaction when Jimmy invited him along was positive. But then he experienced a kind of flash. Without understanding why, he suddenly found himself saying, "I'm sorry, I can't."

Jimmy also telephoned me, asking me to go with him, but I was leaving for Mexico that afternoon.

All week long Jimmy had tried desperately to persuade Lew Bracker to come with him to Salinas. But Lew had another interest besides cars—football—and there was a big game that weekend.

"I have tickets for the USC-Texas football game Saturday night, and there's no way I'm going to miss that game," he told Jimmy.

When Jimmy asked his photographer friend Sandy Roth to accompany him, Roth immediately agreed: pictures of Jimmy racing would fit nicely in the magazine article Roth was shooting.

One of Jimmy's last telephone calls Thursday afternoon was to

Monty Roberts in Salinas. He asked Monty if he and Rolf could stay in the guest house on the ranch while they were in Salinas, and perhaps they could look at the ranch Monty had been negotiating to buy for him.

"I want to go into escrow right away, while I'm in Salinas," Jimmy said. "After the race I'm going to go to San Francisco and then New York, but I want you and Pat [Monty's wife] on the place within a month with the best cattle and the best horses."

At six o'clock Thursday night Jimmy decided to give the car a test run and also put more mileage on it before the race. He picked up Bill Hickman, and they headed north on the coast highway intending to really open the little racer up. They were chased part of the way by a Highway Patrol car, but easily outran it. The fog closed in just before Santa Barbara, and they turned around, finally arriving at the Villa Capri for a late dinner at around eleven. Jimmy did not get to bed that Friday morning until almost three.

Early on the morning of Friday, September 30, Jimmy drove by Bill Bast's home to show off the Spyder. Bast asked Jimmy if he wanted him to stop by his house and feed Marcus the cat while he was away.

"I gave Marcus away," said Jimmy.

"How come?" asked Bast.

"You know what a crazy life I lead. What if I went away and never came back?"

Jimmy arrived at Competition Motors around eight. Rolf Weutherich checked the car out one last time and was satisfied. All that remained to be done was to attach the safety belt to the driver's seat; a safety belt was not considered necessary for the passenger side because Rolf would not be riding in the race.

At around noon, Winton Dean and Charles Nolan arrived. Jimmy wanted to take his uncle for a ride in the Spyder.

"Take your dad," said Charles.

"No, you go ahead," Winton said. Jimmy and Charles drove around the block a couple of times and returned in a few minutes.

While Weutherich went off to change clothes, Jimmy and his father and uncle walked half a block up Vine Street to the Hollywood Ranch Market for doughnuts and coffee. When they returned they sat in Jimmy's station wagon and talked. Jimmy asked them to say goodbye to Marcus and Ortense, who were preparing to drive back to Fairmount.

When Rolf returned dressed for the trip in light blue slacks and a red-checkered sport shirt, it was time for Winton and Charles to leave. Charles put an arm around Jimmy.

"Be careful," he said. "That car's a bomb."

Jimmy giggled. "That's my baby."

Sandy Roth and Bill Hickman arrived. It was agreed that instead of towing the Spyder on a trailer behind the station wagon, Jimmy would drive the car in order to put a few more miles on it and gain confidence in his ability to handle it.

Five minutes before they left Competition, Jimmy called Lew on the phone. "Well," he said, "we're leaving. So are you coming?"

"I can't, Jimmy," said Bracker, "I'm still going to the football game."

"Okay, Lew," replied Jimmy. "It's your funeral."

The last thing Jimmy and Rolf did before leaving was to pose for Sandy with their arms raised over their heads in the traditional victory pose.

Jimmy clipped a pair of sunglasses over his prescription lenses and tucked his red jacket behind the seat: it was the same one he had worn in *Rebel*, which he now considered his lucky jacket.

Jimmy led the way to the freeway and then headed east to Ventura. Driving Jimmy's station wagon, Hickman occasionally pulled abreast or ahead of the Spyder so that Sandy Roth could take pictures. Rolf, who had left his sunglasses behind at the dealership, relaxed in the passenger seat with his eyes shut, trying to get a tan.

Jimmy gave the mechanic very little rest, however. He chain-smoked his Chesterfields, and since there was no lighter in the Spyder, Rolf had to hunker down under the dash and light them for him with Jimmy's chrome Zippo.

Rolf and Jimmy were soon thirsty from the hot sun blazing down on them in the open car, and a few minutes after three, they pulled into Tip's, a diner near the top of the ridge outside Newhall. Jimmy ordered a glass of ice-cold milk and insisted that Rolf drink a soda.

As they were sitting at the counter nursing their drinks, Rolf, who had been a test driver for Porsche before coming to America as a mechanic, gave Jimmy some tips on driving in the Salinas race. "Don't try to go too fast. Don't try to win. Drive to get experience."

"Okay," said Jimmy.

A moment later Jimmy told Rolf he wanted to give him something. "Why?" asked Rolf. "To prove we're friends," said Jimmy, who pulled a ring from his finger and gave it to him: it was a ring with a Pan American Airlines emblem that Jimmy had gotten as a souvenir. Rolf tried to put it on his ring finger but it was too small, so he settled for his little finger.

Sandy and Bill came through the door as Jimmy was paying the check. Bill told Rolf not to let Jimmy drive too fast, he could barely keep him in sight at sixty mph. "No, no, no," said Rolf. "That is all settled."

A waitress asked the mechanic if his friend was Jimmy Dean. Rolf nodded, and she ran off to tell her friends.

Rolf checked the various fuel levels of the Spyder while he and Jimmy waited in the parking lot for Sandy and Bill to finish their sandwiches.

Both cars headed north on Highway 99 (now 5) where they crossed the Los Angeles county line into Kern County. Here the sun-browned hills dipped into flat dusty plains. Jimmy began to accelerate and was soon going seventy down the divided highway called the Grapevine, the last stretch of steeply descending mountain highway just before Mettler Station. The posted limit was fifty-five.

It was nearly 3:30 P.M. when California Highway Patrolman Otie V. Hunter saw the Spyder and clocked it at seventy mph before noticing the station wagon towing a trailer following closely behind it at the same speed. Hunter, traveling in the opposite direction, made a U turn across the gravel median and took up pursuit. He slipped his Oldsmobile patrol car between the two vehicles, flashed his lights, hit the siren, and motioned for both drivers to pull over onto the shoulder.

Hunter walked over to the Spyder and politely asked Jimmy for his license, then told him he was being cited for excess speed. The name James Dean meant nothing to the officer, who asked Jimmy for his place of business. "Warner Bros." replied Jimmy. While writing out the ticket, Hunter asked Jimmy about the car: the patrolman had never seen one like it before. Jimmy told him that it was a racer, and he was on his way to the races at Salinas.

Jimmy signed his name on the ticket. Hunter cautioned him to slow down, and then cited Hickman in the station wagon. That ticket was for sixty-five, but Hickman was driving twenty miles over the speed limit because the vehicle code specified forty-five mph for vehicles towing trailers.

Before driving off, Jimmy told Sandy and Bill that they'd meet for dinner at Paso Robles, about 150 miles north.

Fifteen minutes later Jimmy drove through Bakersfield where he enjoyed the stares of the townsfolk. Though Bakersfield was the locale of several races each year, the Spyder attracted attention.

They passed through Bakersfield on Highway 466 (now route 46) and found that the road ahead was nearly empty. Just before 5:00 P.M. they reached Blackwell's Corners, a gas station and grocery store at the junction of routes 466 and 33. Jimmy noticed a dark blue 300 SL Mercedes Gullwing parked in front of the store and recognized it as belonging to Lance Reventlow, a racing aficionado and the twenty-one-year-old son of Barbara Hutton, the heiress with whom Jimmy had had a one-night stand earlier in the year. Jimmy knew Lance from racing and he pulled off the road to say hello and stretch his legs.

Lance, who was also racing that weekend, was going to Salinas with his fellow driver and best friend Bruce Kessler, whose father, Jack, had founded the Rose Marie Reid swimwear company. Rolf went to the edge of the highway to flag Sandy and Bill down while Jimmy chatted with Bruce and Lance: they had also gotten a speeding ticket on the Ridge Route. They were both impressed when Jimmy bragged that he had gotten the Spyder up to 130 mph. (He had, in fact, averaged seventy-five miles an hour from the time he had been ticketed, which meant that his boast about doing 130 mph in some stretches was probably right.)

Rolf signaled the station wagon to stop. When Jimmy told Bill how fast he had gone, Bill warned him, "Be careful of the cars turning in front of you. The Spyder's hard to see because of the color and it being so low."

Jimmy took the cigarette from Bill's mouth and lit one of his own. "Don't worry, Big Bastard," he said, and laughed.

"What do you think of the Spyder now?" Sandy asked.

"I want to keep this car for a long time, a real long time," said Jimmy, who went into the grocery store to use the telephone. He called Monty Roberts to tell him that he and Rolf would be arriving in Salinas early in the evening, and to have a pot of chili on the stove.

Sandy had bought two bags of apples and gave Jimmy one. It was getting a bit chilly so Jimmy put on his red jacket. As he got into his car, Jimmy shouted to his friends, "Nonstop to Paso Robles!" He accelerated out onto the highway without fastening his safety belt.

It was nearing 5:30, and the setting sun was shining directly into his eyes as Jimmy approached the Y intersection of Routes 466 and 41 east of Cholame at the point where the highway splits. There had been several fatal collisions at the intersection in the past.

John R. White, a fifty-year-old CPA with the prestigious accounting firm of Price Waterhouse, was driving with his wife on the highway when Jimmy passed him at a speed White would later estimate in excess of eighty-five mph, possibly as much as 110. White also noticed a two-tone black-and-white Ford sedan some distance ahead preparing to turn left into the highway in front of the speeding car. Certain there was going to be a collision, he said to his wife, "Watch this."

Jimmy also saw the Ford sedan about to make a left turn into the highway. "That guy up there's gotta stop," he told Rolf. "He'll see us."

"That guy up there" was Donald Gene Turnupseed, a year younger than James Dean and a student at California Polytechnic. By the time he saw James Dean's Spyder racing toward him it was too late. He slammed on the brake pedal. The rear wheels locked, and the Ford slid thirty feet. John White watched in horror as the Spyder swerved although its brake lights did not flash. Then the two cars hit. Turnupseed survived the collision dazed and bruised. The occupants of the Porsche were not so lucky.

Weutherich was thrown from the little racer and suffered a broken jaw and crushed left femur. Jimmy, trapped in his seat behind the wheel, his head practically severed from his body, was dead on arrival at the Paso Robles War Memorial Hospital, where a doctor issued a report that he had suffered "a broken neck, multiple broken bones, and lacerations over his entire body."

Chapter Sixteen

THE IMPACT

Los Angeles • At almost the same moment the accident happened, Maila Nurmi and Jack Simmons were sitting in the living room of her home on Larrabee Avenue in Hollywood. The curtains, as always, were drawn: for privacy, for intimacy, for that certain sense of gloom Maila thrived on. Suddenly, the room filled with light. There was something so eerie and unnatural about it that Jack felt unaccountably nervous.

"It's creepy in here," he said. "Let's go out."

Drawn to the light—she thought it fascinating and beautiful—Maila didn't want to leave, but she finally agreed, and the two of them went outside for a fifteen-minute walk.

New York • Natalie Wood, Nick Adams, and Sal Mineo had just seen Richard Davalos in a performance of Arthur Miller's *A View From the Bridge,* and together with Davalos and his wife they were sitting in the China Doll, an Oriental restaurant on West Fifty-fourth Street, just across the street from the Warwick Hotel. For the most part, they talked of Richard's performance, but they suddenly changed to the subject of Jimmy, and for a few moments they joked and laughed loudly. Then Sal said, "I think he's racing this weekend." The others fell silent.

"He knows what he's doing," said Richard.

THE IMPACT

They all agreed, picked up their menus, and began discussing their dinner order.

Los Angeles • It was a few minutes after six in Los Angeles when the telephone rang at the Warner Bros. studio gate. The studio switchboard was closed, so the call came in on the night line. A studio policeman took the call, which was from the War Memorial Hospital in Paso Robles. A female voice, speaking clearly and matter-of-factly, informed him that James Dean had been killed in an auto accident.

The policeman hung up the phone, thought for no more than a few seconds, and then quickly picked it up again to call the publicity department. Steve Brooks, who was editing still pictures, answered. Although numb from shock, he immediately called the hospital to be certain the report was accurate and not a hoax. He then tried to reach his boss, Max Bercutt, who was out for the evening. Brooks then took it upon himself to call Henry Ginsberg, who was at his home in Palm Springs for the weekend.

Ginsberg knew that George Stevens and some of the film's cast, including Elizabeth Taylor, Rock Hudson, and Carroll Baker, were watching rushes in a studio projection room. Jimmy was on the screen when Stevens, sitting behind the others at a console near the projection booth, answered the phone. The color went out of his face. His reaction was such that Baker thought something bad had happened to his son, George Jr., who was in the air force. Stevens got up and walked out of the projection room for a few moments and then returned. In hushed tones, his words pained and slow, he relayed the news: "Ladies and gentlemen, I have an announcement to make. There's been a crash. Jimmy Dean has been killed."

Elizabeth Taylor gasped and collapsed across the chair in front of her. Both Baker and Hudson rushed to her side and tried to calm her, but she was obviously lost in grief. Then she suddenly composed herself, stood up, and left the projection room in search of dialogue coach Bob Hinkle, who was also a friend of Jimmy's.

Meanwhile, Brooks notified the wire services, the city editors of the three Los Angeles newspapers, and the Hollywood film trade papers, giving them what news he had. He knew that Ortense and Marcus Winslow had been in Los Angeles visiting Jimmy, so he called the home of Arthur Loew, Jr., hoping he might know how to reach them.

Loew was out for the evening at the Interlude, a popular club, and it was Stewart Stern who answered. From Ginsberg's voice Stewart knew something terrible had happened. "What's wrong?" he asked.

"The boy is dead!" exclaimed Ginsberg. "The boy is dead!" Stewart understood immediately, and even in the moment's shock recognized Ginsberg's unintentional paraphrasing of Jimmy's line from *Rebel*: "Mom, Dad, a boy was killed tonight!"

Stewart put out the cigarette he had been smoking; he was not to light another for six months. He went out to find Arthur Loew, Jr., and when he had found him and sat him down and told him, he got back in his car and drove aimlessly around Hollywood. There was no one he could talk to, nowhere he could go. For the next hour or so he was one of the few people who knew that most terrible of news. He knew he couldn't tell anyone—he himself didn't believe what he knew—so he kept driving up and down the streets of Hollywood.

Elizabeth Taylor stayed at the Warner Bros. studio until after nine that evening with Hinkle, phoning frantically to the police and various newspapers, trying to prove to herself that it was a false report, that Jimmy wasn't really dead. They learned that the reports were true.

When a distraught Elizabeth was getting into her car in the studio parking lot, she saw Stevens and went over to the director and said, "I can't believe that Jimmy is dead."

Stevens looked at her for a long moment and then retorted, "He had it coming to him."

She was shocked. "What do you mean?"

"The way he drove," said Stevens, "it was inevitable."

In a rage and speeding at up to one hundred miles an hour, Elizabeth drove over the canyons to her home. Only later did she decide that when Stevens said "inevitable" it was his way of expressing his own particular kind of grief.

THE IMPACT

* * *

Dick Clayton wasn't feeling well. He wasn't sick, but he sensed something strange, something just wasn't right. So he had left his office and gone home, and he was there when the telephone rang a few minutes after six.

Jack Ordean, his boss at Famous Artists, called and said, "Are you sitting down?" Dick sat down. "George Stevens just called me," said Ordean. "Jimmy was killed in an accident."

"Are you sure?" asked Dick.

"I'm sure. The studio checked it."

The shock of the news left Dick fighting for air in his lungs, but he knew what had to be done, and quickly. He immediately called Jane Deacy at the Chateau Marmont and arranged to meet her within the hour at Frascati's restaurant on the Sunset Strip. First he wanted to get to Jimmy's father before he heard the news on the television or radio. He got in his car and drove out to Winton's apartment. When he walked in, Winton and Ethel were laughing.

"I'm sorry to have to tell you this," said Clayton, "but Jimmy has just been killed."

Winton paled. "Oh, no, he hasn't," he said, and started to cry.

"I wish it wasn't true," said Clayton.

Brooklyn, New York • Leonard Rosenman was visiting his parents at their home in Brooklyn when Jane Deacy telephoned. "I want to tell you that Jimmy was killed in an automobile accident tonight," she said, sobbing.

Deacy's phrase was to stay with Rosenman for weeks afterward, his mind repeating it—"Jimmy was killed"—over and over with gradually decreasing intensity.

The Rosenmans' next phone call was from Lew Bracker's father, Joe, who had heard that Jimmy had been in an accident and, like many others that night, feared that Lew had been with him. For the next few hours, the Rosenmans' grief for Jimmy was mixed with their frantic concern for Lew.

Los Angeles • When Dick Clayton and Jane Deacy met at Frascati's they agreed not to discuss Jimmy with the press: he had been too close to both of them personally.

New York • Chris White was alone in her apartment. Her acting career had finally begun to show promise: she had a part in the Broadway production of *A Hatful of Rain* directed by Frank Corsaro. The phone rang. It was someone from the Actors Studio who asked if she was sitting down.

"Why, what's the matter?" asked Chris.

"Have you heard the news on the radio?"

"I have out-of-town visitors and haven't been listening to the radio," said Chris.

"It's about Jimmy."

"Good or bad?" asked Chris.

"Very, very bad."

Chris sat down.

"Jimmy's dead."

Chris gasped, moaned, and dropped the phone.

She was glued to the radio for the rest of the night listening for scraps of news. "It didn't sink in," she said recently. "It was like watching a play and somebody gets their lines wrong. There was no way I could think of this guy who was moving all the time as being dead. It was just impossible."

Lee Strasberg was at his apartment when Jack Garfein called him from Hollywood with the news. At that moment, Strasberg wasn't upset and shed no tears: somehow, it was something he had been expecting. The tears were to come later, when he saw *Giant*. Then he cried, not because of Jimmy's death but because of the waste, the terrible waste of so much talent.

Salinas • Monty and Pat Roberts were waiting for Jimmy and Rolf to come for dinner when they heard the news on the radio. Monty started to cry. "I felt like I had lost a brother," he later said.

Los Angeles • The news bulletin about Jimmy's death was repeated over and over again on local radio. Jim Backus and his wife, Henny, were driving in their car and listening to the radio when they heard the news.

THE IMPACT

* * *

Kenneth Kendall was in his studio on Melrose Avenue. He hadn't seen Jimmy since his visit with Tony Lee, the one-legged girl, but when he heard the radio announcement, he immediately began making a matrix for a bust of James Dean.

Still driving around Hollywood, Stewart Stern began to notice people acting strangely, and he realized the news was out. Outside the popular hangouts Googie's and Schwab's—places where Jimmy had long been a familiar face—young actors and actresses stood in groups, some silent, some weeping. Stern went back to his home on Lookout Mountain and threw himself onto the bed. He was confused: although he and Jimmy had never been great friends, he found himself grieving, grieving more than he ever had for anyone.

Beverly Long was at home, packing her bags for a trip to Las Vegas: she and her actor boyfriend, Bob Dorff, were going to elope that night. A girlfriend called and said she had heard on the radio that Jimmy had been killed.

"That's really cruel," snapped Beverly.

"It's true," said the girlfriend and hung up.

Beverly turned on the radio herself and heard the news. With the bags left unpacked and the wedding postponed, she and the other young gang members from *Rebel Without a Cause* called one another, asking for details—there were none—but most of all they were seeking to share their grief and their shock.

Across town Dennis Hopper was sitting next to his agent in a theater, watching a play, when the agent was summoned to take a call in the lobby. When he came back, he said, "I have something to tell you, but you must promise me that you won't leave the theater." By the look on his agent's face Hopper was certain someone in his family had died.

"James Dean was killed in a car accident," said the agent.

Hopper hit him and then babbled, "Liar."

* * *

Janette Miller was home alone when she heard the news on the radio. Did I hear that right? she thought. Am I hearing that right? But within moments the phone rang. It was Ursula Andress.

"Have you heard about Jimmy?"

Janette then knew she had heard right. "Yes," she replied.

Ursula and John Derek came to Janette's apartment and stayed with her, and the next day the three friends saw each other again.

New York ● By 11:30 dinner at the China Doll in New York had ended, and the five friends were saying good night. Natalie had to get back to her hotel for some rest—she was in New York to appear along with Jo Van Fleet in an ABC special of *Heidi* to be telecast live the next day. She and Nick Adams were both staying across the street at the Warwick. On the way up in the elevator, Natalie asked him to stop by her room and say hello to Maggie Waite, her chaperon from Warner Bros. on the trip.

"Did you kids have a good time?" Maggie asked as they walked in, but Nick could tell from the way she looked at him and spoke that something was wrong. Maggie waited until Natalie had left the room to make some hot chocolate and then, handing Nick a folded piece of notepaper, said, "Here, take this, read it, but don't say a word to Nat. She'll be awake all night if she knows, and she's going to need every minute of rest she can get. You'll have to tell her in the morning."

Nick unfolded the small piece of paper and looked down at it: "Jimmy was killed tonight—in an auto accident in California at 5:30 P.M."

He was shaken and felt weak, as though he had been physically struck. When Natalie came back with her cup of hot chocolate, he made a date to meet her the next morning at eight for breakfast. Then he excused himself and went up to his room. He spent that night staring out the window, unseeing, past the neon lights.

Los Angeles ● On Larrabee Avenue, Tony Perkins had dropped by Maila Nurmi's house, and he, Maila, and Jack were in her living room when the phone rang: it was Randy from the Villa Capri, who told Maila the news.

"You must be joking," she said and looked up to see that one of the pins holding up a photograph Jimmy had given her of himself had dropped to the floor. The picture was swinging back and forth like a pendulum.

Late that night Elizabeth Taylor called Stevens and said, "I can't work tomorrow. I've been crying for hours. You can't photograph me tomorrow."

"What's the matter with you?" asked Stevens.

"I loved that boy. Don't you understand?"

"That's no reason," said Stevens. "You be on that set at nine o'clock tomorrow morning, ready to shoot."

Lilli Kardell made the final entry in her diary, for the first time writing in English instead of her native Swedish: "James Dean, my only love, died on his way to Salinas for the races tonight. Auto crash. Please take care of him, God, and let him be happier now than before. I can only hope I will find my Jimmy in some other person. My thoughts will always be with you, Jimmy.

"Goodbye . . . forever. I love you, will never forget you and our memories."

Dennis Stock was having dinner at the Villa Capri with Arlene Sachs when Mario Marino, the maitre d', came over to their table and bent over so only they could hear what he was about to say: "Jimmy's been killed in a car crash." They both stood up, left their dinner uneaten, and went to the bar where they talked about Jimmy. Like so many of Jimmy's friends, they needed to be together and talk about him, keeping him alive for as long as possible. They were also worried about Lew Bracker. No one had heard from him, no one knew where he was.

At 11:30, Lew walked into the restaurant to a greeting of loud exclamations of relief and even a few hugs: everyone told him they thought they were seeing a ghost. Lew had heard nothing of Jimmy's death and had come to the Capri for a late dinner. After the joy at seeing him alive, someone sat Lew down and told him. Lew said very little. He left the Villa without eating and went home where he locked himself in his room for three days.

Arlene, who had left before Lew, was in her car driving up and down Sunset Boulevard repeating out loud to herself, "What's the point?"

Fairmount, Indiana • Late that night, as Marcus and Ortense Winslow pulled into the drive of their farmhouse after their long drive from California, friends met them with the shattering news. Ortense began crying and Marcus put his arm around her. But he said nothing, and his eyes, without tears, stared off into empty space.

New York • Bill Gunn had learned of Jimmy's death on Friday night from Robert Heller, who had heard it on the radio. Early Saturday morning the two of them met a few other friends, and they all went to the apartment Jimmy still kept on West Sixty-eighth Street. One of the group easily picked the lock, and they entered. They searched through Jimmy's belongings and took away whatever pictures they thought might be embarrassing to Jimmy's memory.

As they left the apartment, they passed a few teenage girls on the stoop. The girls asked if James Dean lived there. "Yes," said Gunn. Some months later Heller recognized one of the girls at a James Dean fan club meeting.

On Saturday morning, at eight o'clock, Nick Adams went downstairs for breakfast. He found Natalie and Maggie waiting for him in the hotel restaurant. When he sat down at the table, Maggie excused herself and left.

Natalie could see from his face that something was wrong. "What is it, Nick?" she asked.

He reached across the table and took her hand. "Nat, something has happened to someone we both like."

Somehow she knew. She grew suddenly pale and stood up. "Jimmy." It was less a question than a statement.

He nodded. "He was killed last night in California. An auto accident."

Natalie walked across the room between the tables set for breakfast, some of the patrons looking up to watch her pass. She went and stood by a window, and even from where he was sitting Nick could see she was crying. But she wasn't making a sound.

THE IMPACT

* * *

Farther uptown, Montgomery Clift was just waking up in the West Side brownstone of his friend, jazz singer Libby Holman. They had just returned from Europe and had been staying in her house. Each morning she woke him with coffee and the morning newspaper. On this morning she found him already awake as she came into the room, so she began talking. "Isn't it terrible what happened to Jimmy Dean? He was killed in an automobile accident. He was driving his silver Porsche. His neck was broken, and his chest was crushed when it smashed into the steering wheel."

Clift sat bolt upright in the bed and vomited across the white satin sheets.

Around nine o'clock that morning, Adeline Nall was busy at work at the reception desk of the Biltmore Hotel. She had taken a leave of absence from Fairmount High and left Indiana to go to New York in the hope of beginning her own Broadway career. In part she was inspired by Jimmy's success, and in part she was embittered by it. She had read in a fan magazine that Jimmy had paid $4,000 for a Porsche Speedster, more money than she earned in a year. And she believed that doors would open for the teacher of the great James Dean. She arrived in New York on August 9, 1955, went to see Jane Deacy, and got herself a room in the YWCA. She had taken the job in the hotel to support herself while she made the rounds.

That morning she got a call from the hotel's personnel manager, who knew of her relationship to Jimmy. He told her he had just read in *The New York Times* that Jimmy had been killed. Adeline felt cold chills run down her back, and her mind went completely blank.

Barbara Glenn was sleeping late at her parents' home when her mother came in and said she had a phone call, adding, "I hate to wake you this way, and I don't want to get you upset, but it's not good news." Marty Landau, who had heard the news from a friend, was on the phone. Marty intended to tell Barbara about Jimmy's death in his own way. He hoped someone else had already broken the news, but if that were not so he didn't want his voice to reflect anything. But as soon as Barbara heard his voice she said, "Jim's dead."

To this day Marty still doesn't understand how Barbara already knew why he was calling.

Frank Corsaro had been feeling uneasy since the night before. He was in the middle of rehearsals for *A Hatful of Rain*, and that Friday night he looked around his apartment for some records he wanted. In doing so he came across the record of Chaliapin that Jimmy had given him for Christmas. The record was completely smashed. Corsaro took great care with his records and couldn't understand how the record had been broken. Looking at the shattered record gave him a strange apprehension.

When he walked into the rehearsal hall that Saturday morning, he found Ben Gazzara seated reading a newspaper.

"Well," Gazzara called out to him, "guess who died last night."

"Who?" asked Corsaro.

"An old pal of yours," said Gazzara. "Dean."

"How did he do it?" asked Corsaro. He realized later that Jimmy's death was something he had always expected.

Los Angeles • Elizabeth Taylor was on the set of *Giant* Saturday morning, but when she started to rehearse she went into hysterics, and an ambulance had to be called to take her to the hospital. After five days in the hospital she was finally able to return to work on her last scenes in the film.

Saturdays were workdays at Warner Bros., but Rhea Burakoff had the morning off. That Saturday she slept late and had a dream about Jimmy. In the dream she was looking at a newspaper headline that read, JIMMY DEAN MARRIES WAITRESS. In the dream she was distraught by the news and said over and over, "No, no." She was terribly disturbed and kept thinking, "It can't be."

She was awakened from the dream by the ringing of her phone. It was a friend from the studio, who said, "I guess you've heard."

"Heard what?"

"Heard about Jimmy Dean."

"Don't tell me he's married a waitress, for heaven's sake."

"No," the friend said. "He's dead."

It was the only dream Rhea had ever had about Jimmy.

San Juan, Puerto Rico • Dizzy Sheridan was working as a dancer, and that Saturday afternoon she was sitting in a movie theater. Somehow, from the street outside, she heard the voice of a paperboy hawking his wares with that morning's headline news about Jimmy's death. It was a cold and lonely ending to her relationship with Jimmy.

Los Angeles • That morning, Mercedes McCambridge and her husband, Fletcher, were driving along Highway 466 to San Francisco. To celebrate the end of her work on *Giant*, she had reserved a room in the Fairmont Hotel overlooking the bay, and they were making their way north slowly. In need of gas, they stopped at a small grocery store with two gas pumps in front and a garage with a big metal sign reading CHOLAME GARAGE. While Fletcher saw to the gas, Mercedes went into the store to buy some Cokes. She overheard a girl tell Fletcher, "We have Jimmy Dean's sports car in the garage." Then another girl appeared at the counter in front of Mercedes and pointed out a window. Mercedes followed the girl's indication and looked out to see the Spyder, a heap of folded and smashed aluminum marked by dark stains.

"They said they'd never seen a body so limp and broken," the girl said.

"Oh, my God," Mercedes cried out.

Fletcher and Mercedes drove in stunned silence to Paso Robles, where they found the Kuehl Funeral Home. "He's in there," Mercedes said to her husband. She wanted to go inside but a crowd had gathered. Fletcher numbly circled the block a few times and then got onto the highway to San Francisco.

Lew Bracker was home, but he wasn't taking calls. He didn't leave his room until Monday, and when he finally left the house it was to go see Janette Miller. Since he didn't have her phone number, he just showed up; she wasn't surprised to see him. They spent the day together and that night got in his car and headed for the beach. They stopped at Castle Rock, an outcropping a little above the highway level. There they sat on the ground near each other and looked out at the ocean. They didn't talk.

After dropping Janette off at her home, Lew swung by Jimmy's house. He found the key in its usual hiding place and went inside. He could tell instantly that someone had already been there because some of Jimmy's personal items, such as his race trophies, were missing and he wondered if, perhaps, Winton had already been to the house and removed them. But the mess on Jimmy's desk was much as he remembered it, and he filled a wastebasket with letters, Jimmy's notes and date pad, and photos plus other items that he planned to give to Winton.

On that same Monday, Bill Orr was faced with a problem. The public service commercial about safe driving that Jimmy had done with Gig Young was scheduled to be aired that night during an episode of the *Cheyenne* television show. An executive of ABC called and insisted on pulling the commercial, claiming it was in bad taste. Orr argued with the executive, claiming that sometimes bad taste is justified to get across such an important message. Finally, Leonard Goldenson, head of ABC, telephoned Orr and said, "Get the spot with Dean out." Orr spent the rest of the day getting prints back and putting in another spot as replacement.

Lew Bracker had had second thoughts about the things lying around in Jimmy's apartment, so he decided to go back and inventory them for Winton. He later gave me a copy of the inventory.

Here is an excerpt: Bongo drums. Paints and pastels. Checkers set. Radio innards. One small metal box enclosing one gold St. Christopher medal, cuff links, and an envelope containing a lock of black hair. White apron. Miscellaneous small busts of famous composers. Record collection. One Rolleiflex camera. Hemp rope in a box. Motorcycle equipment. Sketches and drawings. One scrapbook with sundry clippings.

Later, I saw the contents of the scrapbook, and noted them

down. I had once given Jimmy a book of poems by Emily Dickinson, and he had torn out one and pasted it in the scrapbook. It read:

> *I died for beauty but was scarce*
> *Adjusted in the tomb*
> *When one who died for truth was lain*
> *In an adjoining room.*
> *He questioned softly why I failed,*
> *"For beauty," I replied.*
> *"And I for truth, the two are one,*
> *"We brethren are," he said.*
> *And so as kinsmen met at night,*
> *We talked between the rooms*
> *Until the moss had reached our lips*
> *And covered up our tombs.*

The scrapbook also contained an article by Tennessee Williams on the relation of creative work to the personality of the person who does it; a newspaper clipping about Elia Kazan; a color photograph of a needlepoint sampler reading, HOME IS WHERE THE HEART IS; a dozen photos of babies laughing and poems about children. There was a sentence torn from a newspaper article reading, "The peace and hope and faith that babies have brought since the world began recompense for any hardship and peril and heartache." Another sentence clipped neatly from a newspaper read, "The world and all its good are yours . . . if you can laugh at life." And another sentence underlined in an article read, "People are lonely because they build walls instead of bridges." Tucked into the pages was a short article on "Is It Neurotic to Like Yourself?"

Jimmy had clipped and saved color pictures of bucolic country scenes in winter and summer. Over the picture of a laughing infant was pasted, "The child that cries is your master; and he is master again when he smiles." There was a story about Abraham Lincoln in which some words in one sentence were crossed out. The sentence was "The mould disappeared after his humble birth," and in place of "his humble birth" Jimmy had written, "2/8/31 JD," his own birthdate. Another sentence clipped from a newspaper read, "Every child is filled with a little loneliness . . . and a lot of curiosity." Another short clipping read, "These are the needs: The need for love, the need for security, the need for creative expression, the need for recognition, the need for new experiences, the need for self esteem."

Jimmy had saved two pamphlets: one was on baptismal regeneration, and the other was the entire "Order for the Solemnization of Marriage." Everyplace where the bride's name is left blank, the name "Pier" was lightly penciled in.

Finally, and most moving to me, were three typewritten pages from Chapter IX of *The Mysterious Stranger* by Mark Twain with two sentences underlined: "Life itself is only a vision, a dream," and, "Nothing exists save empty space and you."

EPILOGUE

O n Saturday morning October 1, 1955, a shaken Winton Dean arrived in Paso Robles accompanied by the chief of security from Warner Bros. They drove to Kuehl's Funeral Home, a solid two-story gothic house with a turret and spire, the only undertaking establishment in the town. Bill Hickman, still shaken and unwilling to accept the fact that Jimmy was dead, embraced Winton. Winton signed for all of his son's personal effects, including the $33.03 Jimmy had in his pockets. He selected a simple bronze casket and handed over the suit he had brought for Jimmy to be dressed in. Winton asked that the torn and bloodied clothing Jimmy had been wearing be destroyed.

Winton then made arrangements for Jimmy's casket to be brought to Los Angeles. From there he would accompany it on the plane to Indianapolis and then to Fairmount. Winton had first wanted Jimmy to be buried in Grant Memorial Park in Marion next to his mother, Mildred. But he had talked with Marcus and Ortense, and it was decided to commit Jimmy to the ground in Park Cemetery, nearer to the house where he been raised in Fairmount.

Ironically, on that Saturday night, *Rebel Without a Cause* opened across the country to superb reviews, and would earn Jimmy his second posthumous Academy Award nomination for his performance: the first was for *East of Eden*.

On the following Monday morning, a death certificate was signed by Deputy Coroner John Stander. In it he stated that twenty-four-year-old James Byron Dean, actor, never married, had met his death on 30 September at 5:45 P.M., one mile east of Cholame at the junction of Highways 466 and 41 in San Luis Obispo County. Chief cause of death was a broken neck with numerous other fractures and internal injuries.

The next day, Stander loaded Jimmy's casket into a black Cadillac hearse and began the long drive to Los Angeles on Highway 101. He stopped in Santa Barbara for gas, and soon attracted a crowd of young people who had recognized the significance of the Paso Robles placards on the hearse. Stander removed the mortuary placards from the windows before getting back on the highway.

He met Winton Dean at Los Angeles airport before midday. Security was tight as he signed the body over to airport officials.

At 10:17 that night, a Hunt Funeral Home hearse met the plane returning the body at the Indianapolis Airport. James Dean was taken to Vernon Hunt's store, which was also the town mortuary: it was also the place where, on his trip home in March, Jimmy had posed for Dennis Stock in a casket. Jimmy's closed casket lay in the Winslow living room for one day, and *The Fairmount News* reported, "Friends may call."

On Saturday, October 8, eight days after the accident, services were held for James Dean in the Back Creek Friends Church where Ortense was organist. It was the largest funeral in the history of Fairmount, with three thousand people crowding the church, standing in the vestibule, and overflowing into the churchyard. Included among the mourners were a few of Jimmy's friends from Hollywood.

Lew Bracker had been so despondent since Jimmy's death that Dennis Stock had to take him in hand, make the plane reservations, and then get Lew on the plane to Indianapolis where they rented a car. They arrived at the church late, but one of the ushers recognized Dennis and seated them in the front row on the other side from the family. Others who flew in from Hollywood were Jack Simmons, Stewart Stern, Henry Ginsberg, producer of *Giant*, and Steve Brooks, head of publicity for Warners. Elizabeth Taylor and Edna Ferber sent flowers, as did Barbara Hutton, who sent twenty-four white roses.

EPILOGUE

Dr. James DeWeerd, then pastor of the Cadle Tabernacle, flew by private plane from Cincinnati following his noon telecast there to deliver the eulogy, "James Dean: A Play in Three Acts." Jimmy's pallbearers were high school friends and fellow members of his basketball squad.

At the conclusion of the service, the family went to the back of the church, where they greeted the mourners, who were inching their way out the door. When Marcus saw Dennis he said, "Boy where have you been?" put his arms around him, and then started to cry. "This is the first time he has cried [since learning of Jimmy's death]," said Ortense.

Dennis and Lew went to the internment and then to the Winslow farm with other mourners. After an hour, Marcus came over to them and suggested they go off alone for a while. With Marcus in the front seat of the car, they drove aimlessly around the country roads. Marcus wanted to learn anything they knew about Jimmy's life in Los Angeles. On their return to the Winslow home, Dennis and Lew said their goodbyes: they were scheduled to return to Los Angeles that night. Winton Dean flew home to Los Angeles the next day.

I have often thought that the lives of five of the people who worked together in *Rebel Without a Cause* were a quintessential Hollywood story with all the elements of romance, mystery, and tragedy.

Nick Adams's career never took off despite being touted as "the next James Dean." From 1959 to 1962 he starred in *The Rebel* television series, aptly titled to take advantage of his association with Jimmy. In 1963 he received a Best Supporting Actor nomination for his role in *Twilight of Honor*. However, he will most likely be remembered as the self-appointed "best friend of James Dean." In 1968, despondent over his wife's infidelities and an indifferent career in films, he was found dead in his Beverly Hills home from a drug overdose, a probable suicide. He was thirty-seven years old.

Sal Mineo was nominated as Best Supporting Actor in 1955 for his role in *Rebel Without a Cause*, and had a small role with Jimmy in *Giant*. Five years later, after delivering fine performances in several films, he was nominated again as Best Supporting Actor for his role in *Exodus*. He was making a career change to producer of stage plays with gay themes when, on a February evening in 1976, he was stabbed to death in the garage of his West Hollywood apartment. An avowed homosexual, he lived in "Boys Town," an area of Los Angeles populated by people with alternative life-styles. His killer has never been found, and no motive for his death has ever been given. He, too, was thirty-seven years old.

Director Nick Ray died at the age of sixty-eight in 1979 of lung cancer after a twelve-year battle with the disease. I have always wondered how he survived as long as he did. There were few personal problems imaginable that didn't bedevil him: drink, gambling, sex, drugs, yet he was able to convert his own anguish and dark vision of the world into personal movies. Emotionally he was the most autobiographical of American directors.

Natalie Wood's career took off after *Rebel Without a Cause* and she was nominated twice in the Best Actress category: for *Splendor in the Grass* (1961) opposite Warren Beatty and *Love With the Proper Stranger* (1963) opposite Steve McQueen. Natalie died mysteriously and tragically in a boating accident off Catalina Island in November 1981. She was forty-three years old and left behind a legacy of good performances in a variety of films.

Some of the other people whose lives were entwined with Jimmy's also died tragically. Within a few months of the accident Rolf Weutherich, Jimmy's German mechanic, was well enough to return to Germany, where he became a rally driver for Porsche. In 1956 he filed a $100,000 law suit against the Dean estate "for damages" due to personal injuries "as a result of the negligence, carelessness, recklessness and/or wilful misconduct on the part of decedent [James B. Dean]." The suit was ultimately dismissed because it had not been filed in the required span of time.

Weutherich never recovered physically or mentally from the accident that took Jimmy's life, and he was never allowed to forget it. For years he was haunted by interviewers asking him to relive that tragic day. Weutherich had four failed marriages: after attacking one wife with a knife, he was confined to a psychiatric hospital.

Early in 1981 Weutherich signed a contract with an American book publisher to tell his story about James Dean, and was scheduled to go to America to start working on the book with a writer in August. On the night of July 20, 1981, he went to a bar in his hometown of Kupferzell, Germany, where he had one too many for the road. It was raining and the pavement was wet as he got into his car and raced off. He lost control and smashed into a house. No one else was hurt, but he was pinned in the wreckage. Doctors tried in vain to revive him. Weutherich was fifty-three years old.

In 1958, four years after her "storybook wedding" and three years after Jimmy's death, Pier Angeli divorced Vic Damone, beginning a bitter custody battle over their son, Perry, that was not settled until 1965 when she got part-time custody. She was married again in 1962 to musician Armando Trotajoli. When that marriage ended four years later, Pier openly blamed Jimmy for her marriage problems and told *The National Enquirer* that Jimmy was "the only man I ever loved deeply as a woman should love a man. I never loved either of my husbands the way I loved Jimmy. I tried to love my husbands but it never lasted. I would wake up in the night and find I had been dreaming of Jimmy. I would lie awake in the same bed with my husband, think of my love for Jimmy and wish it was Jimmy and not my husband who was next to me.

"I had to separate from my husbands because I don't think I can be in love with one man—even if he is dead—and live with another."

After living in Italy for many years, she returned to Hollywood early in 1971. Debbie Reynolds gave her a welcome-back party, and she moved into the home of a friend, Helena Sorell. Pier was hoping to find work in television and began making the rounds, but by the middle of August she still hadn't had any luck and was feeling depressed. Suffering stomach problems, she saw a doctor, who also gave her barbiturates to help her relax and sleep.

On the morning of September 10, 1971—only a few weeks shy of the sixteenth anniversary of Jimmy's death—Sorell looked in on Pier and found her unconscious. Her body was warm, but her head was cold, and Sorell could find no pulse. She immediately called for an ambulance.

While the rescue squad was desperately working over her, the phone rang. The person calling was Pier's Hollywood agent, Walter

Kohner: the producers of *Bonanza* wanted her for a lead role in an episode. She would have been acting opposite Lorne Greene, who'd made his movie debut with her in *The Silver Chalice*. The cause of her death was ruled an overdose of drugs although it may have been accidental. Pier was thirty-nine.

As for Jimmy's family: Winton Dean, now eighty-seven, has Alzheimer's disease and currently lives in a retirement home near Fairmount. Ortense Winslow Dean, the aunt who raised Jimmy and whom he called Maw, died at the age of ninety in 1991. Marcus Winslow, Jimmy's uncle and surrogate father, died in 1976. Marcus Winslow, Jr., the young nephew Markie, married his childhood sweetheart and has two grown sons of his own. Like Jimmy, Markie is a car buff, and his hobby is restoring old cars and trucks. He still lives in the Winslow farmhouse in Fairmount, now refurbished and modernized, and like his parents, he is unfailingly polite to the strangers who drop by almost every day of the week wanting to take photos or talk about Jimmy.

Jimmy died intestate. Winton inherited his estate, which consisted of $96,438.44 after taxes. The bulk of the money came from the $100,000 accident insurance policy plus the sale of Jimmy's personal belongings, including $125 for his horse Cisco, $30 for his racing helmet, $475 for his Triumph motorcycle, $2,200 for his Ford station wagon, plus $6,750 from the company that insured the Spyder and $3,256.48 in Jimmy's account with the Chase National Bank of New York.

When the Dean family hired lawyer Mark Roesler, president of the Curtis Management Group, to run the James Dean Foundation six years ago, the first thing Roesler did was register Jimmy's image with the U.S. Trademark Office in Washington. He then copyrighted Jimmy's name, face, and poses. By 1991, more than 250 companies had registered items from the foundation, including a life-sized mannequin made in Japan, jogging suits, T-shirts, posters, pillow cases, and sunglasses.

In a recent interview, Roesler said, "In a homogenous society like Japan, they admire rebels. In England, his appeal is from nostalgia. And the French think he is sexy."

Last year, the Dean Foundation earned almost $6 million for

EPILOGUE

Jimmy's surviving relatives: not bad considering that his salary from *Rebel* was only $10,000.

Young people everywhere are rediscovering James Dean: his appeal is universal. Posters, T-shirts, and memorabilia are hawked on main streets and in souvenir shops in every city throughout the world.

This summer while on vacation in Bangkok I asked a shop owner whether a T-shirt with Jimmy's photo was selling well. "We sell out as fast as we get them in," he said. In Los Angeles, James Dean posters rank with those of Elvis and Marilyn as the number one best-sellers: the same is true in New York, Colorado Springs, Washington, D.C., Hong Kong, Milan, Tokyo, and Athens—all places I have visited during the past two years.

Only last week a friend of mine from Dallas gave his sixteen-year-old daughter some extra money to buy a souvenir while in Paris. She bought a James Dean T-shirt on the Champs Elysées. And there is a popular TV channel in France called Jimmy that features only movies from the 1950s.

Japanese millionaire Seita Ohnishi, who has one of the world's largest collections of James Dean memorabilia and artifacts, recently commissioned a 35-foot-high 120-ton limestone statue of Jimmy to mark the spot on Highway 46 where he crashed. Cost of the statue: $200,000. At a press conference Ohnishi said, "There are some things, like the hatred that accompanies war, that are best forgotten. There are others, like the love inspired by this young actor, that should be preserved for all time."

For the first three years after Jimmy's death, Warner reported they were receiving two thousand letters a week from bereaved fans. According to the fan mail department, which maintains such statistics, the studio still gets five hundred letters a week, increasing daily during the past two years.

Editors and publishers have discovered that there are three deceased stars whose face on a cover can guarantee sales even today: Marilyn Monroe, Elvis Presley, and Jimmy. One of the top films of 1982 was *Come Back to the Five and Dime, Jimmy Dean, Jimmy Dean*, the story of girlfriends who hold a twenty-year reunion of a

James Dean fan club they formed when he was filming *Giant* in a nearby Texas town.

Every September 30 since 1957, thousands of mourners descend on Fairmount to assemble at Back Creek Friends' Church and at Park Cemetery to play out a drama of tribute. Over the years the event has expanded to include a parade and a mammoth rally of old cars.

James Dean made only three films: *East of Eden, Rebel Without a Cause*, and *Giant* before his death; and he made those films in just over one year's time. Even people who don't know Jimmy's name and have never seen his films recognize his face and stance and are drawn to him. Converse Shoes recently bought the rights to an old Phil Stern photograph of Jimmy wearing their sneakers and featured the photo in their ads. Sales to young people rocketed. Stern originally sold the photo for $75, but Converse paid him $50,000 for the rights.

Often called a cult figure or an international cultural icon, Jimmy has lost none of his appeal and stands as a personification not just of the restless youth of the 1950s but of some larger notion, something that embraces all the tragedy and hope of youth, particularly American youth. No one before or since has ever looked better in jeans and a leather jacket. Jimmy doesn't look like anyone else, but generations have sought to look like him.

There is no simple explanation for why he has come to mean so much to so many people today. Perhaps it is because, in his acting, he had the intuitive talent for expressing the hopes and fears that are part of all young people. Perhaps it is because, in his personal life, he was continually struggling with universal conflicts: he wanted to experience all there was to life, yet he couldn't quite face life; he remained an adolescent to the day he died, unsure of the way others felt about him, afraid to form any lasting alliances, and he was in constant rebellion against adult authority. In some movie-magic way he managed to dramatize brilliantly the questions that every young person in every generation must resolve.

Jimmy achieved fame far beyond that of his dreams, in truth a fame that he himself would never have been able to imagine, and one that, I am certain, would delight him and at the same time cause him to giggle because he would consider it a joke. His image

EPILOGUE

is omnipresent today, and given the benefit of perspective and some wisdom, I believe he left his mark not only on our culture, but on those who worked with him and knew him as a friend.

While preparing this book I invited several of Jimmy's friends to my house for dinner, explaining in advance that I hoped we would all share memories of Jimmy. It was a wonderful evening—some of us had not seen each other for decades—and we easily and naturally shared stories and laughed about some of the outrageous things Jimmy did or said.

And we all agreed, like everyone, that when Jimmy died a great talent was lost. More than that, we agreed that when he died so did something that had to do with the dreams that we had about ourselves.

ACKNOWLEDGMENTS

I could have written a book about Jimmy thirty-seven years ago, right after he died. Doing so then would have been emotionally difficult, and the result, I'm sure, would have been more of a lamentation, an expression of grief and sorrow, than a coherent life story. Five days after he died I wrote about him in my column in *The New York Herald Tribune,* and a year later, to commemorate the anniversary of his death, I was assigned by *Redbook* magazine to write a long biography of him based on the fact that he was, even then, becoming a legend.

I went to Fairmount, where the Winslows put me up in Jimmy's room and provided me with information and the names of people who might be of help in giving me insight into the young boy they had raised as their own. Some of what I discovered both intrigued and unsettled me, especially my interview with the Reverend James DeWeerd: I was not prepared to handle what he told me in some detail—I suspect he was proud of what he said about his relationship with Jimmy—and he gave me the first clue about Jimmy's sexual ambivalence.

I left the *Herald Tribune* in 1963, and ten years later I felt it was time to write about my first years in Hollywood. The resulting book, *Mislaid in Hollywood,* includes a chapter on Jimmy: I couldn't tell my own story without making reference to him.

Nearly twenty years have passed since I wrote that book. During that time I've occasionally thought of writing about Jimmy, and friends from that period—people who knew Jimmy—as well as publishers asked me to write about him. No particular incident or memory ultimately led me to write this book, and perhaps all along it was just a matter of enough time passing.

I'm glad I made the decision. Most books require lengthy research and interviews, and this book was no exception, but I never enjoyed the process as much as I did for the past eighteen months because it gave me a chance to visit with friends of nearly four decades ago and to reminisce about years we all considered among the best of our lives, and to talk about a friend who we all agreed was unique and memorable. Those conversations sparked my own memories, which are the heart of this book.

Over the years I remained close to three of Jimmy's closest friends: Lew Bracker, Dennis Stock, and Leonard Rosenman. After Jimmy's death, Lew quit the insurance business and went on to become a stockbroker and entrepreneur. Dennis, who now lives in Provence, France, has an international reputation as a photographer and director of short subjects. The photographs Dennis took of Jimmy for *Life* magazine have become justifiably famous and show up in every corner of the world. Leonard is a successful film composer with two Academy Awards plus two additional Oscar nominations to his credit. I am indebted to each of the three for sharing their personal memories of Jimmy with me.

I began my research by returning to Fairmount, Indiana, where Jimmy's story begins, to update my original notes. A journey to Fairmount is really a pilgrimage. Fairmount has changed very little since my first visit and since Jimmy lived there. The only difference is signs along the road approaching the town that proudly proclaim it to be the birthplace of James Byron Dean as well as the hometown of "Garfield" Jim Davis and "CBS" Phil Jones.

Although the town itself has changed very little, time had taken its toll of Jimmy's family: Marcus Winslow had died in the intervening years since my first visit, and his wife, Ortense, and Winton Dean were in nursing homes (Ortense died shortly after my visit). Marcus Winslow, Jr. (Markie), now forty-eight years old, took me on a personal tour of the Fairmount Historical Museum situated in two rooms of the Town Hall devoted to James

Dean memorabilia that he has supplied. Markie's prime concern was that I not be unkind to Uncle Winton, who, he said, has been much maligned over the years. According to Markie, Jimmy and his father did love each other, and he has the letters to prove it: letters he intends to use sometime in the future in a book of his own about Jimmy.

My second stop was at the James Dean Gallery, run by David Loehr, which displays a remarkable collection of everything available about James Dean, from movie posters to articles of clothing and the Minifon recorder I loaned Jimmy before his last trip home. David, who lives part-time in New York where he conducts an annual walking tour of the places Jimmy lived and spent time in, and his assistant, Jayne Beck Skinner, who grew up in Fairmount, helped put me in touch with many of Jimmy's early friends. All of them were delighted to talk about the young man who made their town famous just by virtue of being born there.

I am indebted to Richard "Dick" Beck, Jayne's brother, who was one of Jimmy's first childhood friends; Bob Pulley, who was Jimmy's classmate from the seventh to twelfth grades and who is president of the Fairmount Historical Museum; Jerry Lee Payne, whose parents put up the newlywed Deans on their honeymoon and who remained friends with the Deans, especially Mildred, until her death.

Some of Jimmy's instructors still recall him vividly, including Hugh Caughell, Jimmy's biology teacher at Fairmount High; and Gurney Maddingly, the former Broadway actor who befriended Jimmy (Jimmy sometimes baby-sat his children), and who gave Jimmy his first stage directions. Although now in failing health and in a nursing home, Adeline Nall, whom I had interviewed decades before, still spoke glowingly of her most famous actor pupil.

James Whitmore, who was Jimmy's first mentor and who suggested he go to the Actors Studio in New York to study, is still active in films and theater.

For Jimmy's life in New York, the city he seemed to have adopted as his real home, I interviewed Barbara Glenn. Although three decades have passed, it is easy to see why Jimmy fell in love with her. She is still petite and beautiful, still married to successful actor and stage director Mark Gordon—the man Jimmy met and

ACKNOWLEDGMENTS

approved so many years ago—and still a working actress. She was generous enough to talk to me about her relationship with Jimmy, a truly personal subject, and in so doing she clarified many of the letters Jimmy wrote to her and some of the ambiguities concerning Jimmy's years in New York. Barbara helped bring that period to life for me.

Also helpful in setting straight some of the facts surrounding that time in Jimmy's life—a period shrouded in rumors and inaccuracies—was Frank Corsaro, today head of the Actors Studio and Juilliard School.

Jonathan Gilmore, one of the first people Jimmy met in New York, had much to offer about Jimmy as both a friend and as an intimate who shared an intense closeness with Jimmy, in New York as well as later in Hollywood. Author of *The Real James Dean*, he allowed me access to some of the journals he kept during that period.

Two of Jimmy's New York friends—veterans with Jimmy of many cattle calls—successfully made the transition from television to movies: Martin Landau and Rod Steiger. Both of them knew Jimmy when becoming established actors was only a dream for all three—something they talked about over cups of coffee at Cromwell's Pharmacy—and both of them thus have a special perspective on Jimmy. They are now world-famous stars, but the early days have a special poignance and clarity, and Jimmy was very much a part of their early lives.

Cromwell's Pharmacy is long gone, but Roy Schatt's studio, where Jimmy spent so much of his time in New York, is still on East Thirty-third Street. What Jimmy saw in him is clear and ever present: creativity marked by a distinctive originality. His photographs of Jimmy are an integral part of how later generations have come to look at Jimmy. Those photographs, together with a memorable text, make his book *James Dean: A Portrait* an important part of the literature on Jimmy. Schatt does not remember Jimmy as a famous actor, but as a friend and student. He and his wife, Elaine, gave generously of their time.

Christine White, who tested with Jimmy at the Actors Studio and was one of his best friends and confidantes, now lives in Washington, D.C., where she is writing her autobiography. Still slim and beautiful, Chris gave me some clear insights into Jimmy as a young man, reminiscences enlivened by vivid anecdotes.

Arlene Sachs continued with her acting career and is now known as Tasha Martel. I had interviewed her decades earlier and was astounded at how little she had changed over the years: still lovely and vivacious, and still in love with her memories of Jimmy, which she again shared with me.

Arnie Langer, Arlene's cousin, no longer drives a taxi as he did when he knew Jimmy and when I first interviewed him. Today he organizes and guides golf tours of Scotland. Arnie's recollections of Jimmy are still keen.

It was Ralph Levy who wrote a letter to James Sheldon introducing Jimmy. Interviews with Sheldon provided the essential background for Jimmy's work in television. In a sense, Sheldon was the first to recognize Jimmy's talent, and it was he who sent Jimmy to Jane Deacy.

Daniel Mann, one of the directors who worked with Jimmy during his early years in New York, told me of his problems with Jimmy during the staging of *The Immoralist*. He recalled Jimmy as graceless and impolite, but wonderfully talented. He died shortly after I interviewed him.

I spoke with Gusti Huber, who co-starred with Jimmy in a television drama in New York while Jimmy was still in the throes of his love affair with Pier Angeli. Gusti knew Jimmy only briefly, but her encounter with him seems emblematic of what meeting Jimmy was like for many people: when he wanted to, or when the chemistry was right, he made quick and often deep friendships. She remembers the day in the rehearsal hall when she gave Jimmy a record of Frank Sinatra's newest hits: he looked at the record, looked at her, and then ran out of the hall. When he returned, he dropped a small package in front of her. Inside, wrapped in tissue paper, was a small box in the shape of a Bible, and in the box was a tiny rosary. His relationship with Angeli may explain the gift, but the impulsiveness is pure Jimmy Dean.

Thanks go also to Hume Cronyn, whose recent autobiography, *A Terrible Liar*, only proves that his talent is not restricted to just acting and directing. Mr. Cronyn's candid memories of Jimmy, though not necessarily flattering, are certainly revealing.

ACKNOWLEDGMENTS

Director David Swift, who was married to actress Maggie McNamara when he knew Jimmy, provided revealing insight into Jimmy's private life during his years in New York along with impressions of Rogers Brackett.

Adele Rosenman, whom Jimmy referred to as his "earth mother," knew Jimmy intimately in New York as well as Hollywood. Now living in Los Angeles, she is an accomplished sculptor.

It was Elia Kazan who took Jimmy to Hollywood. Undoubtedly one of the greatest film and stage directors of our time, he is now a renowned author as well. In his superb autobiography, *A Life,* he provided a candid view of Jimmy and his romance with Pier. Kazan was generous enough to read over the portions of this book that apply to his relationship with Jimmy. Thanks also to his secretary, Eileen Shanahan.

Until now, no one knew Jimmy's whereabouts during his first few months in California for *Eden;* I solved that riddle through pure serendipity. My son-in-law, Paul Husband, an attorney of equine law and breeder of Arabian horses, mentioned that he knew a man in Salinas named Monty Roberts who said he had known James Dean. Roberts turned out to be Jimmy's guardian-mentor who had taken Jimmy in tow, toughened him up, and introduced him to the Salinas area before the film commenced. Monty became Jimmy's good friend and is now a prominent rancher and breeder of horses in Salinas.

Sometimes research can be as easy as picking up a telephone book. Rhea Burakoff was listed on the production credits of *Eden* as Elia Kazan's secretary. Thirty years later she was still listed in the Hollywood phone book with the same phone number. Burakoff provided some telling and humorous anecdotes about Jimmy's relationship with the director.

Dick Clayton, Jimmy's Hollywood agent, who became one of his most trusted friends, is one of the nicest people I have ever met. Now a personal manager with several promising young clients, he was generous with his time and memories. Dick now lives in Hollywood on the site where Jimmy once planned to build his own house.

William T. Orr, vice-president in charge of talent for Warner Bros. in the 1950s, was one of the first to recognize Jimmy's screen potential. He helped guide Jimmy through the politics of studio life. Now living in Palm Springs, he proved to be a fund of valuable information.

Sid Avery was still photographer for Warner Bros. on *Eden* and *Rebel*. Now retired, he has one of the largest collections of studio stills in America and generously supplies them to qualified institutions and researchers.

Max Bercutt was head of publicity at Warner Bros. during the 1950s, during which time he dealt with Jimmy and the problems he created, sometimes on a daily basis. At the end of an interview with Max he gave me the title of this book by describing Jimmy as a "little boy lost."

Tom Pryor, West Coast Bureau Chief of *The New York Times*, was my chief competitor during the 1950s, and later became the editor of *Daily Variety*. He recalled vividly some of his own memories of James Dean.

Julie Harris, whom Kazan described as the "angel on our set" of *Eden*, is still one of Broadway's most enduring leading ladies. Her memories of Jimmy shine with compassionate understanding.

Debbie Reynolds was Pier Angeli's best friend in Hollywood and warned her not to marry Vic Damone. I am grateful to her for insights into the romance between Pier and Jimmy.

Mario Marino was one of Jimmy's favorite waiters at the old Villa Capri and, as such, was privy to many private moments in Jimmy's life with Pier. Now the owner of his own superb restaurant in Hollywood, Marino's, Mario was delighted to revive the past with me.

As Vampira, the voluptuous hostess of a series of horror films on Los Angeles television in the 1950s, Maila Nurmi was every man's fantasy. Her independent iconoclastic style and wit fascinated Jimmy, and they became friends. Maila delighted me with anecdotes about Jimmy, both humorous and poignant.

Kenneth Kendall looks like what he is, a creative and original artist. His feelings for Jimmy are sincere and his recollections lucid. His busts of Jimmy have gained him well-deserved international fame.

Stewart Stern wrote the screenplay of *Rebel Without a Cause*, one of the most successful movies in history, for the princely sum of

ACKNOWLEDGMENTS

$12,000 a week for five weeks. He put much of his life into that screenplay, and Jimmy understood his feelings and made them his own. Stewart gave generously of his time and granted me permission to use some of his original notes on the screenplay. He now lives in Seattle, where he is an instructor in screenwriting at the University of Washington. I envy his students.

A year after Jimmy's death, Arthur Loew, Jr., founded the James Dean Memorial Fund at the Actors Studio in memory of his friend. Over the years he and Stewart Stern still meet occasionally and reminisce about Jimmy. Today Arthur lives in Tucson, where he is involved with the Arizona Film Commission, and spearheads various theater and musical groups.

Faye Nuell Mayo, who was Natalie Wood's double on *Rebel*, became Jimmy's good friend and confidante. Faye allowed me to quote from her own journal of the period. She is now a personal manager and casting director in Hollywood.

Beverly Long Dorff met Jimmy during his first television commercial and went on to act with him as one of the gang in *Rebel*. She recalled many of the behind-the-scenes fun and games during the filming. She owns and operates her own successful casting agency, known as Beverly Long & Associates.

Rod Amateau was stunt coordinator on *Rebel* and did most of the driving for Jimmy: he also taught Jimmy many race driving techniques. Now a successful director of feature films, he took time from his busy schedule to regale me with lively stories about the making of *Rebel*.

John Veitch was production assistant at Warner Bros. during all of James Dean's films. He recalled many humorous and telling moments with Jimmy that added color to this story.

George Stevens, Jr., graciously gave me permission to read portions of his father's voluminous notebooks detailing the making of *Giant*. The notes as well as an oral history of George Stevens, Sr., are now on file at the Academy of Motion Picture Arts and Sciences. Stevens Jr. is now a filmmaker and co-chairman of the American Film Institute.

Joseph Hamilton was the night clerk at the El Paisano Lodge in Marfa, Texas, when Jimmy was filming. The experience for him was memorable and his stories brought to life some of the off-the-set shenanigans that livened up his life as well as the lives of the film cast.

Vernon Scott has been a Hollywood columnist for the United Press since the early 1950s and is probably the last of that era still on the beat. He was one of the few newsmen allowed to visit the set of *Giant* during filming, and his insights and interviews with Jimmy were valuable.

June Levant well recalls the night that Jimmy, along with Liz Taylor, Michael Wilding, Joan Collins and some girls Jimmy had picked up, visited her home, and Jimmy talked with her daughter, Marcia. She confirmed my own memory of the event as it was told to me by Oscar.

Ursula Andress, who now lives in Italy, was in Hollywood on vacation when we spoke. She has changed little physically over the years. Ursula filled in for me some of the gaps in the story of her relationship with Jimmy as I knew it.

Janette Miller was under contract to Paramount Studios when she first met Jimmy, and they became friends, a friendship that lasted until his death. Janette had some perceptive insights into Jimmy. She was also one of the last people to see him before he left for Salinas.

Johnny Von Neumann owned Competition Motors in Hollywood where Jimmy bought the Porsche Spyder. He was also Rolf Weutherich's employer, and as such, was able to fill me in on the mechanic's life after the accident.

Bruce Kessler was a passenger in Lance Reventlow's Mercedes on the drive to Salinas. Bruce, who is now a director of feature films, helped flesh out some of the last minutes of Jimmy's life.

Mr. and Mrs. John Robert White witnessed the accident on the road to Salinas. Mrs. White sent me a copy of the deposition she gave shortly after the tragic event.

Warren Newton Beath lives in central California and was fascinated from childhood with the events leading up to Jimmy's death. His book *The Death of James Dean* contains a complete account of the tragedy, including the inquest that followed.

Leon Raskin, who lives in Baltimore, is a Porsche historian and vintage car racer and has devoted many years to tracking down the various vehicles Jimmy owned.

ACKNOWLEDGMENTS

Bill Dakota never knew James Dean but he was a close friend of Nick Adams's. Over the years, Dakota has become somewhat of an authority on the life of Jimmy, and he gave me access to some of the material he has collected.

Sylvia Bongiovanni, one of the premier collectors of James Dean memorabilia and president of We Remember Dean, International, Jimmy's most active fan club, was a fund of information she readily shared with me.

During a conversation with author C. David Heymann, he told me about Barbara Hutton's diaries and pointed out for me the story about the heiress's one-night stand with Jimmy.

Weaving together these many anecdotes and making sense of the chronology of Jimmy's life required reference to some of the many books that have been written about Jimmy since his death. Also useful were several autobiographies written by people who knew him. I owe thanks to the staffs of the Margaret Herrick Library, Academy of Motion Picture Arts and Sciences, and the Billy Rose Theatre Collection of the Lincoln Center Library and Museum for the Performing Arts in New York. The books and articles I consulted are listed in the bibliography that follows.

BIBLIOGRAPHY

Leith Adams and Keith Burns, eds. *James Dean: Behind the Scene*. New York: Birch Lane Press, 1990.

Warren Newton Beath. *The Death of James Dean*. New York: Grove Press, 1986.

Susan Bluttman. "Rediscovering James Dean: The TV Legacy." *Emmy*, October 1990.

Paul F. Boller, Jr., and Ronald L. Davis. *Hollywood Anecdotes*. New York: William Morrow and Company, 1987.

Patricia Bosworth. *Montgomery Clift: A Biography*. New York: Harcourt Brace Jovanovich, 1978.

Jim Backus. *Rocks on the Roof*. New York: G. P. Putnam Sons, 1958.

William Bast. *James Dean: A Biography*. New York: Ballantine Books, 1956.

Hume Cronyn. *A Terrible Liar*. New York: William Morrow and Company, 1991.

David Dalton. *James Dean: The Mutant King*. San Francisco: Straight Arrow Books, 1974.

David Dalton and Roy Cayen. *James Dean: American Icon*. New York: St. Martin's Press, 1984.

Jonathan Gilmore. *The Real James Dean*. New York: Pyramid Books, 1975.

Alec Guinness. *Blessings in Disguise*. New York: Warner Books, 1986.

Venable Herndon. *James Dean: A Short Life*. Garden City, N.Y.: Doubleday, 1974.

Hedda Hopper with James Brough. *The Whole Truth and Nothing But*. Garden City, N.Y.: Doubleday, 1963.

BIBLIOGRAPHY

Barney Hoskyns. *James Dean: Shooting Star*. New York: Doubleday, 1989.

Elia Kazan. *A Life*. New York: Knopf, 1988.

Eartha Kitt. *Alone With Me*. Chicago: Regnery, 1976.

Mercedes McCambridge. *The Quality of Mercy*. New York: Times Books, 1981.

Randall Riese. *The Unabridged James Dean*. Chicago: Contemporary Books, 1991.

Roy Schatt. *James Dean: A Portrait*. New York: Ruggles de Latour, 1982.

Mike Steen. *Hollywood Speaks: An Oral History*. New York: Putnam, 1974.

Dennis Stock. *James Dean Revisited*. New York: The Viking Press and Penguin Books, 1978.

Robert Wayne Tysl. *Continuity and Evolution in a Public Symbol: An Investigation into the Creation and Communication of the James Dean Image in Mid-Century America*. Ann Arbor: Michigan State University, 1965.

Index

INDEX

INDEX

INDEX

INDEX

INDEX